ET

UP WEST

Do you remember the West End of London during the 1950s? Did you live or work there? If so, I want to hear from you...

This was the advertisement author Pip Granger placed in a local newspaper, and the response was immediate. Soon she was hearing from people who recalled when sweets were rationed; from families who'd been bombed out of their homes during the Blitz; from men who worked in the flower markets of Covent Garden; and from the son of a family who'd opened one of the very first delicatessens in Soho. All have extraordinary stories to tell. Based on these, and the author's own memories, *Up West* evokes a unique and vibrant community and a way of life that is vanishing fast.

UP WEST

UP WEST

by

Pip Granger

Magna Large Print Books
Long Preston, North Yorkshire,
BD23 4ND, England.

British Library Cataloguing in Publication Data.

Granger, Pip
   Up west.

   A catalogue record of this book is
   available from the British Library

   ISBN   978-0-7505-3209-9

First published in Great Britain in 2009 by Corgi

Copyright © Pip Granger 2009
Map copyright © Encompass Graphics Ltd. 2009

Cover illustration © Kerry Norgard by arrangement with
Arcangel Images

Pip Granger has asserted her right under the Copyright, Designs and
Patents Act, 1988 to be identified as the author of this work

Published in Large Print 2010 by arrangement with
Transworld Publishers

Magna Large Print is an imprint of Library Magna Books Ltd.

Printed and bound in Great Britain by
T.J. (International) Ltd., Cornwall, PL28 8RW

I would like to dedicate this book to the memory of those who sadly did not live to see *Up West* completed. I was too late to interview Ray Constantine and Andrew Panayiotes and therefore their testimony is from their initial emails. Alberto Camisa gave a long and fascinating interview and I hope that the fact that his memories run all through the book proves to be of some comfort to his family and friends. Roy Walker, Barbara Jones's husband, also died before I could interview him in depth, for which I am very sorry. Bryan Burrough of the Soho Society was already unwell when we met, but I think of him often when I feed my greedy blackbirds, a little ritual that we shared along with our love of Soho. I am only sorry that I was unable to glean more of Bryan's great knowledge of our favourite bit of London before he left us. I hope that the families and friends of all these people will accept my sympathy for their loss and my gratitude for the help that their loved ones gave to this book.

Acknowledgements

I'd like to express my heartfelt thanks to all the contributors without whose generous testimony there would be no book. It has been an honour to share your memories and thank you for trusting me with them.

There aren't adequate words in the language to thank my husband, Ray, for his support, all the legwork and unstinting encouragement – he is my hero and a star.

Many thanks to Mike Janulewicz for the loan of some very useful books and thanks are also due to the Archivist of the Peabody Trust, Christine Wagg.

Last, but by no means least – here's to those who do all the unsung schlep – work that gets books on to our shelves – in this case my editor, Selina Walker; cover designer, Diane Meacham; editorial production, Judith Welsh; pictures, Sheila Lee; copy-editor, Beth Humphries; map, Tom Coulson and Phil Lord.

Contents

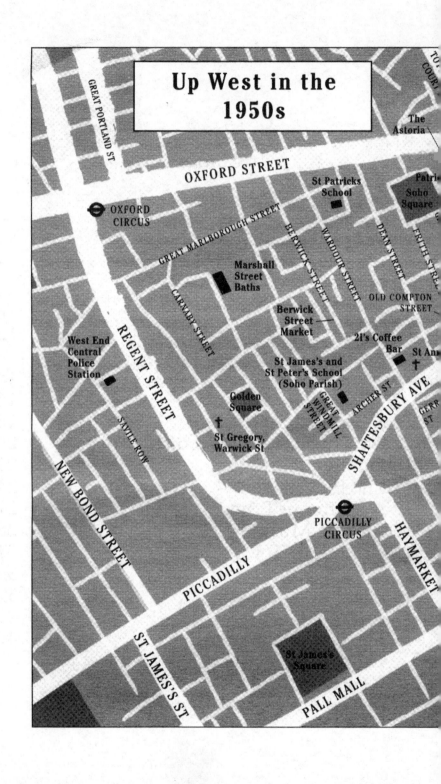

Up West in the 1950s

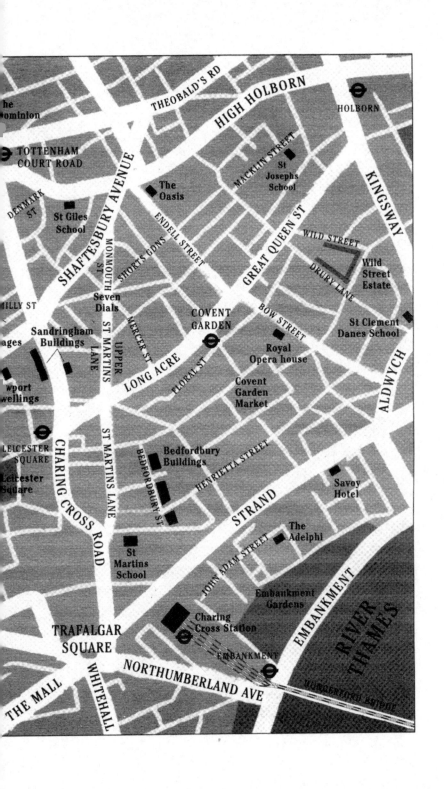

Introduction

I'll own up to two things straight away. First of all, this book is not a 'proper' history, with dates and hard facts and footnotes, although there is a bit of that sort of thing. *Up West* is more to do with people's memories of how things looked, sounded, smelt and felt, about what it was like to work and live in the West End of London in the twenty years after the Second World War. Rather than telling a story in chronological order, I've therefore chosen to present a series of pictures, of impressions, from my life and those of others interviewed for this book, to make what might be called an emotional history.

Secondly, although this book is called *Up West*, it's pretty obvious that my heart belongs to Soho. Covent Garden gets a fair crack, too, but poor old Mayfair, for instance, hardly gets a look in. Although people did live in Mayfair and its West End neighbours, St James's and Knightsbridge, those areas do not seem to have had that mysterious something that made people love them in quite the same way as Sohoites and Covent Gardeners love their 'manors'. They simply don't appear to inspire the same sense of place as the other two.

There's a reason for that, which emerged when

I was researching this book. Literally everyone who was interviewed who had lived in Soho and Covent Garden in the post-war years remembered the life and bustle of the streets, the sense of being 'all in it together', and the fact that most of the people who lived there, worked there, too. Working men and women, artisans and traders, breathe life and soul into a place, and Soho and Covent Garden have always had them in abundance. Some had only to go downstairs to go to work, while others had just a few minutes' walk to get to their jobs in workshops, restaurants, markets or the many small businesses tucked away in backstreets. Of course, the people who lived and worked there brought up their kids there, too, and there were plenty of them. Between them, Soho and Covent Garden could boast more than half a dozen primary schools, their class sizes swelled by the post-war baby boom.

It was this living together, working together, going to school together, eating together in local cafés, even going to the public baths together, that brought people together, and gave them a wonderful sense of belonging that persists long after they have moved away. A really thriving community needs a population that stays put for most of the year, and one that includes the young, the elderly and the middle-aged from all walks of life.

People in the posher parts of the West End never experienced this. According to Judith Summers in her book *Soho*, when the architect John Nash (1752–1835) laid out his plans for the building of Regent Street, his express intention was to separate the streets occupied by the 'Nobility and Gentry' from 'the narrower streets and meaner houses occupied by mechanics and the trading part of the community'. It was the habit of the Georgian upper crust to reside in London only during the season, then to remove themselves *en masse* to Bath or the seaside at Brighton, or hightail it back to their country seats. As a result, the town houses in fashionable Mayfair were shrouded in dust sheets and closed up tight as the place went into hibernation for much of the year. It must have felt rather like a seaside town on a winter Sunday, only without the bracing, salt-laden gales and crashing seas.

As for Fitzrovia, Marylebone and Bloomsbury, the areas north of Oxford Street, Londoners tend not see these as part of the West End, because they lack the concentration of cinemas, clubs, theatres and shops that make a trip 'Up West' a treat for East Enders. Besides, I tend to feel that Fitzrovia is simply the wrong side of Oxford Street. Some Soho natives even refer to it darkly as 'the other side'. There are those who have tried to claim that Fitzrovia is, in fact, North Soho, which would suggest that it has had a bit of an identity crisis for some time now.

By the time the chocolatey remnants of my very first birthday cake had been wiped from my hands, face and eyebrows, I was already a veteran visitor to London's West End, and particularly to Soho's bars, cafés, clubs, bookshops and the snooker halls. Having sent my mother out to work to keep the family, Father was in charge of my care, and as the West End drew him back to its narrow, sooty, fragrant streets like a drunkard to his stash of bottles, that's where we spent most of our days.

This was the case for the first five years of my life. After that, I was a semi-resident of Old Compton Street until I was thirteen. Then, once I had gained some independence, I haunted the place day and night until my mid-twenties. My visits became less regular after that, but whenever I had the time to wander aimlessly, I always chose to do it in Soho. I was happy to be back, soaking up the atmosphere and dropping in on some of the old 'faces', shopping in Berwick Street market, eating and drinking in the area's restaurants, cafés and coffee bars. I developed a deep love and an abiding gratitude for the place and its people, and this love has sustained me for my whole life. For me, Soho is, very simply, my spiritual home.

There are many books about London's West End. Some are general histories of particular areas, while others concentrate on specific sections of the West End community – the Chinese, for example, the bohemians of fifties Soho, or the lesbian and gay scene. Then there is the 'I drank with...' genre of memoirs, books that focus on a selection of the author's famous boozy chums. Here, anecdotes about the likes of Francis Bacon, Dylan Thomas (my own father drank with him), Brendan and Dominic Behan (and them), the Bernard brothers – Bruce, Jeffrey and Oliver – and John Deakin (and, indeed, all of those), tend to feature large.

What appears to be missing is a book that looks at the lives and times of so-called 'ordinary' people who happened to live and work in this extraordinary area – the shopkeepers, the market traders and market porters, the playing children and the working girls, those who lived on the streets and those who entertained on them, and the very different populations of both Covent Garden and Soho by night and by day. It was these people that made the greatest impression on me when I was young, and it is their stories I wanted to tell.

I have chosen to focus on the years from 1945 to the early sixties, partly because I was there for most of them, but mostly because the two decades immediately following the Second World War, from VE Day to the emergence of 'Swinging London' – a scene that was nurtured in the shops in and around Carnaby Street, in Soho's north-west corner – formed one of the most interesting periods in London's long history. What's more, it is all within living memory – just. That is why there's been such a rash of vox pop television, radio programmes and books about the Second World War and its aftermath: the rush is on to record the testimony of those of us who were there, before our memories fail or we kick the bucket eternal.

Nowhere else that I have visited in my life has had such a generous 'live and let live' attitude. From the start, Soho has been a community of the dispossessed, a welcoming home for the marginalized and different, whether they were fleeing persecution or poverty abroad or petty prejudices and hide-bound attitudes at home. Since the eighteenth century, it has opened its generous arms and heart to virtually all comers, and in the immediate post-war years there was a new influx of the displaced peoples of war-battered Europe, and those who simply sought an alternative to the drabness of Civvy Street.

The Lyceum dance hall in Covent Garden, the theatres along Shaftesbury Avenue, the cinemas of Leicester Square and the dazzling, colourful, newly re-lit neon lights of Piccadilly Circus, as well as Soho's cafés, restaurants, pubs and night-clubs – not to mention its brothels and spielers – offered escape from the memory of the horrors of the war that they had somehow managed to survive, the gloom of rationing and restrictions, and the new post-war terrors symbolized by the spectre of the atom bomb. The West End, with its many delights, brought a splash of much-needed, vibrant colour and cheer to the grey drizzle of austerity-bound Britain.

My strange little broken bohemian family, shunned as weird and out of step in the mind-numbingly, narrow-minded housing estates of post-war Essex, was instantly accepted in Soho. Nobody cared tuppence what accent I had, where I had been born, who my parents were, or how they earned their living. In that exotic, fascinating, multicultural and tolerant place, I was seen simply as a child who deserved the pro-tection and love of adults – and I found it. No wonder I loved the place. For me, Soho was, is and will remain, a place of refuge.

I am aware that this view is at odds with that of the majority of outsiders. Many feel that Soho is, and always has been, a very dangerous den of viciousness, violence and vice. However, you will see from the testimony of the people I have interviewed for this book that they never felt threatened, frightened or intimidated as they wandered its night-time streets as adults, or played in its sooty squares when they were children.

It isn't just outsiders, either. The parents of some children brought up in Covent Garden, just next door, warned their offspring – or their daughters, at least – against crossing the Charing Cross Road, especially after dark, as they would be exposed to sin and danger. Of course, that only added to the attraction for some. Those that risked their parents' anger say the same thing as Soho children: that they were in no danger. Personally, I felt – and indeed was – far safer wandering about Soho's streets and alleys than I was in any of the playgrounds of the many Essex schools I attended.

Later, when I was a young woman, if ever I was approached and hustled by an outsider looking for action on Soho's night-time streets, a local would magically appear from the gloom of a doorway and tell the man to 'Piss off, she's Cliff's daughter': if anyone tried to argue the toss, it would be explained in no uncertain terms what would happen to them if they laid a single, unwanted finger on me.

Nevertheless, mention Soho in particular and the West End in general to anyone who has never lived there, and they immediately think of the four Ss – sin, sex, sleaze and shysters. They are unaware of the place's many other, less disreputable qualities. I can, for instance, shock the unwary by mentioning that I have been invited to eat with the Soho Senior Citizens' Lunch Club. I love to see the look of bewilderment metamorphose into disbelief. 'Senior citizens in Soho? Surely not!' It never seems to occur to anyone that people actually *live* in Soho, or if it has, they have assumed that the population is entirely made up of prostitutes, ponces, pimps, gangsters, gamblers, druggies and drunks. Other, more informed, types throw the odd bohemian, actor, musician, artist and writer into the mix, recognizing that alongside the sleaze, Soho has an equally long history of artiness.

What few people seem to suspect is that, within the half square mile or so of streets crammed between Oxford Street, Charing Cross Road, Trafalgar Square and Regent Street, families go about their daily lives in pretty much the same way as they do in the rest of the country. Children go to school to wrestle with the three Rs, while their parents, aunts, uncles, grandparents and older siblings get on with their jobs, trades and professions in order to pay their rent, bills and council tax.

Today, Covent Garden is a tourist trap, and a Mecca for lovers of opera, ballet, theatre, cinema and fashionable shops. In the period covered by this book it was a commercial and industrial centre, with the fruit, flower and vegetable market at its heart giving it a fragrant – and, at times, distinctly pungent – flavour. In Odhams in Long Acre, printing presses thundered out copies of a national newspaper, the *Daily Herald*, while small and large businesses – cigarette factories, bakeries, barrow-makers, printers and so on – thrived in

Dickensian premises tucked away in courts and up alleys.

The well-heeled lived along both sides of the Strand, in the massive art deco block of the Adelphi, or in elegant eighteenth-century town houses, while Hollywood stars and other rich visitors stayed in the area's fashionable hotels. Just a couple of hundred yards away, in narrow terraces of cramped Georgian dwelling houses or blocks of purpose-built, cold-water flats – many without bathrooms or electricity until well into the fifties – lived those characterized by the Victorian philanthropists who built the blocks as 'the industrious poor'. Many were members of families whose roots in the area were several generations deep.

Like me, the people who lived and grew up in the West End during the period covered in this book, who experienced its seamy joys and every-day kindnesses, its bustling, life-filled streets and bleakly glamorous nightlife, and above all its warm and unquestioning embrace, are growing older. My parents, and most of their friends, are long gone, but others survive, and it is their testimony, woven with my own memories and the contemporary writings of those who were equally captivated by this remarkable time and place, that I present in this book, which is at once a history, a memorial and a love letter.

1

A Special Place

It is hard to imagine now, but before Henry VIII got his hands on it, the West End of London was a rural place well outside the city walls. The Abbey of St Peter at Westminster owned land in Soho, as did Abingdon Abbey in Berkshire. The monks of Westminster Abbey also owned a slice of Covent Garden, and they leased land to the powerful Mercers' Company in both places, while some Carthusians had a stake in Bloomsbury. In the 1530s, Henry relieved all three religious foundations of their valuable real estate as part of his campaign to dissolve the monasteries and bring all church lands under the ownership of the Crown. He then parcelled out the same land as estates to his favourites in reward for their services and loyalty.

Although the area remained countrified under the new owners during Henry's reign, things were already changing rapidly enough to alarm his younger daughter by the time she became Queen Elizabeth in 1558. She issued several edicts forbidding building on Soho Fields, and embargoes on unlicensed development throughout the area remained in place when the Stuarts came to power. Even in its gestation period, though, Sohoites showed a fine and customary disregard

27

for the rules laid down by authority. Building carried on regardless, albeit relatively slowly. Soho continued to be used for hunting and for grazing livestock for a while, but was already coming under very serious pressure from a city that had long outgrown its walls, and whose population were keen to 'go west' to find more elbow room and fresh air, and to escape the regular epidemics of plague, smallpox and the bloody flux.

In her book, *Soho* (1989), Judith Summers likened the area's name to 'a short, wistful sigh' and it certainly has that about it, but the name actually has a bloody provenance: 'Soho' was an old hunting cry. A jinking hare would hear the eerie cry 'Soho, soho' as the baying pack and braying hunters tore across the fields, determined not to let lunch get away. Soho was prime hunting country for the well-to-do who, thanks to Henry, had estates there. It was handily placed within easy riding distance of both the court at White-hall, and the city, and the King and his courtiers regularly enjoyed hunting trips and visits to one or another of their newly enriched lordships.

Elizabeth, in her turn, was a version of our latter-day couch surfers, forever foisting herself on her subjects' hospitality, except that she in-sisted on a four-poster bed and the best of every-thing. She made an absolute point of descending on her nobles one after the other, expecting free room and board for herself and her court. Such royal progresses served several purposes. They allowed her to see her country and her subjects and them to see her, which helped to strengthen the bonds of loyalty in both directions, while closing up her court for months on end saved the royal purse thousands of gold sovereigns. Finally, they got her out of harm's way in the summer months, when the open sewers and crush of unwashed bodies set up a stomach-heaving stench, and London was usually in the grip of one life-threatening pestilence or another. The estates to the west were a good starting point for some of these trips, and they still provided sport in the form of hunting. Soho hare was certainly on the menu in 1562 when the Lord Mayor sallied forth on his annual inspection of the water conduits that brought the precious liquid across Soho Fields and into the fetid and smelly city.

Funnily enough, Soho has remained synonymous with hunting of one sort or another ever since; only the nature of the quarry has changed. It has long been known as the place to go for a good time, whether you're looking for entertainment, an exciting nightlife or the thrill of illicit sex. It has a worldwide reputation for so many other things besides the 'ladies and gentlemen of the night'. It has provided excellent restaurants, a great market and its own quirky brand of retail therapy for centuries. Even today, while nearby Oxford Street and Regent Street supply the usual opportunities of high street shopping, Soho offers an array of small, specialist shops that will supply virtually anything you can think of, from first-rate produce to what one might (sometimes euphemistically) call niche requirements.

There are shops selling freshly roasted coffee, aromatic tea, rhinestone handcuffs, fabulous pastries, perfume, packets of Rizla, fine cheeses,

29

tap dancing shoes, aged brandy, rubber catsuits, olives, titty tassels, cooking pots, excellent wine, violin strings, glittering theatrical fabrics, mouth-watering continental chocolates, bird's nest soup, sequins, oil paints, the *Times of India*, jugged hare, greasepaint, ravioli, real hair wigs, a brace of plump partridge, fake mink knickers, studio pottery, strings of garlic, kinky boots, salami, chefs' hats, chequered trousers and electric dildos. If you're hunting for something tasty, useful, glamorous, wacky, wonderful or weird, chances are you'll find it somewhere in Soho's narrow streets.

In the fields of medieval Soho, lepers were nursed at St Giles hospital, well away from the city's dense and terrified population. Lepers had been outcasts from biblical times, right up until modern medicine found an effective treatment for their disfiguring and contagious condition. They were required to ring a bell to warn of their approach, and the word 'leper' is still used to demean those deemed 'unclean', unwanted and beyond the pale. It seems appropriate that the despised lepers should find refuge in a place that was later to go on to welcome other kinds of outcasts from all over Britain and mainland Europe, as in the following centuries, wave after wave of political, economic and religious refugees found a home in Soho, along with our own home-grown bohemians, oddballs and social misfits.

The name of Covent Garden, immediately to the east of Soho, is a corruption of 'convent garden', and it was there that the monks of St Peter's Abbey grew fruit, vegetables and barley for their tables. The Abbey assumed ownership of the area in the tenth century, and, although the garden wasn't mentioned until around 1200, they must have been doing something with the land during the intervening time. The Abbey's garden has often been seen as the beginning of Covent Garden's long association with produce, which was to last until the sixties, but the area's history as a market is now believed to go back even further, into the Saxon period. It is thought that the Venerable Bede, writing in 731, was describing it when he mentioned 'a metropolis' and 'a mart of many peoples coming by land and sea'.

Archaeological digs in Covent Garden have revealed that it was settled by Saxons some two hundred years after the Romans upped sticks and abandoned Londinium, and Britain, at the beginning of the fifth century. They developed a port on the gravel banks of the Thames where, thanks to the intervention of Victorian engineering, the Strand now stands high and dry. It was here that the 'many peoples' gathered to trade. And, of course, although the produce has gone, people still come by land, sea and, nowadays, air to wander through a modern market that sells souvenirs, trinkets and handmade bits and pieces at bijou little shops and the odd market stall.

Henry VIII took Covent Garden from St Peter's Abbey and gave it – along with the title of first Earl of Bedford – to John Russell to reward his services as a soldier and a diplomat. It was not until the third Earl, Edward Russell, that the family built a mansion on the estate lands. Until then, like other gentry of the time, the Russells had a mansion on the Strand with fine river views

31

and easy access to the Thames, which, in the absence of any roads better than rutted tracks and lanes, was the main thoroughfare for London and its environs.

Bloomsbury, north of Covent Garden, was yet another place that Henry VIII grabbed. This time he ousted some Carthusian monks. The area's name is thought to derive from the name of one William Blemund, who had a manor house there in the early Middle Ages. Henry gave the property to the Earl of Southampton for services rendered. Later, a descendant married into the Russell family, and the properties were amalgamated.

There was originally a nunnery on the site of the parish church of St James at Clerkenwell, east of Bloomsbury, while the Knights Hospitallers of St John of Jerusalem had their headquarters somewhere in the area. Oliver Cromwell lived in Clerkenwell Close, and in the seventeenth century the place became very fashionable. Before it was built up, it was a kind of resort, where Londoners disported themselves at tea gardens, Sadler's Wells and health spas. Clerkenwell Green was the centre of the old village, before London outgrew its walls and crept out to meet it. The term 'green' is a little misleading, as there hasn't been any grass here for three hundred years or more. It is dominated by the old courthouse, an imposing building that is now a Masonic hall. Clerkenwell has long had a mixture of housing, offices, pubs and flourishing workshops that have given it a particular character and identity.

In the 1880s, Clerkenwell witnessed a mass influx of Italians looking for work. Like others who came before and since, they brought their trades with them: making mosaics and terrazzos (mosaic floors), organ grinding, knife grinding and plasterwork, which included making plaster saints for churches and shrines. They also brought roasted chestnuts to our streets, a strong, tasty and fragrant memory from my own childhood.

When grinding barrel organs ceased to bring in a living wage, the grinders turned to catering. Many of the Italians who worked in Soho's restaurants lived in Clerkenwell. By the turn of the twentieth century, it was known as 'little Italy' and the poorer workers lived in appalling slum conditions. There are still workshops in the area that continue some of the traditional trades brought to London from Italy, while St Peter's at 136 Clerkenwell Road, 'the Italian church', still caters for Italian Catholics and keeps the language, culture and customs of Italy alive in the West End.

At St James's, south-west of Soho, Henry VIII, having finally rid himself of his first wife and the Church of Rome, built a new palace for himself and his new consort, Anne Boleyn. Henry's desire for a new queen has long been seen as the main catalyst for all this upheaval in Church and state, although modern scholarship suggests that the situation was far more complex than that. The Church of Rome was far too greedy, corrupt and ambitious for the Tudor king's liking: it had to go. Anne was simply the spark that finally lit a fuse that had been laid for some time. Whatever the reason, getting shot of Rome's influence resulted in the dissolution of the monasteries and Henry taking over ownership of their green and pleasant lands to the west of the city.

St James's had once been very isolated: in the twelfth century there was a leper hospital for women on the site, which later passed into the hands of Eton College. By the sixteenth century though, it was a desirable location near the seat of government, which is why Henry wanted it. Before building commenced, the king, true to form, gave Eton its marching orders, coercing the provost into swapping the land for a bit of Suffolk. Eton College, however, stayed near Windsor.

It could be argued that, despite the six wives, Henry remained a bachelor at heart, always enjoying the pleasures of a single man, including gambling, fornicating, drinking, hunting and hanging out with the lads. In the decades after Henry's death, St James's became a kind of haven for well-to-do single men about town, where they could gamble, booze, swear and play. Pall Mall, St James's main thoroughfare, began life as a court on which young bloods could play the game of pell mell – a cross between croquet and golf – and be as uncouth as only a bunch of young men can be, without the troublesome influence of their women to rein them in.

They all acted pretty much like old Henry, basically, although, rather than the nasty beheading thing he went in for when someone upset him, they had duels. The last duel of honour in London took place in St James's. Once again, there's a sort of eerie continuity about the fact that the place has long been associated with young (and not so young) men, from the days of Eton College ownership, through Henry and his pals and on to the foundation of many gentle-men's clubs there, beginning in 1693 with White's; several of these clubs survive to the present day. This preponderance of testosterone also explains the nature of the shops that St James's has long been famous for: high-class tailors, Lock's hatters, wine merchants, makers of monogrammed silk shirts, bespoke shoes and expensive guns, as well as art galleries.

That small area provided just about everything that a well-heeled chap from the top drawer of society could possibly have ever wanted, includ-ing the baths and bagnios they frequented to purchase sexual pleasure. By Regency times, the area was a favoured spot with dandies and beaux who would ogle any passing female. The ogling explains why there was a lack of upper-class women there, although there would certainly have been servants and prostitutes who simply had to put up with the leers and lechery.

Mayfair, west of Soho, is named after a fifteen-day fair that began in 1686 on the site of what is now Shepherd Market. By 1709, the local gentry had decided it lowered the tone of the place and had it suppressed. The area first became fashion-able with the nobility because it was within such easy toadying distance of St James's Palace and the monarch, and belonged chiefly to the Grosvenor, Berkeley and Burlington families, who all had estates there. Sir Richard Grosvenor, already very rich, decided to increase his stash of cash by developing his land, and began building in 1700. Grosvenor Square, where the American Embassy in London is now, was the centrepiece of his design, which included broad streets and large town houses suitable for his friends and peers. Berkeley Square followed in 1738. Mayfair's third square, Hanover, honoured the new, German, royal family rather than a local landowner.

Mayfair started posh, and John Nash built Regent Street partly to make sure it remained that way. The famous street not only provided a link between the Prince Regent's home at Carlton House and Marylebone Park, but also acted as an effective barrier between 'the Nobility and Gentry' and the hoi polloi who made up 'the mechanics and trading part of the community'. Personally, I've always felt that keeping the lower orders at bay has done Mayfair no favours in terms of having a character and an identity of its own. Being the playground of the super-rich has made it, in modern parlance, a bit 'up itself', content to rest on its exclusive laurels. Even the prostitutes working from Shepherd Market and Park Lane have traditionally been seen as 'a cut above' those in Soho and Covent Garden, and consequently charged significantly more for their services.

Fitzrovia, the area immediately to the north of Soho, across Oxford Street was part of Lord Southampton's estate. When he found he needed to make some quick money, buildings were thrown up rapidly and sold off to service industries as early as the 1700s. The residential property built there in the eighteenth and nineteenth centuries was always let on short leases, which made for a shifting population. This is why the area has never had the same sense of community that both Soho and Covent Garden still enjoy.

Neither did it have the snob appeal that Mayfair and St James's had from their very inception, although some illustrious – and, it was rumoured, royal – names frequented gambling clubs and male brothels in Cleveland Street in the nineteenth century.

The name Fitzrovia was coined in the 1930s by the Bloomsbury Group, some of whom, such as Virginia Woolf, lived in Fitzroy Square – as did George Bernard Shaw. The square itself was built and named for Charles Fitzroy, Lord Southampton, in the late eighteenth century and the Adam brothers were its architects. The area had a strong bohemian and artistic presence. Augustus John drank at the Fitzroy pub with his arty cronies, as did Dylan Thomas when he was in town. Nina Hamnett was quite a fixture there too. There was always a sense, in this regard, that Fitzrovia envied Soho: its loucher denizens even tried calling it 'North Soho' at one point, but the name never really caught on.

In the seventeenth century, those who owned acreage west of London began to see the development potential in land that was so near the King's court and the growing mercantile centre of the city. There was serious money to be made, and Francis Russell, the fourth Earl of Bedford, was one of the first to see it. He set about building the first planned development at Covent Garden. Charles I duly issued the necessary licence to build, despite the monarchy's traditional reluctance to allow building so close to London. Money – perhaps as much as £2,000 – apparently changed hands between Bedford and the King, an early instance of corruption in the West End.

An ambitious plan was hatched to build town houses for the gentry and a large square in the Italian style. The great architect, Inigo Jones, probably played some part in the design, although how much is not entirely clear. When completed, the Piazza astonished Londoners. It was a large open space bounded on the west by the church of St Paul, on the north and east by arcaded houses and on the south by the wall of Bedford House. It served as a meeting place for all comers, rather than a private garden for those who lived around it, as was the case in the other West London squares that were built in its wake.

There were other innovations as well. The haphazard tangle of roads and lanes that had followed the long-gone field boundaries of medieval farms and smallholdings were swept aside in favour of a neat grid of streets lined with smart houses, at least in Covent Garden's initial development. Things developed in a more haphazard fashion around and about, where there was no single landlord.

Russell's plans for Covent Garden were, however, upset by the Civil War. The gentry did not take up tenancies as the Earl had hoped, as it was not safe for Royalists to linger in London. Less exalted tenants were sought and found for the Piazza, and a bustling market developed on its south side. Property development virtually ceased in the nascent West End during the hostilities and the Commonwealth period that followed. When it finally resumed in the eighteenth century, the gentry preferred the exclusivity offered by the squares further to the west of Covent Garden's Piazza and its environs.

By 1776, an anonymous writer, referring to the Piazza, could declare that 'One might imagine that all the prostitutes of the Kingdom had pitched upon this blessed neighbourhood', which shows just how low the area had sunk when compared with the fourth Earl's lofty ambitions. And thank goodness for that, because it created a vibrant neighbourhood, rich in contrasts and interest, that never existed in snooty old Mayfair. Over the years, a whole variety of businesses would settle there and thrive, including the produce market, which soon took on a wholesale rather than retail character, publishing houses, printing works, saddlers, coach builders and so much more.

Theatres, coffee houses, taverns and other places of entertainment were built there, initiating the idea that Up West was where Londoners went for a good time and adding immeasurably to the colour of the place. By the nineteenth century, the burgeoning market, as well as the various commercial enterprises and factories that had moved there, required a large workforce, and this in turn created a great demand for places to live. By the middle of the century, the ordered Piazza and the streets around it had long been surrounded by a hotchpotch of houses, narrow alleys and dingy courts that had grown organically over the previous century. When one hovel fell down – which they did remarkably frequently – another two were built on its footprint. The Covent Garden area contained dwellings for every station in life, from the great houses of the aristocracy along the Strand to truly miserable shacks, shanties and tenements for the lowly. The 'rookeries' around Seven Dials and St Giles church were one of London's most notorious slum areas, where life expectancy was unusually low and infant mortality unusually high even for the times. This state of affairs lasted late into Victoria's reign, when the slums were razed and new, wide streets, befitting the capital of the world's greatest empire were built.

The development of Soho did not have the cohesive initial vision that created Covent Garden, and so it grew in a more organic manner right from the start. In many ways this was an advantage. Although Soho was never as grand as Covent Garden, it never degenerated to the extent that its eastern neighbour did.

The first explosion in property development in Soho came in the fifty years following the Great Fire of London in 1666. The Fire rendered hordes of people homeless, and enterprising types saw a business opportunity in rebuilding houses and business premises to replace those lost. Many men were instrumental in the development of the area, and they have been immortalized in the streets that they named after themselves and their craftsmen – Gerrard Street, Wardour Street, Whitcomb Street, Sutton Court, Lexington Street and Beak Street, to name but a few. Few of these men were landed gentry. They were novices in the building industry, chancers who saw a way to make a few bob. Courtiers and craftsmen began to form partnerships. The former had clout at court, and were able to get the required permission to build, for a price, while the craftsmen could assemble teams with the required skills – bricklaying, plastering, woodworking, paving, roofing – to get the places up and running.

Because the initial building frenzy had been so hurried, much of the stock soon needed replacing. Building and reconstruction work continued into the eighteenth and nineteenth centuries, which accounts for the Georgian character of so much of Soho. The new streets boasted every kind of dwelling, from mansions for a royal bastard, the Duke of Monmouth, on Soho Square and slightly lesser gentry in Leicester Square, to courts and tenements for skilled workers, unskilled labourers, artists and artisans.

And skilled and unskilled workers arrived in their thousands, according to Richard Tames's *Soho Past*. He quotes a survey conducted in the 1890s, which estimated that there were more than four thousand foreigners living in Soho's square half-mile, comprising Germans, French, Italians, Poles, Swiss, Russians, Belgians, Swedes, Austrians, Dutch, Americans, Spaniards, Hungarians, Danes, Turks, Greeks, Portuguese, Romanians and Africans. The countries of origin of the last-named were unspecified, Africa being much of a muchness to the Victorians, apparently. Added to the list were a couple of Persians and a solitary Serb. The Chinese had not yet arrived; they began to trickle into south Soho after the Second World War, then poured in during the sixties.

Like other migrants before them, they brought their delicious food and colourful customs with them. The Camisa family, for example, were immigrants from Italy who have been bringing a taste of Italy to Soho for more than eighty years: 'My father and his brother came over in about 1920, when my father was thirteen and his brother sixteen,' remembered Alberto. 'There was no work in Italy. My aunt was over already, because she married one of the Parmigianis, who came from the same village in Italy, Tarsogno – in Parma ham country. My father was the baby of the family, number thirteen. It took them four days on the train to get here, across Europe; they did not know the language and had no money. They came to Soho because somebody from the village was already there.'

It is remarkable just how many of the immigrants listed in the Victorian survey have descendants still living in Soho. In a few cases, they are still beavering away in the same occupations and trades their ancestors brought from their homelands. Skills have been handed down through the generations. This is particularly true of catering, specialist shops such as delicatessens, wine merchants and pâtisseries, and the rag trade, but it was, in the past, true of all sorts of other highly skilled crafts.

It has been estimated that in the early eighteenth century some 40 per cent of Soho's population were French Protestants, known as Huguenots, who were escaping from religious persecution in their native land. They made and traded in tapestries and clothing in fine silks and wool, were silversmiths and jewellers, made clocks and watches, and sold wine, coffee and pastries. Jews

42

fleeing persecutions and pogroms in eastern Europe brought expert tailoring, among other things, while German refugees made and repaired musical instruments, the Italians and French brought good food and wine, and the Swiss, like the French, were known for their clocks, watches and scientific instruments.

For many, this cosmopolitan mix was the heart of the place. John Carnera came to Soho as a seven-year-old from Italy. 'I could not speak English. It was a new world to me, like being on a different planet. It was only when I went to school that I started to learn English, and in those days we all spoke Italian at home. It was a very happy time for me. I always felt that the best place I ever lived in my life was Soho. It was adventurous; in those days it was simple, and most of the people were foreign – they were either Italian, Spanish, French, lots of Maltese – so they were all immigrants anyway.'

Ronnie Mann's family had a long history in the West End. 'I think our lot came over from Germany in about 1800, from what I can gather; we traced them back to Petworth in Surrey. Apparently they come over to help the local farm, tend the cattle, whatever.' By 1849, the Manns were in business in Covent Garden, and the extended family assimilated people from all over Europe. 'My brother-in-law's name is Broulier; they were French Huguenots and came over centuries ago. My uncle's Schrader, his family's German; they came over in about 1900. My aunt's father was a Russian Jew from God knows where after the pogroms; a tailor, he was. My mate Roy

Harris, his family is Jewish. His name's not Harris – he told me it once, and I was pissing myself laughing – but he was like us, he had no concept of where he came from, or of his religion being important; he was just born into it.'

Pepe Rush's father was born in Soho. Despite his English-sounding name, his family also came from far-flung parts. 'When my grandad first came over, he went into the Post Office, and they asked him his name, and he told them [makes growling, consonantal noise], and they said "Where are you from?" "I am from Rooossia!" "OK, we'll call you Rush then."'

Sonia Boulter, another interviewee, told me that she 'was born in Newport Place, just behind Shaftesbury Avenue. Both of my parents grew up there, too. They went to school together, and eventually married. My mother's parents were immigrants from Italy, about 1900. I'm not too sure about my father's parents, but have always believed my grandmother was French and grandfather English. My Italian grandmother got killed during the Blitz, and my grandfather died when I was about sixteen. He couldn't speak a word of English. Not a word.'

It wasn't just Europeans who were pouring into the West End during the post-war period. Meru Ullah wrote to me that 'My father was the first Bangladeshi to settle in the Seven Dials, and our house, 52 Neal Street, was a place where all immigrants entering London would aim for. From there, they would move to the Midlands.'

I first experienced the West End as a visitor, when

44

my father took me with him on his forays into Soho to pursue his dream of being a writer. The place seemed remarkable and very different to me, even as a toddler. The sense of 'specialness' that hung around Soho could be intoxicating. Paul C, who grew up in a new town in Sussex in the fifties, told me how he loved to take the train to Victoria and walk the streets, just drinking in the atmosphere. 'There seemed to be so much going on. Not so many cars, of course, but lots and lots of people walking in the street, walking on the pavement, just looking. Lots of life going on, different nationalities working and enjoying themselves. You could hear different languages in the air, music, sounds of people working.'

When conducting interviews for this book, I always asked the people who grew up in the West End whether they were aware that they were living in a special place. Some saw it simply as home, but others felt privileged, such as Ann Lee, who grew up on Wild Street, just off Drury Lane. 'The West End was somewhere that people knew about, and there was a feel about it, and the fact that we used to get tourists, American people coming up and asking us the way to Buckingham Palace. The Palace was a walk for us. Down to Trafalgar Square, feed the pigeons, down the Mall, St James's Park, Buckingham Palace. You had the Waldorf Hotel in the Strand, and you'd be out for a walk and you'd see these ladies getting out of cars, fur coats and diamonds, and I'd say to my mum, "Oooh, look" and she'd say, "Yeah, in your dreams."

'If there was a première of something at Drury

Lane theatre, or the opera house, the Queen used to drive up Wild Street, very slowly, and we'd all be out, either side of the road. The light would be on in the car and she'd wave to everyone. That was fascinating. You could go play on the grass and feed the ducks in St James's Park, then Dad would maybe buy a juice between us from the cafeteria. One glass of juice and two straws, and then we'd walk home. Horse Guards Parade was smashing, seeing the soldiers on parade was lovely. That was an everyday occurrence for us. People would travel hundreds of miles to see it, and we just had to wander down the road.

'There was a lot do. Although it wasn't laid on for you, it was there. We even used to go in the art gallery in the winter. We'd go for a walk, go in the National Gallery, to look at the paintings. How many kids of ten or eleven have got an art gallery on their doorstep? I knew about Monet and Constable, because they were my sort of pictures. My brother would rather have been kicking a ball, but I learned about art. You could go to the gallery, you could go and walk round a church. We used to go down and walk along the Embankment. I mean, if you walked down into the Strand, down a side turning and down some steps, you're on the Embankment, you can just walk along. There was a lot to see, and it was a bit special.

'We used to think, cor, this ours, you know? You could jump on a bus, it took you to Chapel Street market. You could walk to Berwick Street market, or walk up Oxford Street, because it wasn't that far. Everything was on your doorstep, really. It was lovely, really lovely.'

Mike O'Rouke, who grew up in the Seven Dials, enjoyed the simple pleasures the West End offered in post-war Britain. 'When my grandfather was alive – he died in 1953 – he used to take me out and about a lot. He'd take me down to Trafalgar Square, we used to go down the Strand, he'd take me down the Embankment a lot. We used to like to walk over Hungerford Bridge to see the trains. There was the building going on for the Festival in 1951. I used to love to stand under Waterloo Bridge. The trams used to come out from the tunnel under Kingsway, and I would stand there and watch them change the points, for hours.

'I got a second-hand bike when I was about eleven. I used to go around Kingsway and Lincoln's Inn Fields, places like that. And that was great. That was the first time I found out where the Old Curiosity Shop was, around the back of Lincoln's Inn. I always thought it was a made-up name but I went down this street one night and I saw it on the corner.'

It was only later, when Mike went to grammar school way out in the wilds of West London – there were few places in the West End for those who passed their eleven-plus – that he became aware how special other people thought his manor was. 'We went down to Stukeley Street, just off Drury Lane, one night, to see an Arts Theatre production of, I think, *Julius Caesar*. It was to do with school. The boys were walking back to the station with the teacher, about twenty of us. We walked back past my house, and I said, "See you, I live here." After that, as a teenager, all my school friends would go out on a Saturday night, for a drink or something, or the pictures, and all come round to my place, because it was the centre of London, you know. It used to drive my mum mad: "Oh, no, not them again."'

Although outsiders saw the West End as a homogeneous whole, those who lived there tended to stick to their own side of the Great Divide – or the Charing Cross Road, as the A–Z prefers to call it. Mike O'Rouke 'didn't mix much in Soho until I was older. Me dad used to take me to Chris's, the barbers in Old Compton Street, but growing up, I never really had any connection with the other side of Charing Cross Road. My manor was more the Dials and Covent Garden, you know.'

Jeff Sloneem, who lived in Old Compton Street, remembers the Great Divide from the other side. 'We didn't go to Covent Garden. I remember I very rarely crossed the Charing Cross Road. We went over Shaftesbury Avenue to Gerrard Street, because there was a post office there, but the only reason I'd have to cross Charing Cross Road was that I started collecting cigarette cards when I was a little kid, and there was a shop over there that sold them.'

When I quoted this to John Carnera, he said, 'I know what he means. Going across Cambridge Circus was like a divide, because in those days Covent Garden market was very much active.' The Sohoites tended, ironically, to see Covent Garden as 'foreign', while many in Covent Garden were alarmed by Soho's reputation for sin – although, as we shall see in later chapters, those who actually lived in Soho were rarely, if ever, touched by it.

Ann Lee, who came from a long line of Covent Gardeners, suffered more than most from the suspicions of their neighbours across the Great Divide. 'Us girls, as we were growing up, were told we mustn't go to Soho. Good girls didn't go to Soho. Of course we did go: my friend Alethea and me used to go to this coffee bar in Soho called Le Macabre. We couldn't go very often, because we didn't have a lot of money. If my mum had found out that I'd been to Soho, even though it was literally round the corner, I wouldn't have been allowed out for months.

'You couldn't go to the cinema in Leicester Square. You had to go to the Dominion, Tottenham Court Road, or somewhere else. All us girls that grew up there were told, Oh no, that's not a nice area for young girls to be on their own. We did go, obviously, because we wanted to have a look round. Our mums usually found out if we were somewhere that we weren't supposed to be. Because it was such a close-knit community, someone always knew you, so you couldn't get up to too much, because somebody would tell your mother. That's how it was. But we still did it, just hoped we didn't get caught.'

I'll leave the last word in this chapter with Peter Jenkins, whose father managed a large estate in Covent Garden. 'Where we lived, within spitting distance, was the Theatre Royal Drury Lane. And you had the Aldwych Theatre, and all those on the Strand. It was a very richly cultural place to live, and there was so much history there as well. I had Trafalgar Square, the Changing of the

49

Guard, Buckingham Palace, the Mall and White-hall and everything else on my doorstep, and that became essentially part of my childhood.

'My father was self-educated, and always pushed my interests in those ways. When I walked around the area with him on Sunday afternoons, he would point these things out to me, so I was always conscious I was at the centre of a very special place, and that I was part of the evolving history of a great city.'

2

During the War

Throughout the late forties and well into the fifties, the war and what came with it – rationing and austerity, bomb sites and bereavements, and a sense of drabness and dislocation – dominated people's lives and conversation. Everybody's life was marked out by the phrases 'before the war' and 'during the war', and the events of those years had a profound effect on what came later. And while some people in my parents' and grandparents' generation were adamant that they 'didn't want to talk about' the war, others could not shut up about it.

In the late fifties, when rationing was finally over and a little colour started to come back into Britannia's grey and sunken cheeks, some people started to feel nostalgic for the days of togetherness and the much-vaunted 'Spirit of the Blitz'. Personally, I could not see the appeal of queuing, singalongs in drab bomb shelters or rest centres, and dodging flying masonry on your way to the British Restaurant to eat off-ration. Thanks, but no thanks.

Like me, Ann Lee was a post-war baby, but her family's experience of the Second World War was very different from that of my mother and father. They were living in the Peabody Estate in Wild Street, Covent Garden, when the Luftwaffe accounted for two of the estate's thirteen blocks of flats. 'Everyone always said the war was horrendous,' Ann remembers, 'but the community spirit there was built up by that, so that when I was born, in 1946, that was really strong. Obviously, as I got older, it changed slightly, but it was still very much a community.

'When those blocks were bombed, my mum's family lost their home. They were all safe down the shelter, but when they came out, everything was gone, the whole block. People just picked through the rubble to see if they could find any of their belongings. There was five or six children still living at home with my mum's mum in K block, and they all went and stayed with different neighbours. They put them all up on settees, or an armchair with a chair and a blanket. The blocks were never rebuilt.'

There was a limit to what could be done by neighbours, particularly in the Peabody Estate, where people were already packed in tightly. Families who had been bombed out usually began by going into rest centres, *ad hoc* facilities that

51

were housed in public or institutional buildings; schools were a popular choice, but offices and defunct hospitals and workhouses did just as well, or as badly, depending on your viewpoint. Barbara Jones, who went to St Clement Danes school in Drury Lane, remembers that, 'I went in one day in late 1943 and our cloakrooms were chock-a-block with mostly elderly women and small children. Hardly any men or younger women. We were directed not to leave our coats but to go up to the hall. There we were told that the Peabody Buildings had been bombed out in the night, and that our school was the rest centre for these people. They, and everything they still possessed, took up half the school, and we operated in the other half.'

Families who lost everything in the raids were re-equipped by voluntary organizations. Anne Payne tells us that her mother, who died in 1944 – of natural causes rather than enemy action – 'worked for the British War Relief Society, which evolved from the Bundles to Britain scheme. Clothes, bedding and so on were sent from America to help families who had been bombed out. She worked at their depot helping to sort consignments and allocate them to those in need.'

Ultimately, the goal was to rehouse people, especially those in key occupations, in the local area. Sometimes this meant a considerable upgrade, as the local authorities tried to meet the need by commandeering the more or less luxurious apartments in Bloomsbury and Mayfair that had been left empty when their wealthy tenants or owners had elected to sit out the war somewhere a bit less bomby. Families from the cramped and

52

narrow streets around Covent Garden market found themselves with addresses in Tavistock Square or Gower Street. Sonia Boulter recalls, 'My parents were bombed out of Newport Dwellings twice – it might have been three times. My mum told me we were housed somewhere in Park Lane, but because they had been brought up [in Soho], they didn't want to stay in Park Lane – more fool them!'

Long after the war was over, there were physical reminders in the shape of damaged people in the streets, and the damaged buildings – or rather the places where they had once stood. The words 'bomb site' entered everyday language. Right outside the kitchen window of my father's flat in Old Compton Street was St Anne's church tower, now without its church. By the time I got to know St Anne's churchyard, the church had been gone a while and the rubble cleared away. What I saw from our window was the tower, on the left as I looked out, a few trees in the churchyard and, on the side next to Wardour Street, opposite the tower, black metal railings and a gate that was left open during the day.

I used to play on a path and a paved area just in front of the tower. Either side of it were table tombs that I would climb over and sit on. There was a shed opposite, tucked away a bit in the corner, for the gardeners' tools. Gravestones lined the perimeter. On the Dean Street side of the tower was the bomb site, where the church had been. For a while, early in my memory, part of it was flattened for a car park, and there was a man there who had a bookstall laid out on a trestle table. He kept some stock underneath the stall, for 'the more discerning gentleman', who liked a bit of smut.

One of my interviewees, Leo Zanelli, was at home in Romilly Street in September 1940 when St Anne's Church was bombed. 'There were three distinct sounds,' he remembers. 'Whump, whump, whump, on the ground. We knew something had happened nearby. When we first came out in the morning, I looked up at the front of the church, and it looked all right, except the window looked a bit strange. As we crunched our way through all this broken glass towards it, I realized suddenly that I was looking through the window into the sky. The roof was gone.

'For many years after, the kids would play in the church, in the rubble with all those mosaic tiles. Halfway up the tower there was a room with one wall off, with silver or pewter plates on the other, and a big oak chest, and of course, being kids, we opened the chest and it was full of papers, absolutely full. Some of them were old, the ink had gone brown.

'I still have nightmares about this: we took armfuls of these things away, and we were trying to read them, then suddenly someone said, "If they catch you looting, they shoot you," so everybody crapped themselves and threw them on the fire. I don't know what happened to the plates and such.'

The unfortunate outcome of this adventure did not deter Leo and his friends from playing in the ruins. 'Some time after we went up the tower, we found an opening in the ground. Somebody said,

"Anyone got a torch, we've found this ladder going down." Of course we immediately assumed there was treasure down there, and that it belonged to the King of Corsica, who'd got this gravestone in the church. Much later, I discovered that he was someone who'd done something for the Corsicans, and they couldn't pay him so they gave him the title and an illuminated manuscript. He had died destitute, and people clubbed together to bury him.

'Anyway, my house was closest, about fifty metres away, so I ran back, got a torch, and we went down the ladder. It was all cold, pitch black and cave-like. So we switch on the torch and there are coffins on shelves, just a foot or so away. You've never seen people move so quickly. In the blink of an eyelid everybody was standing up top again. How we all got up the ladder at the same time, I don't know. We'd found the crypt, obviously.'

Leo and his mother generally took shelter during air raids in the Empire snooker hall across the road. The slate-bed billiard tables in the basement snooker hall – with no windows to be blown in – provided more protection than could be found in conventional Morrison shelters.

One of the abiding images of wartime London is of people sleeping on Underground tube stations, and although the stations in the West End did a roaring trade as shelters – Piccadilly slept up to four thousand people, for instance – few locals, it seemed, used them. Some used the newly built Lex Garage, others backyard Anderson shelters, or Morrison shelters set in the living room or under the stairs, while others used imaginative alternatives, like the Zanellis, or simply toughed it out. Because space was so scarce, safe shelters could not always be dug. Many schools had to improvise. 'I remember,' wrote Ray Constantine, 'when I was at school, sitting in the sandbagged areas by the coat hangers and sinks during the air raids.'

Although the East End, the City and the docks took the brunt of the Luftwaffe's attacks on London, the West End did not escape unscathed. Far from it. Sticks of bombs fell across Covent Garden and Soho, demolishing not only St Anne's Church, which copped it again in May 1941, but also part of Newport Dwellings and chunks of Old Compton Street.

A Civil Defence bomb incident photograph shows the aftermath of the raid that brought down part of Newport Dwellings in the early hours of 17 April 1941, killing forty-eight people, including Sonia Boulter's grandmother. Sonia pointed to the AFS man seen from the back in the foreground of this photo. 'I often wonder if that was my dad. He wasn't in the forces because he had TB, but he went into the Auxiliary Fire Service and I wonder if that can be my dad.'

Many men who were for one reason or another excluded from active service joined the AFS, fire-watching through the long nights of the air raids, often from high, exposed places. Volunteer labour like this was at a premium in the Blitz. As Sonia Boulter's schoolfriend, Maria Mechele, recalls, 'I was born during the war and remember going to the air raid shelter in Berwick Street. My dad was in the heavy rescue, and used to go out and help

56

dig the people out of bombed buildings.'

It must have been a desperate and harrowing job, digging through the rubble listening and looking for signs of life, but most of those who lived in London through the Blitz and the later doodlebug raids had nightmares to forget. The bombs left scars in people's minds, as well as on the landscape. On Saturday, 8 March 1941, one of the biggest raids of the Blitz scored a direct hit on the Café de Paris nightclub, killing bandleader Ken 'Snakehips' Johnson and more than thirty others. All told, that night's raids killed 159 people.

Newspaper reports concentrated on evoking the 'spirit of the Blitz'. *The Times* of 10 March reported that 'people living nearby made tea, and passers-by contributed handkerchiefs', while soldiers, who gravitated to the West End on a Saturday night, helped the wounded by applying field dressings. 'All agree,' *The Times* account went on, 'that there was the utmost coolness and much gallantry. "Don't bother about me," people with less serious wounds said over and over again. Rescue work began almost immediately. There were many wonderful escapes, and a fair number of people were able to walk out of the damaged building with no worse hurt than a bruised back or some cuts.'

One can hardly blame the newspapers for putting the best gloss on things, for emphasizing the positive, but things often looked different from ground level. An image from that day still haunts Leo Zanelli, who was ten years old at the time: 'My mother's brother, Uncle Peter, was an ambulance driver in the war. He was always coming to see us in Romilly Street after air raids to make sure we were all right. I remember once he came in, and he was in shock for ages. He'd gone into the Café de Paris. The bomb had fallen straight through the skylight on to the dance floor. My uncle had picked up his best friend's head. He used to stay awake at nights after that. Of course, he had to tell his friend's father that his son had just died, but the bomb had taken his head off cleanly. Head in one corner, body in another.

'He always remembered how, by the edge of the dance floor, there were a couple, still in their seats, and the man was offering the woman his cigarette case. You'd expect, a blast like that, people would be all over the place, and some were, but these two, although the concussion had killed them, they were just sitting there, natural.'

Leo carries other vivid nightmarish images from the war. 'I was in the snooker hall,' he remembers, 'so I didn't actually see it, but after a bomb, a soldier came down the street away from the scene covered in blood. When they took off his jacket to see what the damage was, there was a terrible scream, because his arm came off with it. The jacket was OK, not torn at all. Blast is a funny thing.'

The bombing was not all there was to fear. The blackout also claimed its victims. 'Where the La Capannina restaurant is now,' Leo remembers, 'on the corner of Romilly Street, there used to be an oil shop, a general hardware shop, and in the morning they found a soldier impaled on the railings outside. It must have been a burglary: he just stepped off the roof in the blackout. I didn't see it, but I heard people describe it to my mother; by the time I went out to have a look, they had covered it with a shelter. Apparently it was quite common for burglars to be killed by falling in the dark.'

Ray Constantine was another who experienced the horrors of war at first hand, even though he was a schoolboy at the time. His family had been bombed out. They were living in a rest centre: 'I was walking down Lisson Grove to school one day, when a lorry about four hundred yards away erupted. For an instant I couldn't breathe, then a deafening explosion knocked me over. Some time later, I got up and continued. There was a full arm in battledress on the pavement. I picked it up and placed it in the gutter. I was late getting to school, and said to the teacher, "Please, Miss, a bomb fell on me." There had been no air raid, but nothing more was said.

'I later worked out that the lorry must have been transporting a defused bomb that had somehow gone off. Then, recently, I watched a programme on UXBs. An old man was saying how bomb disposal used to disable the fuse with a large magnet, but that the Germans realized this and added a second, trembler device. He related how they had placed the magnet on a bomb in Marylebone, then loaded it into a lorry to take it to Regent's Park to be exploded. As his fiancée lived in Marylebone, he was excused the trip. The other five members of his team were all killed when the trembler blew it up in Lisson Grove.'

Ray also remembers that, 'in autumn 1944, in

broad daylight, I was riding a bus somewhere near Marble Arch/Oxford Street, and a very little way ahead there was an explosion: a building covering almost a block shimmered, and just collapsed, leaving a cloud of dust, and blocking the road. There was no warning, as it was a V2.'

Of course, living through war scarred people physically as well. One thing I remember vividly from those early postwar years is just how many injured men there were selling things on the city's streets: matches, razor blades, bootlaces, glass animals, hot chestnuts. There were those whose minds had fractured, and there were also the 'walking wounded'. Many ended up as sandwich-board men or pearl divers (washer-uppers) in restaurants, or simply spent their days moving from a doorway to a park bench, from the bench to a bomb site, from bomb site to an alley behind a café that gave its leftovers away. There never seemed to be enough hostels, and dry, warm places to doss down for a night were at a premium.

Barbara Jones and her sister, Pat, were evacuated at the beginning of the war, but her parents stayed behind in their home just south of the Strand. Mr Jones volunteered for the Auxiliary Fire Service. 'My dad,' says Barbara, 'prevented the Royal Society of Arts building from burning down by throwing incendiaries off the roof when the Little Theatre next door went up in flames – and received thanks, and a cheque, from the Society!'

Later in the war, Mr Jones was terribly injured in the bombing. 'He was put with the dead at first,' Barbara remembers. 'When they finally got around to dealing with him, they had to put his skull back on in nine pieces. He was written up in the American version of the *Lancet* as the Man Who Wouldn't Die. My mother was told he would never work again, that he might not see again, or grow hair again, all sorts of things he would never do again. If he had a bang on his head, he'd be dead.'

Barbara's sister, Pat, takes up the story. 'But he grew a shock of hair, he worked, he could see. When he was drunk, though, he would sometimes fall down and hit his head, and of course it would bleed like mad, and I'd be petrified.'

Another consequence of the war, and one that would make its presence felt, albeit in a different way, into the fifties, was how it liberated people sexually. As my mother – who had jostled to near the front of the queue when sexual liberality was being parcelled out – used to say that nothing loosened knicker elastic like the thought that you might die in the morning. For many, the last vestiges of Victorian repression decayed to dust in the face of all that transience. As Quentin Crisp wrote, in *The Naked Civil Servant*, 'As soon as bombs started to fall, the city became like a paved double bed. Voices whispered suggestively to you as you walked along; hands reached out if you stood still, and in dimly lit trains people carried on as they once had behaved only in taxis.'

London in general had filled up with young people – many, but not all, in uniform – looking for some kind of escape from the alternating periods of boredom and terrifying danger that made up military life. The influx of American troops from 1943 on brought a whole new culture and even more sexual openness into the mix, a development that sent Quentin Crisp into raptures. GIs 'flowed through the streets of London like cream on strawberries, like melted butter over green peas. Labelled "with love from Uncle Sam" and packaged in uniforms so tight that in them their owners could fight for nothing but their honour, these "bundles for Britain" leaned against the lamp-posts of Shaftesbury Avenue or lolled on the steps of thin-lipped statues of dead English statesmen... Above all, it was the liberality of their natures that was so marvellous. At the first gesture of acceptance from a stranger, words of love began to ooze from their lips, sexuality from their bodies and pound notes from their pockets like juice from a peeled peach.'

General licence and lawlessness followed this huge influx of people, all of whom were away from home and acutely aware that life could be brutally short and absolutely determined to have a good time while the going was good. After the war was over, the vice lords didn't quietly pack up their working girls and spielers and go home, and their punters didn't necessarily put their wallets away either. But there was a backlash. The fifties became particularly po-faced and judgmental, and would have killed all joy, had there not been strong resistance from those determined not to backslide into what had been before.

For them, the thought of a cheerless copy of their parents' lives, scarred by class snobbery, relentless poverty or 'quiet desperation' of one form or another, would not do. They wanted more, and they often found it by heading Up West. Soho was a magnet for the disaffected who having 'seen Paris' were determined not to land back 'on the farm', as the old song would have it.

The bohemian set that Dan Farson made famous in his book, Soho in the Fifties, were one such group. My father and his friends were another, while the birth of the teenager resulted from a new-found determination on the part of the young to reject the old values and certainties. A direct route may be traced from these post-war renegades through the West End of the fifties to the 'anything goes' attitudes of the swinging sixties.

Trust is one of the first casualties of war, and Soho's multicultural nature, its great pride, was sorely tested by the conflict in Europe. All three members of Soho's Italian community – John Carnera, Leo Zanelli and Alberto Camisa – that I talked to for this book had fathers who held an Italian passport. This was not a good thing to have after Mussolini declared war on the Allies on 10 June 1940, and there was trouble on the streets of Soho as the windows of Italian restaurants were smashed in by groups of people from other parts of London.

Within hours of Mussolini's declaration, Churchill ordered a round-up of Italian nationals as so-called 'enemy aliens', and within four days 1,600 London-based Italians had been taken into custody. No matter how long they had lived in England, all the adult Italian males in the West

End were detained and interned in camps for the duration of the war with Italy. For some, this was a very bitter pill to swallow, as restaurateur Peppino Leoni wrote in his memoir, *I Shall Die on the Carpet:* 'I deeply resented the fact that after thirty-three years in England with no political or police blemish on my record, I'd be scooped up without proper consideration.'

Ennio Camisa, co-founder of the Fratelli Camisa delicatessen, recounted what happened in Judith Summers's book: 'War was declared on Monday. The police came for me and my brother on Thursday, and said, "Just come with us, we want to ask you some questions at the station." We shut up our shop in Old Compton Street and we didn't know what was going to happen to it.'

The Italian men were first taken to Lingfield racecourse, and then on to a disused cotton mill in Lancashire. From there, more than 1,200 detainees, mostly Italian but some German, and nearly 100 POWs, were shipped out to Canada on the *Arandora Star*, a luxury liner that had been commandeered by the navy. On 2 July 1940, less than a day out of Liverpool, the unescorted *Arandora Star* was torpedoed by U-47, and sank with the loss of more than 800 lives, 613 of whom were detainees.

The rest of the Italian detainees were interned on the Isle of Man until 1944, when the Italian Partisans toppled Mussolini and caused Italy to change sides, turning the 'enemy aliens' back into the friends they felt they had always been. In a way, they were the fortunate ones, in being able to come back at all. The loss of fathers, grandfathers, sons and brothers to four years of imprisonment or death on the *Arandora Star* resonated through all the families who had come from Italy to make their lives in the West End.

Another legacy of the war was rationing, which, in the case of sweets at least, lasted to 1953. Peter Jenkins, whose family moved to the Peabody Estate in Wild Street in 1947, remembers sweet rationing very well. 'We took the coupons to a shop on Drury Lane, where we were registered. It was right opposite Clement Danes school, a grocery shop. Mum did a lot of her shopping there. My sweet ration was spent there on penny sherbets and liquorice dips.' Peter also remembers 'food parcels after the war – from your friend in Australia – tinned peaches, blackcurrant purée.'

I remember rationing, too, especially sweet things. In all the comics at the time – or at least the funny ones, such as the *Beano* – the most exciting thing that people could think of was unlimited grub, of golden piles of fish and chips, armfuls of sweets, huge pies with recognizable lumps of cow poking out, or bangers bristling from a massive mound of mash. That was what we kids wanted, more than anything: full bellies and sweet things with which to stop our gobs. The post-war restrictions only fuelled those feelings. So that was another effect of the war. It left post-war people hungry: for experience, family life, entertainment, normality, colour, beauty, all those good things; but also, importantly, for food.

Just as rationing was a hangover of the war, so was the black market that sought to subvert it.

Whenever authority seeks to make something – anything – desirable difficult or illegal to get hold of, there are those prepared to supply it for a price. This was true of booze in America's Prohibition days, it is true of pornography, illegal gambling, illicit sex and drugs, and, during the war, it was enshrined in the 'black market' that arrived hot on the heels of rationing and short-ages. Thieves raided warehouses, looted lorries and pilfered wholesale from the docks to meet the demand for iffy goods. The phrase 'it fell off the back of a lorry' tripped off the tongue of the 'spivs' who were the merchants in that market.

I suppose there must have been the odd black market trader who didn't favour loud clothing, a lounge-lizard moustache and leery behaviour, but I never saw him. No other individuals within society lived up, or down, to their stereotype the way spivs did. 'They used to stand on street corners and sell all sorts of things, anything you could think of,' Peter Jenkins told me. 'They had those big kipper ties, brightly coloured, and very often hats pulled down over one eye. The police used to move them on, but they were an essential part of West End life then. They could get you anything. Or so I believe. I don't know if my parents bought anything. I've got a feeling that my father was too morally upright.'

My father certainly wasn't. He took a pride in being able to lay his hands on little treats for us all when he was feeling flush, especially if, in doing so, he 'got one over' on authority. I am certain that his spiv acquaintances helped a great deal in this cause.

When I think of the Old Compton Street of my childhood, I am struck by just how crowded the streets were. Every doorway seemed to shelter a working girl, a 'man of the road', or gossiping neighbours. Street corners had an endlessly shifting population of men and women, who came and went, returned and drifted in and out to talk, to exchange services and goods. Prince Monolulu would sail majestically to his pitch in Soho Square, Ironfoot Jack would strike sparks from the pavements, and busy spivs flogged anything and everything to anyone with cash and a heartbeat. In this, and in other, more legitimate ways, the war led some people to prosper.

The story of the Constantine family is a case in point. 'In 1940,' Ray Constantine remembered, 'my father was working in an indifferent café in Cambridge Circus for £2 10s., 10 a.m. to midnight six days a week. We were bombed out of our house, very near the BBC, and had to go to the rest centre, which was in the Florence Nightingale Hospital for Gentlewomen, Lisson Grove. The LCC had taken over the basement as a British Restaurant and rest centre for people whose homes had been destroyed. The manager of the rest centre hadn't been able to open the British Restaurant, as there was no staff, so he hired my father as chef and my mother as assistant. They felt like pools winners, with wages of £5 and £3 10s., and a large rent-free flat at the very top of the hospital in the matron's quarters.

'Very early in 1942, they were assigned to the same job for the American Red Cross. An

American millionairess, Mrs Margaret Biddle, funded the whole show. The ARC (American Red Cross) occupied 10 and 11 Charles Street. I recall a lovely marble stairway leading up to the first floor, which was fully open and used as a ball-room. It was oak beamed, with suits of armour spaced along the walls, although the suits were removed and the oak beams were boarded up and wartime posters were stuck on the new walls. There was more affluence; a flat again, and £10 and £6, but both my parents worked more than twelve hours a day, seven days a week for that.'

One of the things that made me want to write about the West End's residents, as opposed to its vast array of visitors, was the sheer resilience shown by its people and the dogged propensity to reach for their goals through persistent hard work. Perhaps it is because so many West End families arrived Up West from somewhere else that it was in their nature to try new things, to roll up their sleeves and get stuck in. It takes courage and a pioneering spirit to begin again in a foreign country with strange customs and using an unfamiliar language.

The Camisa brothers exemplify this. 'My father, Ennio, and his brother, my Uncle Isidoro, came over in about 1920,' Alberto Camisa told me. 'My father was thirteen and his brother sixteen. There was no work in Italy.' Despite not knowing the language, the brothers worked hard enough for their aunt to start them up in their own shop in Old Compton Street. Things were ticking along nicely until the Camisa brothers were marched out of their shop to the internment camps in the

68

Isle of Man. When they saw the shop again, four years later, it belonged to someone else.

Eventually, the brothers took on a building in Berwick Street that the bombs had left semi-derelict. Fratelli Camisa rose again and with an enormous input of hard work, determination and staying power, they built their business up until it was one of the premier West End delicatessens and importers of Italian food and wine.

Theirs is not a unique story: Peppino Leoni rebuilt his beloved Quo Vadis restaurant after returning from the Isle of Man, and locals of every creed, colour and origin picked themselves up, dusted themselves off and started all over again. So that was another effect of the war; it made people work hard, to try to get back what they had had before. It taught them to buckle down. No wonder that almost every story I heard as I was growing up was rooted in time by reference to it. 'Before the war', 'During the war' or 'Just after the war': these words resonate through absolutely everything.

3

How People Lived

People from outside London, and indeed from other parts of the capital, know the West End as a playground or tourist destination, somewhere you go for shops, sights, shows and nights on the razzle. The streets are thronged with office-workers by day and theatre, cinema, restaurant and clubgoers by night. It rarely occurs to these visitors that anyone actually lives there, apart from the odd posh person: of course, the Queen has her place at the end of the Mall, and the Prime Minister is handily placed for a trip to the cinema, while presumably someone sometimes lurks behind the curtains and shutters of the genteel town houses in Mayfair, Knightsbridge, St James's and the Adelphi.

Even today, though, ordinary people live in the West End, usually above the ground floor or tucked away in side streets, or down back alleys. In the post-war decades, there were far more of them. Tens of thousands of native West Enders lived their lives largely out of sight, often in cramped and poky flats above the shops, cafés and restaurants set in the Georgian terraces that lined the streets of Soho and the West End. Although most of these had been built as family homes, very few remained in single occupancy by the end of the Second World War. There were also some late Victorian tenement houses on the Charing Cross side, such as Newport Dwellings (also known as Newport Buildings) and Sandringham Buildings – but very few houses.

Some Covent Gardeners also lived 'above the shop' in eighteenth- and nineteenth-century buildings, or in houses that had long ago been converted into flats. The area contained a great deal of what we now call social housing. This was built following the slum clearances of the 1870s and 1880s, when the Metropolitan Board of

Works used compulsory purchase orders to sweep away the worst of the slums defacing the West End. At the same time they created new streets, including Shaftesbury Avenue, Kingsway, Aldwych and the Charing Cross Road. There were several blocks of flats in private ownership, others run by the London County Council, and two Peabody estates. The last were built with funds provided by a London-based American banker and philanthropist, George Peabody, in the late nineteenth century to house London's 'respectable' (or employed) poor.

One of the Peabody estates was in Wild Street, just to the east of Drury Lane, and the other was in Bedfordbury, which runs parallel to St Martin's Lane. Wild Street was one of the largest of the Peabody estates, with 347 tenements in thirteen blocks, while in Bedfordbury, five blocks were squeezed into a much smaller site. Both had a higher density of tenants than their equivalents in the East End, because the clearances of the Covent Garden 'rookeries' – a generic term for areas where tall, decrepit houses were crowded along dark access alleys no more than three or four feet wide – had displaced so many people.

Despite the great size of many Victorian families, the tenement flats in both the Peabody and LCC blocks tended to be small. Some were just bedsits, and in most the kitchen – equipped with a coal-fired range (also known as a 'black grate') or gas cooker – also served as the living room and an auxiliary bedroom. Every flat shared a toilet, sink and wash-house with the other flats on their landing. There were no bathrooms. Graham

71

Jackson 'used to have friends in Sandringham Buildings in Charing Cross Road, by Cambridge Circus. They were little tiny flats, and my father used to say you could sit on the toilet, cook your breakfast and have a shave at the same time.' The cramped flats and narrow corridors afforded young Graham and his pals the opportunity for mischief: 'The doors used to face each other and we'd tie the knockers together, knock on one door, and of course the woman would open the door, and when she closed it, she'd knock on the door opposite, and so it went on.'

The converted flats in Soho were no bigger, and often no better appointed, than those in the tenements. Toilets were rarely put inside houses, while bathrooms were very much a luxury fitting in new houses until well into the twentieth century: they were rarely plumbed into old houses and flats until after the Second World War. The age of the housing stock in Soho and Covent Garden meant that Victorian conditions persisted well into the fifties, and those interviewed for this book often remembered not only their first bathroom, but also the replacement of gas lighting with electricity in the fifties.

My father's flat, at 61 Old Compton Street, was three floors above a delicatessen. The front door, set between the deli and what, in 1956, became the famous 2I's coffee bar, gave on to a steep, dark staircase that wound up to a flat that had been intended as the servants' quarters when the house was built a century and more earlier. There was a small living room and bedroom at the front, with sloping walls and ceilings following the roof line. At the back, a room had been converted into a tiny bathroom with an Ascot (a gas water heater that exploded into life at the turn of the hot tap), and there was a kitchen with a gas cooker. The kitchen also served as a dining room, although I remember the kitchen table more as Father's desk, with his typewriter, untidy piles of paper and ashtrays overflowing with the oval stubs of the Passing Clouds he smoked when in funds. At the front, the windows looked out on the rooftops of Old Compton Street and Wardour Street beyond, and at the back they provided a view of St Anne's churchyard.

I have many memories of the stream of visitors passing through this small flat, including Father's drinking and gambling buddies, fellow writers, criminals and celebrities, but one of my most treasured is of feeding a pigeon that came every day to the kitchen windowsill for his breadcrumbs and crusts. I christened him 'Crooky', because of his distinctive bent beak. Perhaps the spookiest experience I had while researching this book came during the interview with Chas McDevitt, who briefly lived in the top floor of number 59, next door. He volunteered that he used to feed what was obviously the very same bird, although he dubbed him Ikey.

Jeff Sloneem spent the first eight years of his life just across the road from Father's flat. 'I lived in 62 Old Compton Street, above a greengrocery. We were on the second floor, and basically, you walked in, there was a living room with a kitchen, a little back room, then there was a bedroom, and that was it. It was part of a Georgian terrace that

73

came to an end at my uncle's tailor's shop.' The part of the terrace beyond Jeff's uncle's shop had been blitzed.

Some of the tall, narrow houses above shops or cafés were split between flats and businesses, legitimate and otherwise, which meant that Soho families shared their space with the workrooms of jobbing tailors, tiny offices or perhaps a working girl or two. Janet Vance's situation was typical: 'I grew up at 11 Frith Street on the corner of Bateman Street, diagonally opposite the Dog and Duck. It was a café with flats above, and my dad had a gambling club in the basement. There were two flats on the first floor, two on our floor, and one at the top. Girls, prostitutes, lived in the other flat on our floor, but they didn't interfere with anybody, or work from there. Different girls worked from the two flats on the first floor.'

Ronnie Brace never lived in Soho, but used to visit his mother's sister in Windmill Street. 'My aunt lived about 30 yards past the Windmill on the right-hand side. She had a flat, one bedroom, small rooms, on the second floor; I remember walking up the rickety stairs. She worked for a Jewish tailor who had a workroom on another floor and she would work there, or bring stuff into the flat. She used to repair clothes, trousers.'

Chas McDevitt had several flats in the West End. 'In '58, I lived at the Cambridge Circus end of Old Compton Street above what became a dirty book shop, but was then just a closed-up shopfront, on the second floor. I looked there about fifteen, twenty years later and they still hadn't changed the curtains! Filthy things, they were. I was on the road a lot, so it was just a place to crash. There was virtually a brothel next door, and when the girls knew I was leaving to get married, they wanted to know if they could have my flat.'

For John Carnera and his family, their Soho flat came with a job attached. 'I landed in England on 1 March 1947 with my mother and brother, and we went to live in 45 Dean Street. My father worked at Gennaro's restaurant, and we had the second and third floor above – well, 44 was actually the restaurant, 45 was a bar leading into it, and we were above that. We lived there for twelve years, above what became the Groucho Club.

'On the first floor, above the restaurant in 44, there was another large dining room, which was used for functions, and in 45 the first floor was a changing room for the waiters and whatever. The second floor was our bedrooms, and then on the top floor we had our front room and kitchen.

'In the early fifties, the Gennaros kindly built us a bathroom. Before that, we used to use the restaurant's toilets, and wash there. We had to go down to the first floor, through the banqueting room – which was usually empty – to get to the cloakrooms. So that was not convenient. You had to time going to the toilet when the restaurant wasn't open. You were looking at the morning, between three in the afternoon and six in the evening, and then after eleven at night. Imagine that!'

Owen Gardner's family home also came with his father's job: 'We moved from Somerset to live in Upper St Martin's Lane in Christmas 1946, and were there for ten years. My father worked for Page's, the caterers' suppliers in Shaftesbury

Avenue, and the family lived over Page's main warehouse, which occupied a whole block.

'Before the war, the buildings belonged to Aldridges' Horse Repository. During the war, the building was used as a garage for the NAAFI, and they had it completely altered. Page's took it on after the war as a warehouse. Our flat on the first floor was all converted offices. Our toilet had "Ladies Toilet" painted in gold on the door. It was difficult to find anywhere to live in those days, just after the war; although these were just offices, we didn't mind.'

The lack of housing was a pressing problem in the years immediately following the Second World War. In the East End and the suburbs, prefabricated houses ('prefabs') were built on land cleared by the devastating Blitz years, but these were not provided for West End people whose homes had 'copped it'. As a result of this, those West Enders who did have a place to live hung on to it. Peter Jenkins's father was the Superintendent of the Wild Street Peabody Buildings in the late forties and the fifties. 'In post-war London, if you got a flat you were in clover,' he remembers. 'And you didn't do anything to jeopardize that tenancy. You didn't do any deals on the side; that would get you evicted. You didn't sublet – that was one of the strict rules. You couldn't have a lodger. You couldn't co-habit, you had to be married. In all those years I lived there, I can hardly remember a crime at all. You would have been out on your ear.'

It was not just that people were worried about finding somewhere else to live. The tenement buildings themselves inspired a great deal of love, as Sonia Boulter testified. 'Newport Buildings was a tenement building but I loved it. I sobbed my heart out when I left. I didn't move out of there until I was thirty-one, when they pulled it down. I didn't want to move. My parents were born there, my brothers were all born there, and so was I, in 1940. Actually in the Buildings.'

Ann Lee, who lived in the Wild Street Peabody Buildings, also remembers how living close to one another fostered a feeling of togetherness. 'The Buildings were a very close-knit community. There were eleven blocks all together – J and K block got bombed during the war – and about twenty-five flats in each. Some were one bedroom, some were two. Some were what they called a bedsit, just one room, set in the middle of the landing.'

For some, the sense of community was not simply a matter of living cheek by jowl; it was a family affair. 'Everybody in the Bedfordbury had big families,' remembers Ronnie Mann. 'I come from a family of five. My uncle who lived below us had seven kids. I had three other lots of aunts and uncles living in Bedfordbury. They all had more than three. Five or six wasn't unusual. Another aunt lived in the other buildings, in Wild Street. When my brother got married, he got a flat in Wild Street. I was offered one, but didn't take it, I stayed in Bedfordbury.' All five of the Mann children slept in bunk beds in a single room when they were young; as they got older, the family was moved down from 12E on the second floor to 5E on the first floor, and a rare three-bedroom flat.

The way the tenements were setup meant that

people more or less had to get on with their neighbours. Sharing was a way of life. Ronnie Mann again: 'There was five flats to a landing, you had toilets at the end. You literally just had your rooms: three rooms for the seven of us. There was the coal box as you come in on the right, in a little alcove, then the three rooms in a row, no corridor. In the living room was the gas cooker and a coal fire, and a fire in the other two rooms. No inside toilet. The man in the middle of the landing, the three living next door to me and us seven made eleven – we all used one toilet, and shared a cold water butler sink, where you could fill up your kettle or whatever. There was no running water in the flat. Laundry was done by hand in a wash house, where every flat had one day a week. That was all you had, it was as simple as that. You just got on with it.'

Some of the local flats were particularly run-down. An LCC block on Macklin Street had a reputation for being a bit rough, and some of those in private ownership, such as the Bells at the bottom of Drury Lane, were positively decrepit. The Jackson family had been moved from Shorts Gardens in Covent Garden to rather more salubrious surroundings in Bloomsbury following intervention by the Luftwaffe, but Olga Jackson and her much younger brother Graham still remember visiting their gran in her flat in Crown Court, at the back of Bow Street police station. There were three tenement blocks there, named after theatrical types – Sheridan, Beaumont and Fletcher Buildings – 'where the front door would come out on to the balcony, and you'd go in and

78

you'd step straight into the living area, like a bedroom-cum-everything. There was a little scullery out the back, with a toilet, where a policeman used to watch Gran undress. I thought they would have had better things to do than watch her undress.'

Peter Jenkins's father's duties included the collection of rents and the management of a team of porters, who were all residents and worked for very little money, as they had their flats in lieu. They fetched and carried, looked after the general upkeep of the estate – painting and the like – and carried out small repairs. 'Generally,' his son remembers, 'he had to keep an eye on what was going on. He didn't actually do the letting, but his recommendation counted very much. There were a few bad eggs, but basically it was a pretty stable society. Anything illegal, they would have been given notice to quit. You never abused your flat; you kept it in good nick. You made sure your doors were clean, your step was clean.'

For those tempted to let things slide, there were stark warnings of what could happen in the streets all around. 'Drury Lane and Covent Garden was a big tramp area,' Peter remembers. 'At the top of Kemble Street, on the corner of Drury Lane, was Bruce House, a Salvation Army type hostel. Tons and tons of down-and-outs, particularly in the immediate post-war years, would spend their time sitting or shuffling around outside there, or spitting in the corners, things like that. Very sad cases, a lot of them, often ex-servicemen who'd been severely damaged in the world wars.'

There were 700 beds in Bruce House, and a further 344 cubicles in nearby Parker House. Local residents tended to look upon these hostels as a necessary evil. Olga Jackson, who was born not far away before the war recalls, 'You were told, keep away from those places, but at least there was a place for homeless people to go. They might have been infested, because they used to fumigate them every so often, but nobody needed to be without a bed.'

Her brother, Graham, got to know both places pretty well in the sixties. 'When I went into the funeral trade, you had to go in there and get the bodies out – and in the morning they were rank. The worst place of all was down by the Italian hospital, in Old Gloucester Street in Blooms-bury. That was a women's one. That was awful, believe me.'

The hostels were intended for single working men, but naturally attracted the homeless, the damaged and the alcoholic, who would hang around the area during the day, no matter what the weather, cadging handouts from people in the market and passers-by. Graham Jackson remembered that, 'Down Drury Lane there was an electric substation, and the heat used to come out of a vent. The down-and-outs would sit in there: there was like a little alcove, and they used to huddle in there, I often used to see them.'

Then, as now, London was a city of contrasts: just a few minutes' walk away from where the homeless huddled for warmth, there was great wealth. On the other side of the Strand, a little along from the Savoy, is the area known as the

Adelphi, where Barbara Jones's parents moved in the late thirties, when she was a baby. Her father was a caretaker-cum-housekeeper in a business premises behind the Tivoli, and they lived in John Adam Street, in the basement.

'As a family, we had no money and were, effectively, servants,' she says; but their surroundings rubbed off on them. 'I was discouraged from visiting the Peabody Buildings children I knew from school. My parents had to be very cautious because we lived in a business house and had to enter by the front door, along with the rich and influential clients, so we had to be above "comment" at all times! Because we were the housekeeper's children, we always had to be dressed like "young ladies".'

Although she had a prestigious address, Barbara was always conscious of living in someone else's property. It was hardly the lap of luxury. 'There was never daylight in our flat. It was electric light all the time.' There were some perks, though: 'The Embankment Gardens were our garden, and the river was at the bottom of it – although we knew better than to have anything to do with the water.'

Several other people I contacted told similar stories; instead of living 'above the shop', as in Soho, they lived 'below the offices'. Angela Rashbrook told me how, before the war, her parents were jointly employed as house managers in an office building near the Central Hall in Westminster. After he was demobbed, her father was reallocated to be house manager at Norfolk House in St James's Square, and Angela moved

81

into the flat there in December 1945, when she was three. When her father died in 1969, she and her mother had to leave, as the flat was tied accommodation and went with the job.

Andy Pullinger had a similar experience. 'We moved to St James's Square when I was still a baby: my father was a caretaker for Distillers Company Ltd at 21 St James's Square.' Andy enjoyed living in the heart of clubland: 'I had a paper round for a newsagent in Crown Passage. The round took me all over the area from Green Park to Piccadilly, the Haymarket, St James's Palace for the guards and the higher-ups near the Burlington Arcade and Old Bond Street. It was great at Christmas, as the tips were so good.'

Anne Payne grew up in Knightsbridge. Her parents had split up when she was just a baby, and early in the war she and her mother went to live at 41 Montpelier Square, now one of the most prestigious addresses in London. In 2004, number 41 was sold for £3.2million, but during the war it was run as a lodging house, with a colourful collection of long-term residents. Anne's maternal grandmother managed it for the owners, who had found somewhere less likely to be bombed to live in for the duration. Anne and her mother had their own small flat at the back on the ground floor, complete with the luxury of a bathroom. When her mother died she moved in with her grandmother.

'After the war,' she told me, 'my grandmother's job ended when the house was either sold or reclaimed by the owner as a home – I'm not sure which. She got a job just two doors away, working as a housekeeper to Sir John Prestige – of Prestige Kitchens fame – in his London home.' Anne and her grandmother lived at number 43, next to the King George IV public house, until 1957. Her grandmother's job was not too onerous, as 'Sir John only came up a couple of days a week.' The dusting could be a chore, though. 'One of his hobbies was collecting clocks; he had quite a few grandfather clocks. One, in his sitting room, was quite large, in a glass case. It had a sun and moon that moved around, and apparently there were only two or three like it in the whole world. It's quite strange to be in a large house like that, on your own with all these clocks ticking and chiming away.

'We had a small sitting room on the ground floor and two bedrooms out the back, with a private courtyard garden' – Anne was the only West Ender I spoke to who grew up with a garden of her own – 'and the run of the basement. There was a bathroom and toilet down there, and a huge kitchen, which had a double gas cooker, a fridge – the first one I'd ever seen – and one of those dumb waiters: you turned the handle to winch it up to Sir John's sitting room. That was fun. There were several pantries off the kitchen, and a boiler room at the back.' This luxurious house had been a draper's shop until 1927, when Sir John ripped out the double shop-front and installed a front door with a fanlight above and a garage entrance.

Large luxury flats could also be found in Bloomsbury. When the Jackson family was bombed out of their home in Shorts Gardens, by the Seven Dials, they were rehoused in Ridg-mount Gardens, in an Edwardian mansion block. As Olga remembers, 'They commandeered all these vacant accommodations to house people, and that's how we got in. We stayed until 1966. The company wanted the flats back, so you either bought it, or they rehoused you. They were nice flats, quite selective.'

Her brother Graham, who was born in Ridg-mount Gardens, takes up the story. 'They were all seven-room flats. As you went in, to the right, there was like servants' quarters, a bedroom there, and a toilet and a sort of bathroom, and then there was a bedroom and the main scullery and kitchen up that end, and the rest of the rooms, and what they did was split them, so they'd become two- and three-bedroom flats.' The flats that had not been commandeered housed the well-to-do, including celebrities such as Hylda Baker, Jimmy Jewel of Jewel and Warriss, the actress Brenda Bruce and the pneumatic actress and singer, Yana, who made such an impression on young Graham that he mentioned her four times. 'And then,' says Olga, 'there was Koringa, who used to live down in the bottom. She used to keep snakes and things in the bathroom. She used to perform with snakes. I always remember running past her door, because I'd heard stories of these snakes.'

A common stereotype of the posher areas of the West End was the 'kept woman' – a phrase I've never liked, as it smacks of pets in cages – in her Mayfair mews or bijou apartment. It wasn't that far from the truth, as Owen Gardner remembers. 'When we moved out of St Martin's Lane, when it was redeveloped, we moved into a flat in Cavendish Mews South, in Hallam Street, at the back of the BBC. The guy who owned Pages had had one of his girlfriends at this flat. When he died, about 1949, his sister and brother-in-law inherited the business, and along with it these various women. He had one in Cavendish Mews South, one down in Camberwell somewhere and another in Aldford Street in Mayfair – he had them spread all over London.

'Anyway, she was on the payroll, this woman. I used to take her pay packet to her every week – which was quite embarrassing for me. I would hand over the money, she'd say thank you and close the door. Somehow, in '56, they got her out, and my whole family moved in. It was a beautiful flat, and we lived there until my parents retired back to Somerset.'

The clear and steady light of gas – much closer in colour to daylight than any electric lamp – was a defining feature of Victorian London, but its use extended well into the New Elizabethan age. Most of the street lighting around Soho and Covent Garden was gas, with lamps mounted on short posts and lit by hand. The mysterious figure of the lamplighter, a dark-garbed middle-aged man, and his arcane skills with his ladder and the long wand that was the tool of his trade fascinated me as a child. I was not the only one. Peter Jenkins waxed quite lyrical about him: 'The lamplighter, oh the lamplighter! Every night, towards dusk, he came round to light the gas lamps, with a long pole to flick open the casement and light it.' He used to come round in the mornings, too, after sunrise, to turn off any lamps that had not gone off automatically, as they should. I remember seeing him on a winter's morning, his breath hanging in a mist before him as he went from post to post.

I was surprised to find how much lighting, domestic and workshop, relied on gas mantles. These were chemically treated gauze covers that enclosed gas jets and became incandescent when heated by the flame. They gave the most wonderful soft, natural-looking light that was appreciated by the rag trade in particular – colours were easy to match – and by those with ageing skins. Harsh artificial light adversely alters both colours and skin tone. All my contacts at the Peabody Buildings remembered gas lamps being replaced by electric lights at around the time of the Coronation, while, most unusually, Janet Vance recalls that her family moved out of their electric one-bedroom flat in Frith Street in 1959 into a 'two-bedroom place in Pulteney Chambers, an eighteen-flat block off Brewer Street, that used to have the little gas mantles'.

While electricity had largely replaced gas for lighting by the mid fifties, coal remained the number one choice for heating in the post-war decade. Peter Jenkins remembered that 'Charringtons was the coal merchant for the area. In those days, around Covent Garden, everything was delivered by horse and cart, and the coal wagons had big horses to pull the weight.' One of his father's jobs as Superintendent was to arrange the weekly coal delivery to the Buildings, and its distribution to the residents. 'When the coal delivery men came, they would bring it to the bottom of the stairs in each block, and the porters had to carry these ruddy great hundred-weight [50 kilo] sacks up the stairs. There were no lifts, and six floors.'

The residents got through a lot of coal. They all used it for heating, with a hearth in every room, and some also used it for cooking. Ronnie Mann remembers that his flat in the Bedfordbury had a gas cooker, but that his gran's 'bedsit' flat in the same buildings had a range that she cooked on and kept clean with black lead.

Of course, all those coal fires had an effect on the atmosphere. If you weren't there, it's difficult to imagine the smell of the West End in the fifties. Today, nothing much assaults the nostrils apart from traffic exhausts, fast-food joints, pub fumes, the odd bit of decaying rubbish in the summer and an assortment of those sickly scents that bleed from gift and cosmetic shops. Peter Jenkins, however, remembers the particular pong of the Wild Street Peabody Buildings in the late forties: 'The estate had a Lambert & Butler's factory at the far end, which used to blow a lot of smoke out over the estate. The whole place was smelly: Lambert & Butlers, the market smell of green vegetables, earth, potatoes and horse dung, and the general smell of being in an enclosed, smoky place. Especially in the summer. Everyone had coal fires then, and lit them except on the hottest days. When I had an asthma attack, my mother used to take me out and down to the banks of the Thames, supposedly to breathe good air, although the state the Thames was in, in 1947, '48, I do question what I was actually breathing in.'

Virtually the whole of London smelt of coal. When the Victorian tenements were built, coal was the only fuel for heating and cooking, and the estates and the industrial buildings would belch out smoke and soot, winter and summer. It blackened the buildings, and in the winter mixed with the river mist and fog to form sulphurous smogs. These 'pea-soupers' were so thick at times that you literally could not see your hand in front of your face. Buses took wrong turnings and got lost; Alberto Camisa remembers a double-decker chugging along Wardour Street, although buses normally ran only along Soho's boundary streets. Dark tendrils of smog would find their way into houses through cracks and air-bricks, so that you could quietly choke in your own sitting room. Cinemas had to cancel showings because the punters could not see the screens. Literally thousands of people with vulnerable lungs were killed by the 'Great Smog' of 1952, which lasted for five days.

The Clean Air Act of 1956 was a direct response to the smog, and made much of central London a smokeless zone. Londoners could still use their hearths, but had to fill them with more expensive smokeless fuels, and a general switch-over to gas and electric cookers and heaters began later in the fifties.

Coal may have been the dominant characteristic scent of London in the fifties, but it wasn't the only one. My father was a fastidious man. Although there was always a strong note of booze and smoke around him, he made use of his bijou bathroom on a daily basis. The majority of the population did not have this resource, however. They relied instead on a tin bath in front of the fire, with the whole family using the same water, topped up with a hot kettle, in sequence; or they would visit the local public baths, usually on a weekly basis. Ronnie Mann reminded me of the results. 'I might be 100 per cent wrong, but I think all of us smelt. I don't mean you stunk, but you're smelling. Mr Murphy, who lived above us, was an old Irish labourer, and he was up early and used to come home late, and I can't imagine Mr Murphy having a bath every night. Certainly, when I was a kid at the 'Bury there was no bath. We went to the public baths in Endell Street, every Friday night. Me and my dad used to go in one, my two brothers in another and my two sisters in another. My mum never went to the baths, just had a wash behind the coal box, and basically that was it, that was our only way of washing and cleaning.

'Nowadays, if I wear a shirt two days running my wife does her nut, but we'd wear stuff for a week. If everybody has a bath on a Friday, if everybody wears the same shirt for a week – 'cause you can only do your washing once a week as well – then basically everybody smells the same. Some might stink a bit more than others, but in the main you all smelt at a general level, so you didn't really notice that things were different.

'I don't recall, ridiculous as this may sound, ever cleaning my teeth until I was about thirteen, when I started getting interested in girls, and suddenly realized that washing my hair was a good thing. Before, I used to remember putting water in, or grease, but I don't remember washing it. Certainly it was a different concept of cleanliness than we have today.'

It was not until the late fifties that baths came to the tenements, and even then, many preferred to continue at the public baths. Ann Lee remembers the washing arrangements at the Wild Street tenements. 'My mum and dad had a living room and a bedroom, and toilet and a big wash house out on the landing. There were big butler sinks and copper boilers, and everybody shared that and had their one set day a week. There were four or five flats on each landing, and everybody took a day.

'They had to boil kettles for a strip-down wash, or a tin bath in front of the fire in the flat. My mum had this massive great black kettle for boiling water for washing and baths. Outside the door of our flat there was a sink with a cold tap. That's where you got your water from. My dad used to wash at that butler sink in cold water every morning. My dad was tough.

'When I was about ten [in 1956], they put baths in the wash house, and partitioned it, put a lock on the door and an Ascot in it. You're talking about a big stone room, with this bath in it. There were two entrances, one on each side of it. Even though you had this sort of solid screen, you had to make sure both doors were locked, as you didn't really want anyone coming in the wash house when you was in the bath. It was really weird. You'd put your two pennies in and you'd get a nice hot bath. It was lovely in the summer, but in the winter, you got in, you washed, you got out. It was absolutely freezing, but it was still a luxury. But we still had to go out to the toilet on the landing in the freezing flipping cold. We didn't get our own bathroom and constant hot water until I was fourteen, in 1960.'

Things were different at the 'Bury. 'When they first put the baths in the wash houses, they didn't screen them off,' Ronnie Mann explains. 'When my brother came home from work, he'd want a bath before he went out, and it used to be three-pence for a bath full of hot water, but you were right in that bloody wash house. You had a good few years where you had your bath stuck in that rotten corner, and it was freezing. Great big stone things, and you had no double glazing or heating in there. It really was cold. You didn't hang around, I can tell you that. I don't think my mum ever used the bath in the wash house. I don't know if she ever had a bath in her life! [laughs]'.

Getting your own bathroom fitted could change your life. Until he was fourteen, John Carnera used to make the weekly trek from his home above Gennaro's to the Marshall Street baths. 'I remember 1954 was a seminal year for us, because not only did we get our first television, a 14-inch one, but we had the bathroom built; we didn't have to go downstairs to the restaurant! I'll never forget that year. Television, and a bathroom and toilet! Luxury!'

As the Superintendent's son, Peter Jenkins had access to the only private bathroom in the Wild Street Estate, as well as hot water and electricity.

His family also had somewhere to do their laundry. 'We had what we called a scullery with a great big bath in it and a copper – that's a smell of childhood you cannot get rid of, coppers and the smell of washing powder in your house on a Monday – always Mondays. I was asthmatic as a kid, and associate that smell with fighting for breath and reading Charles Buchan's football annuals, in bed. Washing was mangled first, then hung up on a rack on the pulley in the ceiling to dry. Things came out of the mangle in strange shapes. A sheet, especially if it had been starched, you might well have been able to cut bread with it. Everybody else had to use the public laundry places.' In those days before running hot water or washing machines, let alone launderettes, there were laundries for public use in most of Central London's public baths.

Father's bathroom meant I never used the West End baths for anything other than swimming. Like most people in the area, including the Covent Gardeners, I chose to swim in the Marshall Street baths, not far from Oxford Circus, rather than the ones in Endell Street. Marshall Street was not only closer, but its choice of heated indoor pools gave it a natural edge over the open-air unheated pool at Endell Street, commonly known as the Oasis. The temperatures were rarely conducive to outdoor bathing in any case. People did flock to the Oasis in rare heatwaves, but these hot busy spells could be dangerous in the fifties, as Janet Vance remembered: 'A little girl from Peter Street, another Janet, went to the Oasis, and came out with polio, so people from Soho didn't go to the Oasis after that.'

As far as using the public baths was concerned, people tended to choose according to which side of the Charing Cross Road they lived. 'There were baths at Marshall Street, and I sometimes used to swim there,' says Ronnie Mann, 'but Endell Street was probably closer, and I fell into a routine of going there. Met all my mates there, too, of a Friday night.' People used to go as a family, and meet up with their friends, schoolmates, workmates and neighbours. The baths, and especially the queues for the baths, were a good place for a natter, somewhere to plan the evening ahead and catch up with what had been happening all week.

'You always had to queue,' Ronnie continued. 'When you got in you'd shout, "More in number 5" or whatever, and the old boy would come round, and top up the bath. Later, he'd come along, bang on the door, and say, "Come on, other people waiting." You'd have to get out pretty quick. You couldn't stay in there. I had no real concept of time as a kid. It seemed I was in there an eternity, but it was probably only ten minutes – I doubt you got much more than that.'

Saturday morning was bath time for Janet Vance at Marshall Street. 'We had to queue up. They'd give you a towel but you had to take your own soap and flannel. I went in first, then waited outside while my mum went in. It was boiling hot. I think that's why my mother used to chuck me in first! We used the same water to save money. There was quite a few cubicles, with brown tiling things on the floors. They were big enamel baths, not sitting baths, just right for a soak, except there wasn't enough time for lying down.'

Marshall Street was not just about baths. There was a public laundry too, and a children's clinic. The clinic took a proactive role in public health. 'The nurses from there were the nit nurses,' remembers Janet. 'My hair was curly. They came to school with those bloody combs and pulled my head to pieces.'

Ronnie Mann tells a story about the visiting nurses. 'When I was at secondary school, the nurse used to come round for the nits, and also sometimes give you the once-over, top to toe. By that age, I was aware that you had to wash more regularly than I was used to. Once you'd gone to secondary school, you was aware that there was a slight difference between that close community and some of the kids that lived in houses with electricity, and hot water you could turn on.

'One kid in my class was from the Peabody Buildings in Abbey Orchard Street, by the Houses of Parliament, and I don't suppose he'd changed his socks or washed his feet for some time. When he took his shoes off, his feet were black, and mouldy, and the stench was huge.

'I couldn't remember when I'd last washed mine, either, and I'm thinking, "You're next," just one person in front of me, and now it's, "Please God, let my feet be clean!" They were, actually – well, not by today's standards: they were filthy, but they were cleaner than his.'

By the fifties, public health initiatives had become more widespread and had started to tackle the needs of those people who lived on the

94

streets. Graham and Olga Jackson told me about the cleansing house in the same building as the mortuary in Macklin Street. 'People who lived on the streets and in the hostels used to get scruffy and lousy. What they used to do was take them in off the streets, take them to the cleansing house, bath them and delouse them, feed them and shave them, then let them go. It wasn't like they were just rounded up: they were quite happy about it, happy to go along for the free grub, if nothing else.'

In 1948, all of these health initiatives had come under the umbrella of the National Health Service. Some of my contacts remember a time before this, when going to the doctor was as much a financial as a medical decision. Pat and Barbara Jones told me they went to the doctor in Bow Street, when Mum could find the necessary 7s. 6d., a lot of money in those days. Then, after 1948, when it was free, I could afford to go to the dentist. It was in William IV Street. I saw either Mr Palmer or his partner, Mr Moss – who was the father of Stirling Moss.'

There was a GP at 42 Montpelier Square, between the two addresses where Anne Payne lived. Her grandmother took her there occasionally, 'but she preferred to go to the pharmacist, Mr Giles in Montpelier Street'. Mr Giles was an old-fashioned chemist, who dispensed advice as well as medicines to many on the Montpelier Estate. Before the National Health Service came in, local chemists' shops were often regarded in the same light as tribal societies would see the wise woman's hut, as a first recourse in times of trouble. The pharmacist was a more affordable alternative to the doctor as both a diagnoser and a treater of minor ailments. Several of my husband's legions of uncles and aunts remember that in the pre-NHS years the local GP was often resented by the poorer people, while the chemist was sometimes looked up to as a father figure (it was always a man) in the community.

An alternative to finding the money for a visit to the GP – let alone for any medicines – was to use the medical services of a charitable institution. Some only offered rudimentary treatment, but others had exacting standards. When Olga Jackson was growing up in Shorts Gardens in Covent Garden, she used to spend a lot of time at the Medical Mission just down the street. 'I think the Medical Mission was set up by a husband and wife. The idea was that, if you couldn't afford to pay to see a doctor, you could go to the Medical Mission and see a missionary doctor home on furlough. When the National Health came in, it wasn't needed any more. There used to be a pharmacy, too, run by a lady called Miss Morton. She helped run the clubs. There was a girls' club, where you could go and play table tennis, even do keep-fit in those days. She used to take us out on Saturdays; we used to go on holiday together.

'In some ways it was very much a religious Mission. They didn't have services, but they did hold these meetings, spreading the Christian message. I can remember a photo I saw from the thirties: it was all men, lots and lots of them, assembled in the Mission for this meeting. Not down-and-outs, just local people – although of course everyone

96

there was fairly poor in those days.

'On the other hand, we used to have Sunday School outings, and there were Italians, Greeks, Jews, Chinese, Indians, you name it, all off to Christian Sunday School – although the Catholics could not go any more after the age of seven, because they took communion.'

Religious faith never touched me personally. My parents were fervent atheists and I found no reason to rebel against them. For those West Enders with religious faith, though, there were ample opportunities to indulge it, in synagogues, churches and temples from Brompton Oratory to St Clement Danes. Some places of worship were in decidedly secular buildings. Myra James, who grew up in a Welsh-speaking home above her parents' café in Pollen Street, remembers how she and her family 'attended a Welsh chapel which met on Sunday mornings in Studio One, the cinema in Oxford Street, because the original chapel in the City had been bombed in the war'.

Another diligent, if apparently reluctant, churchgoer was Owen Gardner. 'Our local parish church was St Martin-in-the-Fields, but you could never get in there, because it was always full of visitors, so my mother hooked up with St Paul's, Covent Garden, the actors' church. It wasn't well attended. An old Shakespearean actor was the vicar, and he couldn't get anybody in the church, so my mother volunteered me – I had been a choirboy in Somerset – to go there on a Sunday morning, unlock it, take the collections at the Communion first thing and at the eleven o'clock service and put the money in the safe.'

After that, he and the vicar would go to the hospital at the back of the market to give Communion to anyone who wanted it, before returning to the twelve o'clock service, where Owen again took the collection before going home to his well-earned lunch. In those days, in most of Britain, everything closed on Sundays.

Some establishments opened seven days a week in the West End, but for most of those who lived and worked there, it was a welcome day of rest. 'My father worked six days a week, sixteen hours a day,' John Carnera remembers. 'He was up and gone by seven, pushing a barrow down to Covent Garden to get the day's fruit and veg. He'd work at the restaurant all day, until five or half-past, then have a break for an hour or so, come up and have dinner with my mother, and then start at seven in the evening as a barman at Les Caves de France, a club two doors up from us. He worked there until about eleven. Sunday was his day off. We saw our dad really only on Sunday.'

John's father was not unique in this. The struggle to make ends meet forced many family breadwinners in the West End to take several jobs. As Sonia Boulter recalls, 'My dad worked behind the bar at Maxim's for quite long hours. Bar work was his trade, and he could tell you anything about it, but he wouldn't drink himself. My mum worked with him, occasionally, in the cloakroom. It was just a bit of money for her. And when she did that, I had to look after my younger brothers. I was only young myself, so it was quite a lot on me, but I had to do it.

'I remember at one stage my dad had two or

three jobs, because he wasn't very well. He'd had TB and couldn't settle into a permanent job and money was very short. I can remember him doing night work, coming home for a couple of hours' sleep, then going to work at another job. It was very hard going. He worked at a cartoon cinema in Windmill Street a couple of days in the evenings to earn extra money, just letting people in, taking tickets, taking money occasionally. He did lots of things to earn extra money. When I was about fourteen, he got a job with Wall's, selling ice cream from trays on the trains. I did that with him to earn a bit of pocket money. Going to Southend, walking up and down on the train selling ice creams from the icebox in the guard's car.'

Ronnie Mann learned to double up on jobs at an early age. Eventually he would work in the family business, a picture-framer's in Monmouth Street, but he had wide experience before then. 'When I was at school, I worked in the late afternoons and Saturdays half-past nine to about half-past three in the butcher's, or delivering for the greengrocer or the dairy. Saturday morning I did a paper round from seven o'clock to about half-past eight. I think a lot of the kids did them jobs. Some stayed on when they left school. Littlewoods – an ironmonger's and paint place in Drury Lane – supplied the whole area with paraffin and all that. I can remember two blokes working there from while they were in school to into their twenties and thirties.'

Ronnie elected not to stay in retailing. When he left school he went to work in the market, doubling up with jobs behind the scenes at local theatres. 'Most of the people in the 'Bury worked locally,' he remembers. 'A percentage worked in the market, and a few in the theatres as well. Others worked in the British Museum, the National Gallery or the auction house in Garrick Street. My uncle was a lavatory attendant in Charing Cross Road. I can't recall anybody having to go more than a small bus ride away.

'Moss Bros employed quite a few people, storemen and drivers – not necessarily serving, that was probably a stage too far for the 'Bury – and the print used to take a lot of people. There was Harrisons bang opposite us, a huge print-makers and stamp-makers. Both my sisters went in there. If you were lucky, you got a job down Fleet Street, or Odhams in Long Acre, where the *Daily Herald* was printed. Some of the girls worked as waitresses, as Nippies down in Joe Lyons or wherever. A lot of them became sales assistants in the shops around.'

All this hard work made West Enders appreciate their leisure time, but they tended to spend it close to home. Just as hardly any of my fellow West Enders grew up with a garden, very few of them spoke of going on holiday on a regular basis. I don't think they were being shy about it: they just didn't go. Peter Jenkins's parents presented an exception to the rule. His father insisted on taking his family away for two weeks in a boarding house in Exmouth, every single year. This made young Peter feel very special. 'So many people did not get away, because they couldn't afford it. In comparison with the people on the estate, we were well off. Nobody else from round about went away for a week, let alone a fortnight. They stuck around the estate, and went places for the day; Southend, or the south coast from Waterloo, sometimes Sheerness from Victoria.

'We used to take day trips of our own, to Little-hampton, Brighton or Bognor Regis, which was exciting in its own way, but there was such a lot of anticipation about the two weeks in Devon: we sent the trunk ahead for a start. Passenger Luggage in Advance. You'd put the labels on your trunk, and that was ever so exciting, because it meant holiday time was near, and then the week before you were going, you walked across Waterloo Bridge with Dad to the station, to buy the tickets.'

John Carnera's father, Secundo, was another who could not bear the thought of going without a holiday, but while the Jenkinses went to Devon, the Carneras had other destinations in mind. 'My dad only had two places he wanted to go on holiday ever in his life. One was Sequals, in Italy, where we came from. We used to go every three years, because that's all we could afford, but when we went, it was for two or three months. We'd go in August and stay through the harvest period. That's when it was best to be in Italy, at harvest-time: the wine harvest, the corn, and all the rest of it.

'And if we didn't go there, we used to go to Brighton. Dad loved Brighton, and I loved the piers. I used to save up every year to spend time on the penny machines. My week's holiday at Brighton was spent on those machines. I used to hate the shingle beach, where you were – ow! ow! ow! – limping all the way down to the water's edge because of the stones, you know, then you'd get in and it was stone cold, absolutely freezing. It wasn't my idea of fun at all. I just wanted to go on one of the piers and spend all my pennies. I used to love that. There was the Executioner, where they cut off the bloke's head, shooting games where you had to shoot cats with a pistol, ones with ghosts coming out of cupboards and laughing policemen. One year, I saved three shillings and tenpence. You can't imagine how rich I felt, like a multimillionaire, and I could not wait to get on those machines. That three and ten was burning a hole in my pocket. I got rid of it in about two days, I think.'

As I researched this book, I came to realize that I was not only collecting stories about the way people lived in the forties, fifties and early sixties, but also stories of earlier generations, passed down from parents and grandparents and often taking them deep into the area's past. Ann Lee, for example, can trace an ancestor back to the Bow Street Runners – the family retains custody of the truncheon – and Mike O'Rouke's family were Covent Gardeners back to at least 'great-grandfather days'. The Mann family business was set up in Monmouth Street in 1849 by Ronnie's great-great-grandfather.

I heard about the way people came to England with little or no money and no English at all, looking for work, working hard and setting up businesses. I heard stories of sacrifice, hard work and humour, of people doing the best they could to get by and to bring up families with pitifully

102

few resources. Olga Jackson, for example, remembers how her grandparents lived: 'My grandfather was a painter and decorator, and my grandmother did anything she could, and must have done that from a very early age, because she was so poor. I think she was a wet nurse at one time. She did everything. They lived in a flat in an apartment house, in Shelton Street. There was no running water, or toilet, or anything upstairs. They were four floors up and they had to go all the way down to the bottom just to get water. Every drop had to be dragged upstairs and lumped down again.'

Ann Lee told me about her mother's mother, who had brought up a large family in the Wild Street Buildings, despite being rendered briefly homeless when Hitler demolished J Block. The more I heard of Nan Glover, the more I liked her, and she'll turn up again in this book. For me, she sums up the stoicism, sensibilities and spirit of the working-class Londoners who lived through the wars and tried to make the best of the peace for their children and grandchildren. 'My nan was such a darling. Cissie was her name, Cissie Glover. Well, Jessica really, but everybody called her Ciss. She had it hard, but I never, ever, heard her complain. She used to do three cleaning jobs a day to keep her family. Her husband cleared off and left her with seven kids. Well, he cleared off and left her with five, and came back twice and left her with another one each time. And then he cleared off for good, to live, as my mother so delicately put it, with his old tart up at the top of Drury Lane. I never met him, I wasn't allowed – well, nobody had anything to do with him. But when Nanny talked about it, you could see she still loved him.

'My grandfather died when I was thirteen. And his old tart came to my mum and said, "Your father's died," and my mum said, "Yeah, and?" "Well," said his tart, "he's gonna need burying." "Let him have a pauper's grave then," my mum said. "We don't want anything to do with him." My mum, she hated him.

'But then we went down to see Nanny and my mum told her "The old man's dead."

'Poor lamb, I'll never forget my old nan's face. It was a mixture of sadness and relief, and I said to her, "Are you all right?" and she went, "I'm all right, love. At least I know where he is, now."'

4

Playing Out

One of the greatest contrasts between being a child in the fifties and today is how much freedom we enjoyed back then. We roamed all over the place and our free time was nowhere near as organized as kids' time is today. Lucky children might have had riding lessons, music lessons or dance, but most did not. The freedom to roam was possible because there was so little traffic. Even in Central London, seeing a car coming towards you as you played hopscotch or football in the street was the exception rather than the rule.

If we weren't at school, we spent very little time amusing ourselves at home. It wasn't just a case of there being no such things as computers or video games; lots of people didn't even have a television. Because television had been in its infancy when the war began, and the authorities had simply switched it off for the duration, it took a while to get going again. Most people had no access to one at all until Coronation year, 1953. Even if your family did own a TV, there was hardly anything on. In the fifties, broadcasting hours were very limited indeed. Toys were at a premium, too, because materials and labour had been missing for so long. Once again, it took a while for imported materials to come through, although limited production did begin again in the late forties. Indoor space was limited for many families, especially those who had taken in homeless relatives who had been blitzed out of house and home. All these factors meant that the fifties child was an outdoors child.

Allowing your children to play and roam about outside must have come as a huge relief for parents, too, especially those who had watched their children being menaced by the Blitz. Children were taught to be wary of strangers, men mostly, but there wasn't the dreadful anxiety that there appears to be today. I understand that the actual numbers of children being abducted by strangers has not changed radically since records began, but back in the forties and fifties, when the media was restricted to newspapers, radio and newsreels at the cinema, we really didn't hear about such things very often. That also contributed to our freedom. Our parents were less afraid for us, especially once the bombing stopped.

Ann Waterhouse had a fairly sheltered upbringing in Knightsbridge, and went to school in Mayfair. 'I saw quite a lot of the West End area,' she remembers. 'In those days, we had the freedom to roam around in our dinner hour, more than would be considered safe these days.' Where Ann lived, there were no other children, and excursions with her school friends, or visits for tea, all tended to be arranged and scheduled. She was an exception, though. Almost all of the people I talked to spoke of the joy of spilling out on to the pavement on the morning of a school-free day not knowing what's going to happen, but knowing you have the whole day to find out.

London's children had, of course, always played out in the streets, back alleys, parks (in those they were allowed to enter) or, where it could be found, waste ground. In the first decade or so after the war there was a lot more waste ground around in the West End, courtesy of the Luftwaffe. Some of the bomb sites were put to use. Many, for instance, were turned into car parks, while one in Dean Street was used as the venue for the annual Soho Fair, which in those days lasted a week. Janet Vance, who grew up in Frith Street, remembers this well: 'There would be floats going around the streets and a proper fairground, with stalls and rides, on the car parks, on the old bomb sites.'

Those sites unsuitable for car parks tended to become impromptu playgrounds, and soon became irresistible attractions to local children. Ronnie Mann, from his base in Bedfordbury, east of Trafalgar Square, got to know them all. 'I reckon we played more in bomb sites than we ever played in normal games. There was a big one in St Martin's Lane, and the other side of the Strand was bombed from Villiers Street all down to the Embankment Gardens. Leicester Square was bombed, Shaftesbury Avenue was bombed, Floral Street in the market was bombed, so you had huge, massive areas that didn't completely disappear until – well, in the case of Floral Street, not until 1970.'

John Carnera came from Italy soon after the war to live in Dean Street. 'There was a bomb site straight across the road from us,' he remembers. 'On one side they'd made it into a car park, but the other remained as it was, no building, just basements and cellars, all bombed out. It was just this hole in the ground, and we used to run up and down playing Cowboys and Indians in it. We used to have stone fights on the bomb sites. Chucking them at each other. Ludicrous.'

It never occurred to children that they were playing in the ruins of people's lives, homes and workplaces. Why should it? Ignorance of the past is one of the joys of being young. 'We'd go to a bomb site,' remembers Ronnie Brace, 'put two coats down for a goal, and there we were. Playing among the debris was part of our lives. We didn't know about the war. I mean, I remember it, but I didn't know the context. Bombs, well, they were just a frightening noise, going under the bed, knocking over the piss pot or something; going down in the tube and all that, but it didn't ring, not at that age; I mean, at school, you have people

107

you like and don't like, but you don't think of nationalities fighting.'

While some sites were clear enough to serve as a rather bumpy impromptu football pitch, others were better suited to more adventurous – in fact, downright dangerous – games. Ronnie Mann again: 'St Martin's Lane was like an assault course – talk about training commandos. You had to climb up the scaffolding and go across, probably a 20-foot drop, on to stone. We all did it. It was a wonder no one got killed.' The element of danger and foolhardiness was something everyone remembered, although they didn't seem to have thought about it at the time.

Peter Jenkins, who lived in the Peabody Buildings in Wild Street, recalls that, 'Me and my mates used to use bomb sites for exploring and making dens and playing adventure games. How on earth we ever survived I don't know, what with all the health and safety risks, all the smashed glass and of course run-ins with the down-and-outs, who were using the ruins as dosshouses.'

It wasn't just the boys who were attracted to these melancholy relics of the war – girls were also drawn to the large crater left by part of Newport Dwellings that took a direct hit. 'We used to play in it,' Sonia remembers. 'My mum used to go mad and shout at me to get out of there, but we really enjoyed it. Once, we were moving some bricks and wood, and we saw this box: Ooh, what's in this box? So we got it out of the rubble and opened it up, and it was a whole box full of make-up – mascara, rouge, lipstick, hairbrushes, everything to do with what women wanted in those days. Somebody said we've got to call the police, and they came and they looked at it. They thought it had been looted from somewhere during the Blitz, then dumped, so they told all of us kids to share it among ourselves. That was my first taste of make-up. It was brilliant. You just thought, "Oh God, I've got some make-up". I must have been all of nine. I remember it very vividly: we thought all our birthdays had come at once, having the hairbrushes, everything – brilliant!'

Sonia also remembers the ruins of St Anne's Church. 'We used to go in over the gates in Shaftesbury Lane. There was like a little chapel and, as children, we used to go in there and play priests and congregation. We'd go in there from school, and one of them would be the priest, standing at the altar, and the rest would be on the few pews that there were. Then, one time we went in there, someone kicked some wood and there was a dead cat underneath, full of maggots. I never went there any more.'

In the fifties, West End streets were full of children. Most of them were as streetwise as they needed to be and as grubby as they could get away with. Today we might call them street kids, but that phrase wasn't in use then. Nor was 'streetwise', come to that. 'Urchin' was the word Raye Du-Val used to describe his youthful self, while Ronnie Mann recalls with laughter that 'we used to play with the kids of a posh family, somewhere round the Adelphi. It never lasted long. The family didn't want us there. There's a limit to what you'll put up with from ruffians and guttersnipes, as we were called.'

Out in the streets, then as now, there were boundaries that some children and young people – posh kid, guttersnipe, urchin or one of the many shades in between – did not cross: some young Covent Gardeners, for example, were forbidden to go into Soho, while several Sohoites knew nothing of the territories across the Charing Cross Road, partly because the busy road was a formidable barrier to young pedestrians, and partly because it was the dividing line between catchment areas for schools.

In the heart of Soho, though, virtually all the streets were safe to play in. No buses and hardly any trucks ventured within the area bounded by Shaftesbury Avenue, Charing Cross Road, Oxford Street and Regent Street, and although there was traffic in the main streets through Soho, it was moving slowly enough not to cause a problem. In Covent Garden, much the same applied. There were lorries in the streets around the market in the mornings, but for much of the afternoon and evening there was little to worry about, particularly in the backstreets. The estates had it easy. Peter Jenkins remembers that 'we didn't play too much in the streets because we had this whacking great space in among the blocks. We could play football, although you had to be careful because of the windows. Our ball games were played in an enclosed space, looked down on by a whole community. No cars came in: we were safe.'

Mike O'Rouke grew up in the Seven Dials and played in the streets around his home. 'You had

110

to be a certain age,' Mike remembers, 'before you could go out and about. My grandfather bought me a little three-wheeler, a tricycle, for my fifth birthday, and that was my prized possession. I used to go up and down Mercer Street on that. One of my relatives would be sitting on the doorstep while I rode up and down.

'A bit later, there was a bunch of us, kids you go to school with and play with after school. We played around the streets. There weren't many cars. We used to play football or cricket in Mercer Street, put an orange box up for a wicket. It wasn't until it was getting quite dark that maybe one car would creep into the top of Mercer Street, up by Long Acre, and park there. We used to play until it was dark.

'There was always people about to look out for us. Everyone knew who we were. Of course, it meant we couldn't get away with anything. You'd get a clip round the ear if you played Knock Down Ginger, anything like that.'

The games that Mike and hundreds of others played in the West End streets ranged from those for just two or three people through more or less formal team games to thoroughly informal adventure games or brawls that sometimes involved great swirling mobs of boys. Sonia Boulter and Peter Jenkins, for example, both recall 'endless games of hopscotch', which of course was so much easier to chalk out on a pavement laid with rectangular stones than it was on the tarmac surfaces in the grounds of the estate.

Others remembered 'run-outs'. Mentioned by several Covent Gardeners, it is explained more

111

fully by Tricia Bryan: 'There were two teams. You both ran off, then would have to try to get back to base without them seeing you. You didn't have to be tagged, you could just say "I spot Trish behind the telephone box". It was how many from the team got back unseen. We used to play that in the playground behind St Giles-in-the-Fields. Although there was a park keeper, Mr Chivers – like the jelly – it was just a playground with swings and a slide, no flowers. You walked through the churchyard and you were in.'

The labyrinth of streets, alleyways and yards around Covent Garden made it just right for games of tag, hide-and-seek, and their many variants. Tricia also remembers Tin Tan Tommy, 'another game of tag with a base, usually a dustbin. The base was guarded by Tin Tan Tommy, and he had to come and find you but at the same time guard his home. If he tagged you before you touched the dustbin lid, you would be out. We would all make a break for the lid. Whoever touched it first without being tagged was the next Tin Tan Tommy. I'm sure that name came from the home being a dustbin lid. We played that in Shorts Gardens, in the flats there next to the Medical Mission, where we all went to Sunday School.'

The Bedfordbury Estate had been jammed into a much smaller space than its sister estate in Wild Street, but the 'Bury kids gleefully took over the roads outside. 'We played Cowboys and Indians, mostly,' remembers Ronnie Mann, 'or whatever was on at the local pictures: Tarzan, pirates, general mucking about. And we used to play 'ares and 'ounds down there. There might have been twenty or thirty kids on each side, and the idea was that after a while you had to get back to the lamp post or whatever it was as home.'

My main playtime was spent in St Anne's churchyard, because it was behind the flat where I lived and was enclosed by buildings and, on the street side, railings, which made it seem safe. It was overlooked on two sides by lots of windows. It made a good playground: there was a paved area in front of the tower and the table tombs could be made to be all kinds of things: a desert island, a ship, a house, a raft or simply 'home' in a game of Tin Tan Tommy and a place to park all those players who were 'out'.

I learned to hula-hoop in St Anne's, and there were skipping and two-balls to master as well. There were seasonal things such as five stones or jacks in summer, when sitting about on the ground, in the heat, had a certain appeal, and hopscotch, skipping and all that energetic stuff when the air was a bit sharper. Two-balls was another summer game. You could play it alone and hone your technique or you could play with others.

'Everything used to close on a Saturday at about one o'clock,' Ronnie Mann recalls, 'so from then until the lorries started to open the market on Monday morning, there was no traffic in the West End. Local people didn't have cars, and anyone coming up to the West End had no problem parking in the Strand or Piccadilly, so they didn't park in Bedfordbury.

'The garages of Harrisons, the printing works,

had shutters. They were the goals. On Sunday morning, all the kids would be playing a game. Cricket was in Coliseum Court, between Charing Cross and Bedfordbury. You had the two telephone boxes; we used to play football and cricket down there.'

John Carnera also had the imagination to turn a back alley into a sports stadium. 'We would play cricket or football in Bateman's Buildings, on the way home from school. There was a lamp post at either end. The one nearest Soho Square – the Hospital for Venereal Diseases on one side, and a factory on the other – was the wicket when we played cricket, and in the winter we played football there.'

One of the advantages of street football was that it required a minimum of equipment. Discarded jackets or pullovers served for goalposts if there wasn't a handy wall to be marked out. You did not even need a ball, as Leo Zanelli remembers: 'The trick was to get a cigarette packet, stuff it full of paper and stick it together. It would slide quite nicely. It wouldn't last very long, though...'

You hardly ever saw one of the big heavy footballs being used on the streets. Most street football involved filthy, dishevelled, bare-kneed boys tussling over a fraying tennis ball. Sometimes they didn't bother with a ball, and just got on with the tussling. 'The 'Bury kids always used to fight the Wild Street gang,' remembers Ronnie Mann. 'The irony of it is that a lot of them were my cousins: my aunts lived in Wild Street, my best friend that I sat next to in school lived in Wild Street, but we would all fight each other on

114

the weekend.'

The 'Bury kids weren't always spoiling for a fight, but they did have a habit of going mob-handed, as Ronnie remembers. 'The main thing we used to do as kids was go down to St James's Park and across into Green Park and back. You're talking about, not half a dozen, but in excess of thirty or forty kids across all ages from six to fifteen, when you left school. We'd walk up to Tottenham Court Road, to Euston Road. Don't ask me why! We actually used to walk to Hampstead as kids. I remember getting my pennies to get home, because the little kids, they used to put us on a bus, and the big kids – ten years old – walked home from Hampstead. We didn't think about it, it was just natural to walk everywhere.'

If walking palled, Ronnie and his pals could always improvise some transport. 'We used to make our own scooters. You used to get blocks of wood, tyre blocks, two planks, then you'd screw it through, two screw eyes, you put a bolt in between the two and you had a scooter you could learn on. You used to have the scooter season, and kids would build scooters, and you'd go wherever you wanted on them.'

Life on the streets changed according to the seasons. 'We used to do penny for the Guy at Tottenham Court Road tube station,' Graham Jackson remembers. 'We had two guys, to catch both entrances [laughter]. We used to earn quite a bit. We'd start early, about the middle of September. The only time we'd get chased off was when we went down into the tube station. They let us sit up the top. As Dad was a PC, he used to tell me off,

"You know, that's begging. You could be done for that." He never actually ran us in, though.'

Some people looked at the shifting mass of kids in the street and saw in them the stuff of recruitment. Ronnie Mann talked of the bonuses to be had if you could work the system. 'There was Corpus Christi, the Catholic Church, in Maiden Lane, St Martin's, and the Communist Party HQ on the corner of King Street and Garrick Street. At that time, we had nothing, but if you went to Sunday School, you had the chance to go to camp with the vicars, or on outings, so all the kids, Catholic or Protestant, went to St Martin's Sunday School in the morning.

'In the afternoon, the priests used to come out of Corpus Christi to round up all the Catholics to go to Mass, and they'd have half of us in it as well! Some of the kids from the Buildings used to sit there in rows, not a Catholic in the family, and I used to come away thinking, "This is strange."

'And then of course, the Communist Party mob got the hump. They used to sweep you off the street, take you up into their building and lock the door so you couldn't get out, and show black and white propaganda films! [laughs] I should imagine there was about a million to one chance of any of them getting a sniff of interest from anybody. Oh dear.'

My dear old friend Terry Pizzey and his pals played the same trick in Marylebone, 'We'd go to all the Sunday schools,' he told me. 'The denomination didn't really matter, it was the teas that counted. Round our way the Church of England did the best teas, closely followed by the

Methodists. The Catholics knew who belonged and who didn't, so we all knew there was no point in turning up at the left-footers because they'd sling you out unless they'd seen you at Mass over several months.'

With her parents both working, Tricia Bryan learned how to get about London independently at a tender age. 'I used to walk everywhere. I walked the length of Gower Street to go to school on my own when I was five or six years of age. You didn't worry about it. I used to pick up another little boy when I was seven or eight, and he was probably five. I used to be paid for that every week, for taking him to school and bringing him home. We used to play out after school; didn't get home until seven or eight. I don't know what we did for food – probably went to the chip shop on the corner of Endell Street, six of chips and crackling, or to Dolls, the sweet shop just up from the chip shop. You could take the penny-halfpenny you'd saved from your bus fare and get a bag of black jacks and fruit salads – a farthing each – or flying saucers.'

She felt perfectly safe walking the familiar streets. 'We knew not to speak to strangers, but I suppose we weren't so sure who was a stranger, because we were always on the streets. That's the thing about communities. You knew faces, and you knew there was always somebody you could go to. You knew you could knock on a door and someone would know who you were.'

Jackie Trussler was in Tricia's class at St Giles. From the age of three, she lived with her aunt in a council flat above a shop in Museum Street.

'My aunt used to work the theatres,' she remembers, 'just the cloakrooms and whatever, so she was out in the afternoons and evenings. So, on high days and holidays her son, my cousin, who was eight or nine years older than me and still at school, basically looked after me. I used to tag along. That's when I wasn't off here, there and everywhere with Tricia and the girls.'

Tricia's grandparents were in the greengrocery trade at Seven Dials, and although her parents had been bombed out, and had to move into a flat in Bloomsbury, her heart was in Covent Garden. 'I had a cousin who actually worked in the market. I remember in the summer holidays just running in and out of the stalls, playing, actually when they were working – because they were still there at lunchtime. That was our playground. Even when we weren't at school, that was where we met up to play, at Covent Garden market, because we could all get there; walk, or bus, or whatever. We'd all meet down at Shorts Gardens, and from there we'd decide where we were going to play that day.

'We used to take turns in going to each other's houses for tea. We once went to Christine's house. There were a lot of them, and – well, none of us were rich, but they were poor – and when I asked "What's for tea?" her mother said "Shit and sugar sandwiches," and I thought, I don't think I can eat *that*. We only went to Christine's once or twice.'

The menu improved when Jackie's mother remarried and Jackie went to live with her above a pub in the Gray's Inn Road. 'It was huge,' remembers Jackie, 'and they had these kitchens

118

where we would cook our own tea – eggs on toast, stuff like that. There was this dumb waiter we would ride on. I can remember her mum yelling at us to get out of the dumb waiter, to get out of the kitchen, get out of the pub. Wherever we were, we weren't supposed to be there.' The eternal problem of youth.

Several of the interviewees spoke about their memories of youth clubs. The fifties was when people began to see 'youth' as a problem, and organizations – churches, usually – started to set up clubs to get teenagers off the streets. There were several church-based youth clubs in the West End, including a club in the crypt of St Martin's, where Ann Lee danced to 'La Bamba' by Ritchie Valens, and Graham Jackson played snooker. Another one, affiliated to the Catholic Church in Warwick Street off Golden Square, offered table tennis and snooker, while St Patrick's in Soho Square opened up its crypt as a club. 'We started a football team,' remembers John Carnera, 'as well as a cricket team. A fellow called Gino, who lived in Meard Street, used to run the teams for us, but it was initiated by Father Hollins, at the church.'

Olga Jackson remembers the clubs too. 'The Mildmay Medical Mission in Shorts Gardens used to have a girls' club, run by Miss Morton; everyone went, the Italians, Greeks, Jews, Chinese, Indians, you name it, they all came along.'

Leo Zanelli spoke of two youth clubs in Soho, 'one in Kingly Street and one at St Anne's. I played for Soho United, which came about from

119

the youth club at the back of St Anne's. They got us a set of green and black quartered jerseys.' The team joined the legions of footballers playing on Hackney Marshes.

The club that everyone remembers is the Gainsford Boys' Club in Drury Lane, a sports club affiliated to the Inns of Court. It ran football and cricket teams and had a fully equipped boxing gym, as well as facilities for other sports. It stood on the corner of Long Acre. 'There's a block of flats there now, posh ones,' Ronnie Mann points out. 'You had one of those concrete and tarmac football pitches where you could play, you had the boxing underneath it, billiard tables, table tennis.' Next door to it was a playground with some swings to attract younger children.

Although it was officially a boys' club, girls were tolerated. 'My brother used to play football for them,' Ann Lee remembers, 'and you could go downstairs when the boys had finished training and have a Coke and a packet of crisps.'

Jackie Trussler was even more privileged: 'My cousin who looked after me belonged to the Gainsford, and I was the only girl member. Because he played in the football team they used to let me in. I'd be sat on a stool in the corner – "You're only allowed in if you're quiet!" – and as I was an honorary girl member of this boy's club, I just sat in a chair and kept quiet.'

Peter Jenkins and Mike O'Rouke played table tennis there 'and a game of snooker – if you got a chance to get a table,' added Mike, ruefully. He saw it as more of a social club, 'mainly for the boys in the flats down Drury Lane, but more or

120

less the only place you could meet up and play football together. I was well into boxing at the time. I remember going in there and doing a bit of boxing training, but just a couple of times and that was it.'

Ronnie Mann also went there for social reasons at first. 'A lot of the guys from Wild Street loved the Gainsford. I went there because of mates, not because I particularly liked it. It had a predominantly boxing culture, not really my scene. Boxers thought they were a cut above the rest of you. You know, they were training.

'I remember going in there, fourteen, big for my age, cocky. They decided they were going to knock the stuffing out of me, and put me in with a kid about two or three years older. It was a big difference at that age, between a boy and a man, and he was knocking the shit out of me. We were only supposed to be sparring: I knew the difference. It was elbows as well – wallop, fuck, where did that come from? I realized the geezer's hitting me on the chin with his elbows.

'So I kicked him right up the bollocks – which caused absolute chaos. I was nearly hung, drawn and quartered, I was the lowest of the low, but as I said then, you shouldn't have put me in with him, you should have stopped him doing what he was doing.

'The Gainsford had a good football team that I played for a few times, but again it was too good for me, in the sense that they were competing in really good leagues, and you had to be prepared to train a lot harder than I was. If you didn't do the circuit training, you didn't get on the team. It

121

was as simple as that.'

One person who did play football for the Gainsford was John Carnera, the only Sohoite I found who was a member. 'In fact,' he tells me, 'I used to play cricket for them as well, and sometimes we used to go and have our training sessions for our cricket team at the Inns of Court in the Temple. They had greens there, just off the Embankment. We used to set up the nets and have our training there.' Unlike many other patrons of the Gainsford, John – despite being the nephew of former world heavyweight champ Primo Carnera – was not tempted to take up boxing: 'Much too dangerous. I thought my uncle was a bit mad, to be honest.'

If you wanted to play in green spaces, your choice depended largely on which side of the Charing Cross Road you were. Youthful Covent Gardeners tended to gravitate towards Lincoln's Inn Fields and Coram's Fields, while Sohoites headed north or west to the royal parks.

Ann Lee remembers Lincoln's Inn Fields with great affection. 'It had big open greens, a massive big circle in the middle with a bandstand right in the middle of that, tennis courts, netball, a little cafeteria. You'd go over there with your mum, maybe watch someone playing tennis, have a run round on the grass, and then we'd go to the cafeteria. It was just an old van that opened up, but I can still remember the smell of the tea, and the coffee, and the cakes. You could buy a sandwich, but normally it was cakes, and ice cream for the kids. There was all little tables and chairs dotted around.'

It was also a favourite haunt of Mike O'Rouke, although for different reasons. 'I got a second-hand bike when I was about eleven. I used to go around Lincoln's Inn, because you've got 400 metres around the outside, like a track, so you could do a bit of racing round there.'

Tricia Bryan was an habitué of 'The Foundling – Coram's Fields – in Guildford Street. My mother played in Coram's Fields, I played there, and later I took my son there. You were always safe, because adults were not allowed in without children.'

Children were, of course, allowed in without adults to sample the delights of the Fields. 'We used to use the paddling pool in the summer,' remembers Margaret Connolly, 'and maybe take a picnic. I was chief swings attendant for my younger sister and brother.'

For the younger children, there were smaller public parks or playgrounds tucked away around the West End. Mike O'Rouke remembers two of them. 'My mum used to take us to St Giles Gardens, up by St Giles church. It's quite small, but it's a nice play area. We used to go there before I started school. And after school she used to take us up there. There was a little canteen where you could get tea or a fizzy drink.

'My mum's mum used to take me a lot as a child to St Paul's Gardens. There were grass verges either side of the actors' church in Covent Garden, and she used to take me up there after school. That was her favourite place to take me. We used to go down St James's Park now and again,

123

feed the ducks of course, Green Park occasionally: you could get a bus to right outside Green Park.'

Although Covent Gardeners such as Mike would sometimes play in the royal parks – they were only a stroll down the Strand or Piccadilly away, after all, or a cheap bus ride if you were in funds – Soho children tended to treat St James's Park and Green Park as their local parks, and would not think of crossing the Charing Cross Road. Janet Vance was typical. 'We went to the royal parks, but never Lincoln's Inn or Coram's Fields. After my mum picked me up from school, we'd either go to St James's – there was a playground there with swings and that, and we'd feed the ducks – or Green Park. She'd take a sandwich. Or we'd go to Soho Square.'

Right after the war, Soho Square was a fenced-off jungle. John Carnera and others from St Patrick's School risked a caning if they were caught climbing in, but the suitability of the overgrown shrubbery and patches of grass for yet another game of Cowboys and Indians often proved an irresistible lure. Eventually the Square was tidied up and officially opened to the public, and the gardens became a cross between a playground and a crèche for the local children, sometimes under the watchful eye of the flamboyant tipster Prince Monolulu. I loved playing there; the draw was the funny little mock-Tudor lodge that was the backdrop for so many games.

Virtually all of the squares in London have gardens in the centre, but Soho Square was unusual at that time in being open to the public. Andy Pullinger might have lived in St James's Square,

124

for instance, but he was not allowed into the locked gardens, as they were reserved for the use of the directors and guests of the companies situated around the Square. Andy went to play in St James's Park and Green Park instead.

These two parks were fine for duck-feeding and other genteel pursuits, but the powers that be didn't look too kindly on muddied oafs banging a ball around, and the footballers had to look elsewhere. Without the Gainsford's all-weather pitch, games of football that didn't involve dribbling around lamp posts or skinning your knees by diving on concrete were quite hard to find. 'Unless you went to Lincoln's Inn Fields for a bit of grass,' Peter Jenkins remembers, 'or were organized by the school to go up to Coram's Fields, there was nowhere to go to play football.'

That wasn't quite true; although most of the royal parks banned ball games, a 'coats for goalposts' game could be very mobile, as Leo Zanelli remembers: 'In Regent's Park, we'd get chased away every five minutes, but you just go and play in another part of the park.'

John Carnera found a solution a little further afield. 'We went to Hyde Park. We'd get the bus if we had a couple of coppers, but very often we'd walk straight down Piccadilly. About a dozen of us would go, and organize a game of football or cricket between ourselves. We used to get chased out of Green Park. You couldn't play in St James's Park, either, but Hyde Park was fine – big, wide open spaces. I still remember going over to listen to the band playing in the bandstand.'

Most people growing up in British cities in the middle of the twentieth century had their local parks, their places to play, but the West End boasted other attractions, all within walking distance. The parading soldiers always provided a good show at Buckingham Palace, which was but a short walk away. The National Gallery was a great place to go when the weather was bad and the local parks, both royal and otherwise, held no appeal.

Another local amenity was the British Museum. 'We'd go there every Sunday,' Olga Jackson remembers fondly. 'Straight off to the mummies.' Her little brother, Graham, wasn't quite so interested in viewing the exhibits in the echoing halls. 'We lived just around the corner from the Museum,' he remembers. 'Coming home from school we would walk through it, take off our shoes and go and slide on their polished floors in our socks. All through the library, it was shiny lino.'

Graham was not the only one to use the Museum as a short cut. Tricia Bryan remembers that 'We would walk home from St Giles, down Museum Street and into the main entrance of the Museum, walk through, and come out the back for home. While we were in there, we might say, "Let's do the Egyptian room today," and that would scare us a lot.'

Tricia's friend, Jackie, lived in Museum Street, and was an even more frequent visitor. 'I remember in the winter actually playing in there when it was cold, because it was big. We were always being told to be quiet, or being thrown out – "oh, it's you lot again, out you go" – but we used to use it as a playground.'

Tricia and Jackie were very keen on making the most of the local amenities, and ranged far and wide. 'On high days and holidays,' Tricia says 'there were funfairs on Hampstead Heath we used to go to, and there was Battersea funfair, which was a permanent fixture. And we knew a place in Regent's Park where the railings were loose and we could get into the zoo, never paid to get into London Zoo.'

There were also the perks that come with being in the right place at the right time. Tricia would hang around Carnaby Street when she was twelve or thirteen, in 1963 and '64, looking in shop windows. 'I saw the Beatles filming *Hard Day's Night,* playing somewhere up by Goodge Street, Mortimer Street: we were passing, and we were asked in off the street to come in and sit in the audience.'

Then of course there were the shops, something that most West End kids took for granted. We may not have had the money to pay, but the windows were an endless fascination, a screen to project our dreams on. Like me, Tricia spent a lot of time yearning at the displays at Gamba's, which sold ballet shoes from a shop on the corner of Dean Street and Old Compton Street. 'The people there knew my name, knew who I was, because I was always looking in the window, just hovering around there. I used to love it there. I was going to be a ballerina. I was in Anello & Davide's almost as much. If they threw me out of one, I would go to the other.'

The food shops also caught my attention. Hunger had sharpened my nostrils and honed my taste buds, and the windows of Camisa's, Lena Stores, Pâtisserie Valerie, the chocolate shop and the Algerian coffee store were wonderlands to me. Inside was even better. Salamis and hams hung from metal frames by means of wicked-looking S hooks and scented the air with garlic, paprika, mace and fennel. The spices and herbs mingled with the deli aroma of freshly ground coffee beans and vanilla pods. In the Algerian Coffee store, light gleamed on the copper and glass fixtures and fittings. Exotic printed labels declared the tea to be from India, Ceylon and China, and the coffee from Jamaica, or Central or South America, and gave me a quick geography lesson while they were about it. It was the same with the paper shop up the road. So many different languages and scripts were on display in their newspapers and magazines that outsiders and visitors would be bewildered; they simply couldn't believe there were so many languages.

Another memory for me was Hamleys toy shop, especially around Christmas, Easter and Guy Fawkes night, when they had special displays in the store and – most importantly to me – in the window, where I could see them easily. Once rationing was over, the windows were gorgeous to the greedy eyes of toy-starved kids. I remember huge displays of things made with Meccano or Bayko, mountains of cuddly toys, dolls that had yellow hair and said 'Mama' and, in the late fifties, lots and lots of things that needed batteries; dogs whose tails wagged and eyes lit up, robots... Dolls' houses were also popular. I remember having one that had 'electric lights' – torch bulbs that lit up when you connected the wiring to the little battery at the back.

The swimming pools at Marshall Street and, in the summer, the unheated outdoor pool at the Oasis in Endell Street used to draw kids from all over the West End. Although Graham Jackson lived closer to Endell Street, he always headed for Marshall Street. 'You had a big pool and a small pool, and they'd alternate, men and women. Sometimes we'd have the whole small pool to ourselves, about half a dozen of us kids. And when you were finished, you'd get an ice cream or something, wander up through Soho, and go home with your towel tucked under your arm.'

I have memories of going to the Oasis, but not of swimming. All I can remember is people sun-bathing, grown-ups mostly, and lots of posing in bathing suits. Marshall Street seemed better suited to swimming and mucking about, and perhaps that's why Graham preferred it. Children find the courtship rituals of young adults really boring, and that's how I recall the Oasis, as a place for young grown-ups to eye each other up.

Ronnie Mann made the trip across Charing Cross Road with some of the other 'Bury kids: 'We used to go swimming up Marshall Street, then nick stuff coming back through Berwick Street market, anything you could get; apples, ice creams, bananas. [laughs] It's a wonder we didn't all end up on bleedin' Dartmoor.'

Angela Rashbrook and Andy Pullinger both made their way to the baths through Soho from their homes in St James's, where their parents were housekeepers. 'My friend Liz lived in St James's Palace, also in tied accommodation,' Angela remembers. 'She and I and both our mums would spend Saturday afternoon at Marshall Street baths. We would swim while our mums sat and knitted and nattered. When we were older, we would be allowed to go alone, and would stop to buy chips in Berwick Street on the way home.'

And, of course, there was something else we had in the West End that no other kid in the country had: Soho. Andy Pullinger remembers that, 'I was an altar and choirboy at St James's Church, Piccadilly. Morning and evening, every Sunday. After the evening service, the choir went to sing for the patients at the Ear, Nose and Throat Hospital, Soho Square. When we had finished singing, my friend, Robert Hoyles and I would roam around Soho looking at the working girls, wondering what they did, and play pinball in the arcade on Greek Street. We did this every Sunday. It seemed to make up for the rest of the day.'

The West End provided its children and young people with seemingly endless opportunities to explore their world. It is hard to imagine a playground that offered more opportunities for fun and games, even the innocent ones. If it snowed, the London child could head off to Hampstead Heath or Primrose Hill with a tin tray for a toboggan. If they had to travel, buses were cheap for kids and scooters, go-karts and skateboards –

130

literally, a roller-skate with a board attached – were knocked up in yards and the raw materials filched from Covent Garden market at night, from the alleys behind shops or from those mother lodes of useful bits and bobs – bomb sites.

And if it was too cold, wet and grim to play outside, there was still no need to go home. The galleries, museums, churches and department stores offered sanctuary, lots of stimulation and even a little education.

5

School Days

I didn't go to school in the West End. My parents split up just before I was due to start, so school was somewhere I went to from the string of houses my mother rented in Essex, while my father's flat in Old Compton Street, Soho, was my home at weekends and in the school holidays. I can't help but think that things would have been better if I had gone to school in Soho, because I never fitted in in Essex.

Virtually all of the people interviewed for this book, though, did go to one of the many primary schools in the West End. I was surprised to find just how many schools there were in the area, tucked away down side streets, out of sight, or indeed my memory. Ironically, all of them – in what outsiders insist on seeing as a godless and sinful place – were associated with churches. The people I spoke to went to St Martin's (just off Trafalgar Square); St James's and St Peter's (now known as Soho Parish) in Windmill Street; St Giles-in-the-Fields in Endell Street; St Clement Danes in Drury Lane; St George's (Hanover Square) in South Street, Mayfair; St Patrick's in Great Chapel Street, Soho: Notre Dame in Leicester Square or St Joseph's in Macklin Street, Covent Garden. The last three were Catholic schools. St Giles, Notre Dame and St Patrick's have since closed, but the others remain.

All of the schools had been built in the late nineteenth century, and thus had to be fitted into a neighbourhood that was already crammed full of buildings. This meant that they were short of space, especially outdoor space for the children to play, which led them to embrace some ingenious solutions. Leo Zanelli, who was born in 1930, had experience of three of them; 'I was at Notre Dame in Leicester Square in the war. A landmine landed on the roof, so for a few days we went to the school at Windmill Street, and then we ended up at St Patrick's. I went from a school with its playground in the basement to one with a playground outside, and from there to a school with one on the roof, completely caged in.'

There were other rooftop playgrounds, at St Giles and St Clement Danes. In the latter, boys were confined to the ribbon of tarmac playground that ran around the tall school buildings while the generally more decorous girls were allowed free rein on the roof, which was fenced, but – because girls don't play ball games – not caged in. There

132

was a strategic advantage to this that had not occurred to me. 'When it snowed,' Barbara Jones remembers, 'we used to make snowballs and lob them over the fence, in the hope they would land on the boys in the playground. We'd make them at break, then lob them over at lunchtime. It was a really cold winter in 1947.'

No boy I knew would let such an insult go un-avenged. Barbara agreed. 'The boys made theirs at lunchtime, and under the old system they got out five minutes before us, at three thirty. And there they would all be, waiting at the gate laden with these iceballs. But I would just walk away with my nose in the air because I had Owen, my knight in shining armour, who would just bat them all away from me.'

Although I heard tales of strict discipline at some of the schools – child cruelty by today's standards – St Joseph's in Covent Garden, a school run by nuns from the Sisters of Mercy, had by far the worst reputation. Mike O'Rouke was a pupil there from 1949 to 1955. 'It was certainly run by sisters, but they weren't very merciful. The headmistress down there, when I first started – my father remembered her well from when he was there – was called Sister Camillus, and her nickname was Sister Come-and-kill-us. That tells you something about them, doesn't it?'

Margaret Connolly, who grew up in Northing-ton Street, in Holborn, remembers Sister Camil-lus's successor, Sister Dominic. 'School was a very long walk away. My mother, with three or four children in tow, had to get the pram across Theobald's Road, *en route* to Macklin Street. She was invariably late getting us to school, and Sister Dominic would be there with the cane, ready to hit us across our knuckles. My mother never made any comment – in those days the Church was always right! My form mistress was Miss Angel, and she was OK. Less aggressive.'

The nuns' fearsome reputation spread beyond St Joseph's. Olga Jackson, who went to St Clement Danes, was 'terrified of the nuns from that school in Macklin Street, if we saw them out. The kids who went there, they used to say how strict they were. Barbaric.'

The Sisters' savage discipline often proved counterproductive. Ann Lee, who went to St Clement Danes, remembers that 'My mum was brought up a Catholic, but the minute she was able to change her mind, she did, because she said the nuns at Macklin Street school were evil. They were supposedly Sisters of Mercy but there was no mercy at that school. My mum said they would hit you across the knuckles with a ruler, but the edge side, not the flat side.'

One of the transgressions punished at the school was left-handedness, which was seen as a devilish characteristic. It wasn't only the Catholic school-teachers who saw the red mist rise when children picked up pens or pencils with the wrong hand. 'I wrote left-handed,' Janet Vance recalls, 'and they used to put the cane across my knuckles. Even in the senior school, they would take my pen out of my left hand and put it in the right.'

Janet's primary school was St James's and St Peter's. 'The headmistress was Miss Hudson. She was an evil cow. Once, when I was five or six, I was

134

running from the playground to the loo, and she caught me running and stopped me and gave me such a clout across the back of the legs that I wet myself. So I ran out of the school and went to my dad, who was working in Bateman Street. When I got there, I still had the finger marks on my legs. That done it. Dad marched me back to the school, went into the office and got hold of her by the lapels of her jacket and said, "If you want to hit her in future, you keep your hands to yourself. Otherwise I'll do exactly the same to you."

'Afterwards, Mum and Dad talked about taking me out of there, but it was handy for my mum's work and that, and they thought she wouldn't touch me again. Well, she didn't, but she had to put her hands down a few times.'

I can sympathize with Janet. A headmaster at one of the primary schools I attended would walk into a classroom and whack the head of whoever was sitting by the door, on general principles. He was also a firm believer in the ruler, edge side on: he thought a few thwacks across the knuckles was a handwriting aid. We were supposed to be learning the Richardson style of cursive script, and because of all those assaults with the ruler, I still don't write that way. It is the first time I can remember being wilfully disobedient. Nothing that monster could do would have made me write the way he said. I was quite firm about that.

John Carnera remembers that the standard punishment at St Patrick's was 'six of the best on the hand, with a cane. You had to rub your hands before you got the cane so you'd feel less pain. It was all hot. There were various techniques. It sounds terrible now, but to be honest I don't think it did me any harm. If you did something wrong, you remembered it. It taught us values.' Although St Patrick's was a Catholic school, this time it was not members of the Church who were handing out the discipline. 'All the teachers were laymen and women. We had some ... interesting ... characters there. There was a Spanish teacher, Mr Benitez. He was always very sharp on the [mimes a cane] and used to chuck chalk at you if he caught you talking while you were supposed to be listening to him, or creep up behind you and smack you on the shoulder with a ruler or something.'

Violent punishment was also meted out to very young children. Ronnie Mann was on the receiving end of some of it at St Clement Danes: 'I remember Mr Jones, the headmaster, as a sadistic bully, but he may well not have been. One of his tricks was, if you talked in assembly, it didn't matter how young you were, he used to pick you up by your hair, lift you off the ground and walk you down to the front, and then cane you. Excruciating pain. It was unbelievable. And one of the lady teachers had a "magic wand", which was the cane. Bear in mind you're dealing with young kids: five, six or seven. OK, we were probably disgusting little bastards if the truth is known, but if you had snot running down your nose you got walloped – and certainly I didn't have a hanky. If you talked, you got walloped. If you got mucky fingerprints on stuff, you got caned.'

I remember the casual, institutional violence of my schooldays well, but when measured against today's standards it seems appalling. Ronnie apparently took things in his stride, and came to the same sort of conclusion as John Carnera. 'I felt that by the standards of the forties, St Clement's was a good school. It taught you how to read and write. It didn't give you a great deal other than that. I think they assumed that most of us kids would be leaving as soon as we could, for whatever reason. They tended to concentrate on the really clever kids. No one ever said to you, this is what you've got to do, because you had apprenticeships to fall back on. Most of the people there were expecting to be in menial jobs, that was the crux of it.'

Other pupils of St Clement Danes seemed to have only positive memories of the place. 'St Clement Danes was lovely,' Ann Lee told me. 'When they put the new bells in St Clement Danes church, our class was standing around the bells on the floor singing "Oranges and Lemons" to christen the bells before they actually went up.'

Ann is one of many who went there from the Peabody Estate in Wild Street. Barbara Jones got to know many of the 'Wild Street Brats' – as the children from the Peabody and other local blocks of flats were colloquially known – at St Clement's. 'There were lots of children, big families, with no adult males at home and perhaps an elderly grandmother trying to hold things together. The boys had to take turns wearing the shoes so they could come to school. In the summer, the girls would wear just a bag-washed cotton dress and plimsolls. Socks – just forget it for everybody. I was seen as "posh" at St Clement Danes because

137

I wore knickers, even in the summer!

'We left for school all bandboxy, with hats and gloves matching, socks all pristine, hair perfectly groomed. By the time I'd finished playing football with the boys in the playground below, rather than tag on the roof with the girls, I'd lost one pigtail ribbon, my coat's split, my socks are all dirty, my knees are probably all skinned, I've lost a glove, and now I'm walking home, and my mother's been known to see me coming along the Strand and cross the road to miss me in case I meet the bosses. A lady went to school, and this urchin came back.'

'Dad wouldn't walk down the same side of the street as her,' her sister, Pat, chimes in, laughing. 'I went to school as a lady, and came back as a lady.'

St James's and St Peter's had an enclosed playground surrounded by tall buildings – including the Windmill Theatre. 'The girls at the Windmill used to sit on their roof in the summer, just across the playground,' Sonia Boulter remembers. 'That could be distracting. We didn't know the Windmill girls, didn't talk to them, but they used to wave to us girls in the street.'

Sonia has nothing but affectionate memories of her schooldays. 'My first teacher, in the reception class, used to wear all black and one of those Old Mother Riley hats, mob caps. She was lovely. We had a woman who used to look after us in the playground. She was very old-fashioned. She used to wear a hat with a bonnet that went up [sic] instead of a peaked cap, the peak was up here. It was great fun there. The school wasn't barred in like it is now, with the tall gates there. You could just walk in.'

St James's and St Peter's didn't suit everyone, though. Andy Pullinger told me that, 'After a couple of years at Great Windmill Street, I was transferred to St George's in Mayfair. I think my mother felt that St James's was a bit too rough.'

Angela Rashbrook's mother agreed with Mrs Pullinger. 'I went to St George's Hanover Square,' Angela recalls. 'My mother considered the primary school in Great Windmill Street, the nearest to us, to be "too cosmopolitan".'

St James's and St Peter's cosmopolitan nature was not exaggerated. 'It was all nations,' Janet Vance remembers. 'You had the Italians, the Greeks, the Jews. You had the Catholic priest come in, the rabbi, the Church of England vicar and every morning they used to take us in a crocodile down to St James's Church, Piccadilly. The Catholics would go to Warwick Street or, if the priest from St Patrick's came in, to Soho Square, and the rabbi would come in and they would stay at the school.'

Jeff Sloneem was one of those who stayed at school with the rabbi – or, in his day, a Miss Klausner. 'She was effectively paid by the synagogue to take the Hebrew class while the assembly was going on,' Jeff remembers. 'There were quite a lot of Jewish children there, actually. We were all sat around one table, but it was quite a long table. I should imagine there were about thirty, over all the years. I would think that St James's was probably the first multinational school.'

Jeff may well have been right, but the same

melting pot effect could be seen at other schools in the area. 'All the races were mixed up in Soho,' says Leo Zanelli. 'Even though there were a lot of Irish and Italians there, one of my best friends at St Patrick's was Paddy Nichopophoulos. We even had Gibraltarians, sent to get them out of harm's way in the war.'

Ronnie Mann remembers that 'The Catholic schools, like Macklin Street, were a bit uptight about you being a Catholic. St Clement's, my school, was Church of England, but it took everybody. Protestants, Catholics, Jews, Greek Orthodox, Russian Orthodox, any old Orthodoxy, and they didn't give a shit.'

Tricia Bryan found it was much the same at St Giles School. 'One thing that stands out is that St Giles was a very multicultural school. I had classmates from Turkey, Greece and the Middle East. Most had families who ran restaurants in the area. One name that springs to mind is Lloyd Zokay, which seemed so exotic.' Tricia embodies that multicultural background. 'We're Polish Jewish on my mother's side, and my father's family were Catholic. So my brother and I had a Catholic father, a Jewish mother, and went to a C of E school: we went to church every Wednesday.'

As with several of the other schools in the area, the links with the Church were real, but not stifling. 'All the primary schools were affiliated to some religion or other,' Tricia remembers. 'The vicar at St Giles, the Reverend Taylor, had a big apartment in our school. He had two daughters, who went to a private school! St Giles was not a bad school at all, though. It may have been small, but the staff were all very dedicated. We were taken every week in a crocodile to the basement of the YWCA in Great Russell Street for swimming. Netball was in Lincoln's Inn Fields, and we walked there. We walked everywhere, no school buses.'

'Coram's Fields for games, country dancing and everything,' chips in her classmate, Jackie Trussler. 'Always walking. We must have gone for the afternoon, then walked home from there.'

The school that Mrs Pullinger and Mrs Rashbrook chose for their children was a cut above St James's and St Peter's. St George's (Hanover Square) had migrated from its original location down to a patch of land between handsome mansion blocks in South Street, just west of Berkeley Square, in the heart of Mayfair. As a council school in a very upmarket area, it attracted a particular type of child, as one of their number, Ray Constantine, remembered. 'Many of the children had parents who were caretakers to embassies, and some VIPs in the Mayfair area. There was one girl whose father managed a pub in Whitehall. A small number had single mums who were call girls in the Shepherd Market area. There were two sisters whose father managed some part of the park, and lived in a lovely cottage near Hyde Park Corner. Their dad was using Italian POWs to maintain the park.'

Before the reforms of the post-war Labour government, the distinction between primary – infant and junior – and secondary schools was not so clear-cut. Some children went to grammar

141

schools, often, but not always, fee-paying, at eleven or thirteen, but the rest generally stayed at the same school. This wasn't always a good idea. Although he later went to university, Leo Zanelli recalls that 'I had virtually no teaching as a child. I stayed at St Patrick's until I was fourteen, then left. No one was bothered. In the war, there were just two teachers for the whole school. There was Mr Rook, the head, who seemed to spend most of the time with his bookie, a nun, and a woman who married a Belgian. That was it for five or six classes. Most of the time, you sat on your own. They'd give you something to do, but most of the time we didn't do it. Several kids never learned to read or write.'

John Carnera from a later generation of St Patrick's pupils, fared a bit better. 'I went to school there from seven until I was fifteen; got a basic education. There might have been 120 or 150 pupils. No more than that, fifteen or so in each year. We all did the eleven-plus. If you passed it, you went to other schools. Most of us just stayed on.

'Ours was a very unusual school, in that it was more or less run by the Church. We used to start the day with Religious Affairs. That was from nine o'clock to half-past. They'd teach us the catechism, and the Bible, stuff like that, then ask us if we'd been to church, been to confession. If you hadn't, you were frowned on, you know.'

Although some of the primary schools, such as St George's and St Patrick's, maintained an upper school, where children could continue after they had taken their eleven-plus, there was only one

142

secondary modern school, St Martin-in-the-Fields, in the Soho and Covent Garden area. Grammar schools were even harder to find, so for some of those who did pass their eleven-plus success was a mixed blessing. A grammar school place meant a daily tube or bus ride to go to school. This could curtail your social life, as Mike O'Rouke remembers: 'I passed my eleven-plus, and there was only a handful of us from St Joseph's that did at that time. I went off to Shepherd's Bush, to go to school there, right on the borders of Holland Park. You come home, do your homework, go to bed. I lost touch with a lot of the people I went to primary school with.' Barbara Jones got into the Greycoat School in Victoria, and others we spoke to went further afield still, to Primrose Hill or Chelsea.

St Martin's got mixed reviews. Janet Vance, for example, turned down both St Martin's and a secondary school at Millbank because, although they were closer than the school she eventually attended, 'they had bad names'. Graham Jackson remembers, 'I went to St Martin-in-the-Fields, and this curate took a fancy to me. He used to come on and say "Hello Graham", put his arm around me. It was a joke, a standing joke. Anyway, there was a club there called Five Farthings – from the rhyme, St Martin's five farthings. They used to do snooker, billiards, that sort of stuff, there was a coffee bar beneath – it was in the crypt. One day, the curate touched a guy who was bending over the table, and this kid's turned round and hit him with his cue. He was from St Martin's School, and of course there's a big hoo-hah, and when he's called into see the head-master, he's said, "If you want to know what [the curate's] like, ask Graham."

'So, I'm sitting in the class: "Graham Jackson out," left-right, left-right, down to see the head-master, and I'm saying, "What am I doing, what's happening?"

'And they ask, "Have you got a problem with this curate?"

'And I've gone, "Well, yeah."

'They dismissed it. "You don't know what you're talking about. Rubbish. He's a friendly bloke. We've had a word with him, and you've got the wrong idea." It was all sort of passed off. Years later, you start thinking, they're all the same. They cover things up by saying you don't know what you're talking about. 'Cause we're, what, fourteen years old, it's easy to get us to think we're the ones that are in the wrong.'

Ann Lee first chose Millbank over St Martin's, but 'I was only there about a year and a half, and my mum took me out. A teacher there abused one of the children, who was my friend. We used to stay behind for music lessons, and this particular day I didn't want to, so I made the excuse that I had to go to the dentist, and I left her on her own with him. The next day, when I went to school, she wasn't there, and neither was he. When I got home that night, Mum had had a call from her mum saying that he'd abused her, and within weeks it was in all the newspapers. My mum decided to take us out, and we went to Starcross in Gray's Inn Road, just off the Euston Road, and that's where I stayed until I was fifteen.'

Ronnie Mann learned several things at St Martin's. One of them was that, just because you were getting older, they didn't stop hitting you. 'At St Martin's,' he remembers, 'discipline was strong. When the whistle went, you stopped; if you didn't, you got the cane. There was no arguing. If you talked in class, you got the cane. If you swore at a teacher, you got the cane; second time, you got expelled. Simple as that. There was no half-measures.'

Yet there was something about this regime that Ronnie found liberating. 'At St Martin's, it was a totally different concept from St Clement's. I think that the headmaster, Mr Tomlinson, although at the time I didn't appreciate him, was really far-reaching. I don't think I started learning until I was about twelve and a half, thirteen. I fully deserved to fail my eleven-plus, because I had no concept of nouns, verbs, adjectives, no concept of anything. I was great at maths, but that was about it.'

As well as schoolwork, there were social lessons to be learned, and put into practice. 'It was a mixed school. You didn't sit next to the girls, because that would have been too effeminate, but certainly they sat in front of you, or behind you, and we had dance lessons together. When you got to thirteen, on a Friday evening there was an hour where they taught you the basics of ballroom dancing, if you wanted to. Bear in mind this was around the advent of rock 'n' roll, Bill Haley was just coming in, but you still learned the basics, and by the time I left we'd already advanced to jiving. It was great for me.'

Anyone educated in the fifties remembers harsh discipline, lots of learning by rote and endless hours spent copying work, with one's right hand, preferably, from the blackboard. It seems, however, that most young West Enders didn't resent the system that much and one thing is for certain, a West End education prepared the young learners to live in harmony with cultural, religious and racial diversity – a very useful lesson that anticipated the world we live in today.

6

The Market

Few parts of the West End have changed their character quite as much as the Piazza in Covent Garden. Today, it's a tourist trap, full of shops, cafés, restaurants and street entertainers, while dominating the whole thing is the new Royal Opera House. When I was growing up in the fifties, the buildings that now house boutiques, antiques and flea markets, the London Transport Museum and the Theatre Museum were home to a wholesale fruit and vegetable market, the largest in the country.

The contrast between the old Covent Garden and the new is startling. I remember a noisy, incredibly crowded place with porters dashing about with stacks of boxes and baskets on their heads, roll-ups hanging from their lips and language riper than the fruit on sale. Incomprehensible (to me, anyway) shouts filled the air as wholesalers and punters haggled over prices in a variety of accents from nasal cockney, through all the regional variations and on to Italian, French, Yiddish, Chinese or Greek, and everything between. It depended on who was selling, who was buying and who was delivering. It really was an extraordinary cacophony, but somehow, with much gesticulating, understanding was reached and business done. Some of the hand signals were reminiscent of the tick-tack men that bookies used on the racecourses, a private language that could only be read by those in the know.

The surrounding streets were just as confused. Locally crafted barrows teetered with boxes, baskets and sacks either coming or going. Horses still shackled to their carts waited patiently, snuffling in nosebags full of oats. Some had their heads down, foraging for stray apples, turnips and carrots, or slurped water from a battered old bucket as they were loaded up with the morning's haul. The gutters ran with water – horse, flower and rain – and the cobbles were strewn with dung, bruised fruit, battered spuds, broken blooms, straw and bits of cabbage, while horses and traders alike waded through it all.

When trading was done for the day, the mess would be cleaned up, to be replaced the following day with more of the same, but before the cleaning squad arrived, the pickers darted into salvage anything worth eating, flogging or popping in a vase. I have often wondered what happened to the daily piles left by the horses at the market.

Elsewhere in the country, people nipped out with a bucket and spade to collect any offerings left by horses pulling wagons delivering bread, milk or coal – it was so good for their gardens. Due to the scarcity of petrol, horse power was much in demand in the forties and early fifties, and there was always a plentiful supply of fresh manure in those narrow Covent Garden streets. Perhaps it went to the London parks, for their roses.

The market was centred around the Piazza, which was laid out by Inigo Jones in the 1630s as a smart, public open space in the Italian style, with the back of the Duke of Bedford's mansion on the Strand marking out the south side and fine houses and St Paul's church on the other three. The Duke had ambitions to provide gracious homes for the elite, and an elegant square for the important business of promenading. It was vital to see who was in town, what they were wearing and so on: being seen was equally important, as was picking up news and scandal.

Given this, it's surprising that the Duke should allow a rather ramshackle market to set up shop on the south side of this handsome public amenity. A daily general market started there in a small way in 1649, selling, among other things, local produce and crockery, from temporary stalls and a few hardly more permanent buildings – sheds, basically – erected on the south, up against the wall of the Bedfords' gardens. A century later, the market had more or less taken over the Piazza, supplying much of West London with many of the necessities and one or two of the luxuries of life, including caged birds, cooked food and 'Geneva and Other Spirituous Liquors'.

From the start, the market was a chaotic, congested affair, almost entirely conducted in the open air. By the 1830s, the managers of the Bedford Estate, which still administered the market and collected tolls, had engaged a man named Fowler to design some permanent market buildings. Fowler had made his name designing an elegant basilica-style home for nearby Hungerford market (where Charing Cross station stands today). His buildings at Covent Garden, with a frontage to the west uniting three ranges of buildings running east to west, still stand today, although they have been smartened up quite a bit. The Clean Air Act of the fifties, the lack of horses and the absence of tons of discarded fruit and veg have all helped to keep them that way.

The managers of the Covent Garden Theatre built the Floral Hall as a private flower market in the 1860s. It was a commercial failure, and was bought by the Bedford Estate in 1887 to be a foreign fruit market. The Estate made further improvements, culminating in the opening of the Jubilee Hall in 1904, before selling out to the newly formed Covent Garden Estate Company in 1918. They remained in charge until 1961.

Although the very occasional visits I made with my father are imprinted on my memory, I cannot pretend that the market was ever central to my life. It was, after all, across the Great Divide of the Charing Cross Road. I was mainly aware of it from its customers: the little old ladies who sold bouquets and buttonholes at street corners, or to theatre and cinema queues – London's flower market was also in the Garden, along the north side, where Great and Little Hart Street had been renamed Floral Street in its honour; and the men who trundled their barrows along Old Compton Street in the early morning on their way to setup their flash in Berwick Street, Rupert Street or the pitches in the side streets just off Oxford Street.

My main memories from my few youthful visits are of the great press of people and vehicles in the narrow streets, and the way the smells of the countryside – horse dung, cabbage, mould and earth – predominated in the centre of the city. I also remember how, in the hours up to lunchtime, the lorries that filled the streets around the market helped my stumbling efforts to read by having exotic addresses painted on their cab doors: Wigan, Bridgend, Daventry, Ammanford – they could have been Budapest or Timbuktu as far as I was concerned. Men – often young men in mufflers, with the inevitable ciggies stuck to their lower lips, or dogged and tucked behind their ear for later – swarmed over the backs of the trucks, building teetering loads of boxes, crates and cartons, all held together with faith, ropes and tarpaulin.

For the children who actually lived in Covent Garden, of course, the market was a vital presence at the very centre of their daily lives, one that everyone I talked to looked back on with great affection. It was often part of their journey to or from school; a mysterious, echoing and empty space when the market was closed, and a fascinating, noisy and jam-packed one when it was open. It was a place of opportunities to be exploited, where they could fill their senses with rare and exotic sights and scents, and often the source of their family's livelihood.

For some, the market, empty or working, was part of an urban playground. Mike O'Rouke, who lived on the corner of Shelton Street and Mercer Street, remembers it clearly. 'I was always up there,' he told me. 'We used to go down where the main Piazza is, we used to get boxes and piles of sacks, you know, and you could climb up those, and play run-outs – you could hide for hours on end down there. We used to play run-outs round the streets, all up and down Long Acre, Langley Street, Neal Street.'

The back yards and alleys of the streets near the market also provided places for young Mike to play. 'On Mercer Street, where my grandparents lived, there was – still is – a big opening behind them, and we used to have sacks and boxes there, and you could squeeze through the gate and you could make camps, climb about – just climbing in general, you know.'

'Covent Garden market was a playground to us,' Ann Lee remembers. 'It was only up the road. Mum knew a lot of the people that worked there, because they all sort of grew up together – I should imagine there were some who worked there who weren't local, but I didn't meet any.' In fact, in the fifties, a lot of the market's workforce lived south of the river, but a fair few lived locally. Mike O'Rouke's family, for instance, had been involved in one way or another for generations.

The O'Roukes were mostly porters and

151

traders, but there was plenty of work supporting the market, too. Ann Lee remembers that 'Mum had a little cleaning job actually in Covent Garden market, and she used to take me into the office with her – you know, the old-fashioned telephones, and the old-fashioned typewriters... I can see myself sitting at the desk – and as she walked through, it was "Morning, Kit", "OK, Kit?" and "Goodnight, Kit", and I thought, "My mum knows everybody", but it was because a lot of local people worked there, in the market.'

It wasn't just the locals who saw the marketplace as entertainment. The everyday business of the market was a tourist attraction in itself, and I suspect that was why I was there with Father (well, that, and the out-of-hours drinking opportunities): we were tourists from across the Great Divide. Several guidebooks recommended a visit. Paul C, for example, on one of his trips to London to sample the delights of Soho, remembers that, one early summer morning after a very late night, 'I went to Covent Garden, just to look round. It was a most extraordinary display of vegetables and flowers, and it was full of "characters", doing business, all furiously smoking and with a pencil behind the ear. They were shouting at each other in a language I could hardly understand, but obviously had something to do with money. And there were other guys in very expensive overcoats running around pointing that they wanted things, holding up fingers to show how many. I was absolutely fascinated just to watch it, and to see so much activity in a fairly small area.'

Even in the nineteenth century the area was

congested. Covent Garden had been laid out for pleasure, not commerce, and the narrow streets were easily overwhelmed by the traffic. The market was so busy that the buildings could not contain all its business, which spilled into the adjoining streets. King Street, Henrietta Street, Russell Street, Southampton Street and Tavistock Street were usually lined with parked lorries, waiting horses and wagons, while others tried to inch their way past. As it was sited so close to the river, when the railways came to London, they could not get near it. Charing Cross was basically a passenger station, and besides only gave access to a few southern counties.

By the fifties, trucks and lorries coming direct from farms, London rail termini and, increasingly, airports, were making virtually all the deliveries to the market, but for the buyers it was a different matter. A lot of the market's customers relied on manpower or horsepower to get the goods home. 'In a way it was like Victorian London, just after the Second World War,' Ronnie Mann remembers. 'The lorries and trains used to bring stuff up to town, but I would say that 75 to 80 per cent of the local traffic – you know, fruit and veg people, all the local people, even as far as Tottenham – would come by horse and cart.'

I loved those horses: some were shire-like with great shaggy hooves, others were titchy – and rather tetchy – Shetland ponies, but, big or small, they all clip-clopped over the cobbles utterly unmoved by the chaos around them. The delicious smell of warm horse continued to provide a base to anchor the fruity and floral top notes of the market's perfume through the fifties, although Ronnie Mann told me that the horses had virtually gone by about 1960. 'From the time I was five or six, until I was about eighteen in 1960, I'd seen it go from 75 per cent horses and carts to maybe two or three. It was only older people kept the horse and cart.'

The market's influence and business spread way beyond the Piazza. The streets across Long Acre and up around the Seven Dials were full of small wholesale concerns. Some of them were virtual Aladdin's caves. 'Off Seven Dials there were lots of little warehouses,' Barbara Jones told me. 'They were all part of the market, and one of the girls at school, called Jean, her family were among the first to get hold of bananas when they came back into the country after the war. I remember standing at this very small warehouse thing – like a greengrocer's, only it wasn't a shop at the front, you know – and the shutters were back, and there were boxes and boxes of bananas. They weren't on the ration but they were so scarce that the greengrocers used to ration them, one a week for every child's ration book.'

Alleyways and arches between the shops, houses and warehouses led to little yards and lock-ups where, until the late fifties, horses were housed next to their wagons. 'Down the other side of the Strand, right by Villiers Street, you had Hungerford Lane, which is now closed off. That used to be all stables,' Ronnie Mann recalls. 'You could go down there, and there was horses and carts there, right up to 1960.'

The buying and selling began in earnest at six or seven in the morning and of course deliveries arrived a good deal earlier.

Barbara Jones remembers the market in full flow very well, as she had a paper round before school for a newsagent in New Row. 'In the market there are all the scenes that you see from *My Fair Lady* or whatever, only more so. And I can remember Mash & Marram, Turner & Turnell, and all sorts of names like that, and they'd be parked from New Row, all round King Street, all over, everywhere.'

Fruit was hard to come by after the war, and for much of the fifties. It was even more out of reach for those on a limited income. When the children were on their way to school, and the market was still thronged, the stallholders' wares could provide a virtually irresistible temptation. Ronnie Mann's route from Bedfordbury took him through Garrick Street or King Street into Henrietta Street, then Tavistock Street. 'One of the things that happened in the market,' he recalls, 'was when they were unloading, they weren't allowed to pick a banana or fruit, but if a thing dropped it was classified as wasted or spoilt, and the porters were allowed to pick it up and take it home. What we used to do was rush in, grab it, and run off again, and they would do their nut.'

Local children had been grabbing and running for decades. Graham Jackson recalls his mother, who was born in the area in the early years of the twentieth century, telling him that 'One would run through with a knife and slit the potato [sacks] open, and others running behind would pick them up.'

A more ladylike approach could work wonders. Barbara Jones, who walked along the south side of the market on her way from her home in John Adam Street to school at St Clement Danes, recalls how 'the market men soon got to know that I wouldn't touch a thing on their stall – or carts, with their lovely little Shetland ponies – because I was very strictly brought up on that point. In consequence, they would *give* me lots of fruit as I walked past, so I arrived at school with pockets crammed – and splitting, to my mother's despair! – and shared it all out with my friends, including those who'd managed to pinch just one piece of fruit on the way to school.' This rather begs the question of why the others kept on stealing: it must have been the thrill of the chase and triumphant escape.

When the market closed in the afternoon it became a very different place, hushed and echoing, full of parked and empty barrows, stacks of baskets covered in tarpaulins and the wooden frames that would support the night's displays. Children going home from school at St Clement Danes or St Joseph's often found a route that took them through the Piazza and the surrounding streets, so they could play in and around them, whooping through the open arcades, examining abandoned or discarded fruit or simply satisfying their curiosity. Some collected the discarded paper wrappers from around oranges, lemons and other exotic fruit. I remember these wrappers well. They were often beautifully printed with colourful scenes, not unlike the labels on wine bottles, but flimsier, like tissue paper. Some were real works of art, and they provided a splash of colour in an often dingy day-to-day world.

Ronnie Mann recalls that 'when we came back from school, and [the market] was all cleared up, we'd scout and pick up potatoes, cabbages – nick 'em, maybe break a box open. I mean, everybody nicked around there. It sounds ridiculous now...'

Ann Lee also played in the empty market. 'The buildings, when the market was closed, it was very quiet, very eerie; but quite exciting. We just used to go round in places where you couldn't go when the market was alive, you could go round and have a look.'

As the afternoon turned into evening, and the last errant street kids went home to their tea, the atmosphere changed again. Barbara Jones relished it. 'Walking through in the evening, when it hadn't started up again yet, there were all these grilles, big manholes, and the strips in them were really quite wide and long, and the smells of the fruit would come up from there, and of course this was the time, after the war, when there wasn't a lot of fruit around, and that was the atmosphere; slightly cabbagey, but fruity as well.'

Thunderously noisy most of the time, the Piazza could be so quiet on a winter's evening that a shout or the clatter of high heels on cobblestones would bounce around the empty buildings. Barbara Jones again: 'When it was closed, there was this strange feeling to the air that affected the acoustics of the market. If somebody in anything other than rubber soles walked down one of the other aisles, you could hear their footsteps, and your own footsteps, echoing all around. It never troubled me, but I can imagine a situation where someone thought they were being followed. You could hear people in the other aisles, but you wouldn't know which direction they were, because the sound would bounce around. You couldn't tell where it was coming from.'

Around ten o'clock, the first of the workers would arrive to stir the market back into life, to open things up and get ready for the early deliveries. As theatre- and cinema-goers caught the last trains and buses home, the legion of night workers at Covent Garden headed the other way. For Barbara Jones, this, too, was a special time of night. 'We'd go to see our friends in Great Russell Street, by the British Museum, and come back via the market at eleven or midnight, and they'd all be there setting up ready for the morning; the lights were on, the smells of all the fruit, everyone hustling and bustling, carrying those round baskets on their heads. It was all there. It was all going on.'

John Carnera, who lived in Soho, never accompanied his father, Secundo, on his early morning trips. He remembers the market from the other end of the day. 'Late at night, that's when the fruit and veg would be delivered from wherever, and that's when the market would start up, in the middle of the night, sorting out the fruit and veg ready for the buyers first thing in the morning.'

Rolling up at Covent Garden in the early hours was part of any night out in the West End. There was one pressing reason for this, as John Carnera

158

explains: 'You could get a drink at Covent Garden at all hours of the night, early in the morning. There used to be a lot of drunks about...'

The area around the market was indeed famous – or notorious – because in those days of strict licensing laws some of the public houses in the vicinity opened all night to cater for market workers. They could be very rough and ready places, to suit the clientele. Ronnie Mann remembers 'The Essex Serpent in King Street was a pub with sawdust on the floor. Can you imagine going into a pub nowadays with sawdust on the floor?'

Although the cafés and pubs were open for the convenience of the market workers, they naturally attracted all sorts of night people; club-workers from Soho on their way home, dedicated drinkers, insomniacs and those who'd missed the last bus and didn't fancy a long tramp through dark deserted streets to their own beds. Gary Winkler, who was up virtually all night running the Nucleus coffee bar in Monmouth Street, remembers, 'When I used to go out drinking – which I did a lot – I'd have booze in my office at the coffee bar, have a few drinks and start getting squiffy, and then we'd go down to Covent Garden market for the pubs, because they opened at odd hours. And when they closed, Smithfield used to open, you could get drinks there an hour later. Covent Garden closed, say, at nine or ten, and Smithfield opened then for an hour, then you could come back into town and start drinking at the normal pubs.'

Ronnie Mann, who worked in the flower market in the late fifties, remembers, 'Blokes there – the night shift started at eleven, by the time the pub opened at three or four in the morning, they've done four or five hours' work and they're looking for a drink. They don't go into a café, they go and have a drink. The Bell in Wellington Street, by the Lyceum, that's where a lot of our salesmen used to go. I always used to say they'd be dead by the time they were fifty, and most of them were, 'cause they were all drinking whisky, beer, long hours, they never slept properly, they were drunk eighteen hours out of twenty-four. We used to have pots of tea, they'd have a whisky, all bleeding night. No wonder the prices of the flowers varied!'

There were cafés as well as pubs, of course, where a split sausage or fried egg, smothered in brown sauce and slapped between two slabs of lightly buttered (or, more likely, marged) bread, all washed down with sweet, thick, aromatic tea, made a satisfying meal. In these steamy rooms was a whole different world, one of flat caps, Woodbines and Brylcreem, where you could find small, whippety men with calloused hands, and large and formidable women bundled up in coats, exchanging greetings and gossip, or quietly reading the racing form and the early editions of the papers with the help of their brand new National Health glasses.

Unlike the market pubs, the local cafés would stay open for much of the day for the local trade. Barbara Jones remembers one just to the right of the entrance to St Clement Danes School: 'One of those with a counter all down one side, dark, a workmen's café for the market men and what have you. The kids at school went in there to buy

160

a penny slice of bread and dripping, when they'd had no breakfast, and perhaps even no supper the night before.'

The market was at the centre of the community, the beating heart of Covent Garden, where to be known as a local was to be respected, whether you worked there or not. Graham Jackson's father was a policeman at Bow Street, and knew the Garden area like the back of his hand, as only a beat copper could. 'After he retired [in 1954], he used to go through the market, and many of the people who worked there would acknowledge him – some he had nicked on occasions. They always wanted to know who I was, and would always give me an apple or some fruit if we stopped to speak to them.'

Ann Lee had a similar experience. 'I didn't need pocket money. My mum took me through the market, and I'd come home with two bob, a shilling, ten bob note. They all thought the world of her – they went through the war together, I suppose.'

The strength of the sense of community among the market workers was matched by the strength of their language. Ann Lee again: 'I learned all my swear words from Covent Garden Market porters. Our bedrooms backed out on to a street where the market porters used to wheel their barrows, and if they dropped something – oh, the language.

'My dad used to say, "You've heard it, don't repeat it, forget it." Once they got the big lorries and stuff, you didn't hear them so much, but when I was a kid, they'd be dragging their barrows

161

about and shouting to one another across the street. They were on the go long before I got up and they stayed on the go until after lunch. They quietened down about two-ish, and that was a long day for them. My mum said I wasn't allowed to swear until I was twenty-one, so I had to store it all up.'

The porters seemed a definite type, what my mother-in-law refers to approvingly as 'Real London'. 'My little brother,' said Ann Lee, 'at age thirteen, was Jack the Lad, all "fink", "fought" and "Fursday", and I used to say to my mum, "Oh, Covent Garden market porter that one" – and he was!'

Mike O'Rouke's family were involved in the market for generations. 'My grandfather was a porter for a firm called Bloom and Green in Floral Street, so that goes back a fair while,' Mike told me. 'I got the impression that his father worked in the market as well; that was the main form of making a living back then. My nan, Nanny O'Rouke, she had her own business in Mercer Street, right opposite the Cambridge Theatre. She also had a stall up in Earlham Street, on the Seven Dials; she was in green-grocery all her life. I had an uncle I was very close to, used to live with Nan and Grandad round in Mercer Street, and he worked for T J Poupart up in Long Acre, opposite James Street, a green-grocery firm. He was a porter there.'

Portering was a hard working life. The market was open 364 days a year, every day except Christmas Day, although there was much less business done on a Sunday. The hours could take a toll on family life. Mike O'Rouke's father, who lost a leg in an accident with a lorry when he was just eleven years old, was brought up by maiden aunts. 'Basically,' Mike explains, 'I think it came down to the fact that my grandad worked at the market, and his wife had her own business, and it was Grandad's choice I think. He turned round and said, "I don't think he's going to get the right upbringing being at home." He was saying that his wife couldn't devote the time. They would both have to be up very early, and she'd be busy, whereas the aunts ... in those days, women tended not to work. I suppose Nan was a bit of an exception, having her own business.'

Everyone I spoke to who grew up in Covent Garden had something to say about the market, but the only person who actually worked there that I interviewed was Ronnie Mann. His first job on leaving school in 1957 was at George Monroe's in the flower market. 'I left school on the Friday and started work on the Monday, and I was classified as Assistant Salesman, so you had to do six months in the office, eight o'clock in the morning until whenever it finished, sometimes at midday, sometimes at six in the evening.

'After that, I started at three in the morning until midday. But although the job was called an Assistant Salesman, virtually you was an under-paid porter, because you had to unload the lorry. Monroe's was a non-union firm – that's how I got in it – and I had to lay out the boxes, take the delivery notes up to the offices, enter them in the ledger books, so you knew what you were getting, so the salesmen could see how much they were getting per bunch.'

What everybody seems to remember the most clearly, and the most fondly, were the sensations of the market, the colours, the vibrancy, the jostling busyness, the clatter of hooves and hob-nails on cobbles, the hubbub of voices, but above all the smells, redolent with the peaty, vegetal dampness of the English countryside, the exotic whiffs of foreign fruits and the café scents of fried food, tea and roll-ups. And then, of course, there were the flowers. Anyone who ever strolled down Floral Street – or dodged through the crowds, more like – on a weekday morning remembers the vibrant colour of the dealers' flashes, so welcome among the muted browns, greys and navy tones of a rationed nation, and the glorious fragrance rising from massed lilies, roses or pinks. Banks of violets from Cornwall or daffodils from the Scilly Isles could really perk up a grey March morning.

Part of the appeal was the timelessness of the place. 'The market hadn't changed in a hundred years,' explains Ronnie Mann, talking about when he worked there in the fifties and early sixties. 'It was basically the same. The porters still had the big boxes, they still pushed them on the trolley, they still dressed as they had pre-war, with the scarf round their necks, the flat caps – it was virtually a uniform. It hadn't changed at all, in any shape or form. The market pubs used to do God-knows-what hours. A lot of them used to open nights, or at three or four in the morning, until midday, but were never open weekends, so that was strange as well. It was an upside-down life, really, but I reckon that way of life in Covent

Garden market didn't change, hadn't changed, in a lifetime.'

Ann Lee agrees. 'It was just a lovely atmosphere. You could walk down Long Acre and go into Covent Garden market from that way, or from where I lived you could sort of walk around the corner and you were there.

'When they turned Covent Garden market into what it is now, I bloody hated it, because it wasn't what I knew. Now, I think they've really done well here, but it still isn't my Covent Garden market. When I walked through it there was the stale smell of fruit and veg where it had rained and it was all cobbles, and it had just sat there, but it wasn't offensive, it was what you knew. It was lovely, like bringing the countryside into the town.'

I have to agree with Ann. Although I never lived there, I miss the old market. I've only been to the new Covent Garden once, and it was enough. What's there now may be a treat for the tourists, but jugglers, bistros and chain stores cannot make up for the unique atmosphere of what was once the greatest market in England. Everyone I spoke to used phrases such as, 'When the market came alive' or 'When the market was awake' as if it were indeed a living thing, like a much-loved, elderly relative. And as with a relative or old friend, when the market was gone forever, everyone who had known it and loved it grieved.

7

Trading Up West

A look through the Kelly's Directories for the forties and fifties shows the extraordinary number and variety of businesses that existed throughout the West End. In 1946, a single yard off Archer Street contained fifteen separate businesses, including a drum manufacturer, three die-sinkers, two working ladies' tailors, three men's working tailors, a mantle-maker, a music engraver, a repairing jeweller and an export merchant. That same year, the short length of Windmill Street housed art metal workers, engravers, silversmiths, antique furniture dealers, cabinetmakers, boot repairers, sign writers, ironmongers, embroiderers, mantle-makers, ladies' tailors, plate glass merchants, a laundry and coppersmiths, while a single address in Wardour Street housed a printer, a film agent, the offices of both a film distributor and a publishing house, an engraver, a diamond setter and a manufacturer of costume jewellery.

There were businesses specifically associated with the area: the theatre, publishing, the rag trade, film-making, catering, and so on. And there was a large pool of craftsmen, often from overseas, who had small businesses all over Soho, supplying and supporting these trades: providing wigs and costumes for the performers, bows for the violinists, shoes for the dancers, and pots, pans and pinnies for the restaurateurs. The theatres needed painted backdrops, publishers needed printers, and clothes designers needed haberdashers and specialist seamstresses. Even the street markets had their own support networks, as Alberto Camisa remembered: 'Where the British Library is now, in the railway arches that were there, is where all the barrows and stalls for the markets used to be made. The guy there took great pride in his work. You could go there and buy or hire one. It was like going back to Dickens's time. All his lathes were manual – he didn't have electricity there, he had tilley lamps to work by. It was nice.'

And of course there were the luxury shops, the ones that distinguished the West End from the rest of London. There were tailors, shirtmakers and shoemakers in St James's and Savile Row, jewellers in Bond Street and the Piccadilly Arcades, and the fashion houses and milliners of Mayfair. The bespoke tailors and couturiers were supported by networks of pieceworkers and freelance specialist craftsmen and women. Each had their own speciality, such as making mantles, cutting and sewing trousers, making buttonholes or closing shoes. They worked from their homes in Soho, Covent Garden or Clerkenwell, or from small workshops in single rooms in Soho terraces. 'All the Savile Row stuff came from Soho,' Albert Camisa told me. Both of Andrew Panayiotes's parents worked in the rag trade: his father was a journeyman tailor supplying trousers to Anderson & Shepherd, Sackville Street. Mr Panayiotes was one of three freelance 'working' tailors – as opposed to retail tailors – who had rooms at 5 Old Compton Street, above the Star Café.

Jeff Sloneem's uncle was in the business, too, but in retail. 'My uncle's shop was a few doors down from where we lived in Old Compton Street. He had quite a famous clientele. His was the only tailor's shop in the street. Just round the entrance to Berwick Street market, a few doors up Peter Street, you had Sam the Presser, who had a big Hoffman press at the time. I used to be sent round there to take things for pressing. Then in Meard Street you had a guy called Stevens, who owned a haberdasher's where everyone went for their cottons, zips, buttons and other bits and pieces. Everyone was in easy walking distance.'

Being surrounded by specialist craftsmen and women came in very useful for the locals. Quentin Crisp remembers in *The Naked Civil Servant* that he could accept gifts of clothing 'indiscriminately', as 'I could at any time enlist the services of a certain Mrs Markham, known throughout Soho as the greatest trouser-taperer in the world.'

When the Huguenots fled persecution and massacre in France, they brought their skills as master embroiderers and silk weavers with them. Most settled in and around Spitalfields but Soho also benefited from their presence. French tapestries had long been the envy of Europe and many master weavers also came in that first wave of French immigrants. They headed for Soho, where they flourished by selling their wares to British royalty, the aristocracy and the just plain rich. When, in the late eighteenth century, some of France's nobility fled 'Madame La Guillotine' for London, they brought their dressmakers, goldsmiths, lace-makers and so on with them, to ensure that the pretty necks they had saved remained well dressed and stylish.

Soho's craft traditions were applied to its charitable institutions too. In the nineteenth century, orphans in the Parish of St Anne were offered apprenticeships in any trade they chose when they grew too old for the orphanage. Extraordinarily, and uniquely in Britain, this went for the girls as well. They could become cutlers, milliners, bakers, silversmiths, lace-makers and so on, while their sisters outside the parish would wind up in service, or slaving over a hot tub in a laundry, for a pittance. No other parish in the country offered orphan girls the opportunity to train for a trade that would, once their apprenticeship was done, give them an independent living.

The tradition of immigrant craftsmen coming to Soho carried on well into the twentieth century, as John Carnera remembers: 'I come from the Friuli-Veneto, in the north-east corner of Italy, a part of the world famous for mosaic and terrazzo. My father, my grandfather, for generations back, were all in the same trade. In the thirties, it became very fashionable in London to have terrazzo floors, to have mosaic, and my father was one of a number of workers who were contracted to come over to England to work on various projects and buildings in London. The terrazzo at the front on the ground floor of Gennaro's was all done by Dad, he did it all through. My brother, Elvio, followed my father and grandfather into terrazzo mosaic. In the end, his business was mainly tiling, and he had a shop where he sold tiles, and he subcontracted work from other contractors.'

Although he did not go straight into it after leaving school, Ronnie Mann had an established family trade and business to fall back on. 'It was N. Mann & Sons, picture-frame makers, at 7 Monmouth Street. The business started in 1849, and we've got photographs of them ranging back: my dad, my uncle, my grandad, great grandfather and great-great-grandfather, all the way back. The shop was always in Monmouth Street, although it was called Great St Andrew's Street when it started. The original N. Mann was a Noah. My cousin, who's now dead, was also Noah, poor sod. He was in the navy when he was young, and he had so much stick, he used to call himself Billy.

'Me and my two brothers took over in 1962, because Dad wanted to get out. We only rented the place, it was a repairing lease, and we carried it on for a few years. We done quite well out of it, but gave it up eventually because the whole area had changed – double parking, high rates. Funnily enough, when Covent Garden market moved away, they couldn't sell places, they couldn't give them away.'

In this way, the skills and traditions of craftsmen and women were proudly handed down through generations of French, Italian, Jewish, German, Greek and Swiss families, all of whom had sought and found sanctuary in the same sooty streets that had embraced all corners for

170

centuries. This community established the West End in general, and Mayfair in particular, as the place to go for first-class, exclusive shopping.

This wasn't all that the immigrant craftsmen brought to the area; the French, Italian and Chinese populations laid the foundations for good food and fine dining that has pulled so many people, anonymous, famous and infamous alike, into the West End to eat. All those hotels and restaurants needed easy access not only to ingredients – which accounted for the many delicatessens, specialist food importers and so on – but also to catering equipment.

Owen Gardner's father came up from Somerset after the Second World War to work for William Page & Co., a large caterers' supply store in Shaftesbury Avenue that sold everything from kitchen utensils, glasses, crockery, cutlery and pans to whole kitchens. When Owen left school, he went to work in the buyer's department there, and in time, he became the buyer. 'Page's was such a big shop in those days that people came from all over,' he remembers. 'It was a department store for caterers, if you like. Its founder, Harry Bradbury-Pratt, was a tough taskmaster: he thought he paid the best wages in the West End, but if he saw you skiving, then you were fired, just like that. In those days there were no rules and regulations about employment – if he thought you were hard up, or you were unwell, then you got the best money could buy. He just wanted what he paid for, like most people.

'I don't know where his double-barrelled name came from: he started out as a Billingsgate fish porter, but set up Page's in Great Portland Street between the wars, moved it to Brewer Street just before the war, then on to Shaftesbury Avenue in 1942. In those days there were several shops in Soho selling pots and pans and so on. There was Kitchen Supplies in Brewer Street, Leon Jaeggi and Sons in Dean Street, Page's in Shaftesbury Avenue and Ferrari's, a cutlers in Archer Street.

'There also used to be an auction room in Greek Street and one in Dean Street. And as many restaurants as there were in Soho, an awful lot of them went broke, and all the chattels from these went into the auction rooms, and they used to have auctions every week. Sometimes people would go there thinking they were getting a bargain and would pay more for the goods than they were in our place new. They would get carried away with auction fever.'

Owen learned the catering trade at secondary school: 'I went to Westminster College, at Ebury Bridge. It used to be part of the catering school in Vincent Square, which is still there. It was split in two halves in those days, the chefs and the engineering side, and I was on the engineering side. Just after the war, you could just stay at school until you were fifteen, or change school at thirteen and do a three-year technical course, which is what I did.'

Technical colleges were seen as an alternative to apprenticeship, teaching you a trade much more quickly. 'At St Martin's school,' Ronnie Mann remembers, 'they would assess you after a couple of years, and say you're never going to be Brain of Britain, but you can go to a technical

172

college where you can do electricity, bricklaying, carpentry, decorating. To me, the amount of kids that wanted to do that was absolutely incredible. A lot of the kids who left and went to these places are still doing the same job today.'

It was not just the boys who benefited from this system. 'I learned millinery at Bloomsbury Technical College in Southampton Row,' Pat Jones remembers. 'After two years they couldn't teach me any more, so I got a job at King's Model Milliners in Sloane Square. But after making hats for everybody and being paraded around as their best girl at the college, all I was going to do at King's was make the tea. So my mum went back to my teacher at the college and complained that it was not for me. Then I was offered a job with Hardy Amies, but the money was ridiculous, five shillings, seven and six a week, so I turned that down and got a job at Berman's, the theatrical costumiers.'

After a year or so at Berman's, something happened that upset Pat. 'So in my lunch hour I walked over to B J Simmons in Covent Garden. They were rival costumiers, but they were not so much about the stars; they used to do the D'Oyly Carte, all the shows, the choruses and stuff. I walked in and asked to see the personnel person there, I told her I was seventeen, and I was a milliner who had been working for Berman's – and they took me on.'

A gift for handicrafts ran in Pat's family: 'My mother was a housekeeper for a firm of coal factors; she took over the job from her mother-in-law, but she also worked as a designer of

173

dresses and jumpers – knitwear mainly, and crochet. She would sit up all night making up these patterns, then take them in a huge case to Odhams Press, you know, the women's magazines, to sell the patterns. She would get so many guineas according to who she sold it to. Nine times out of ten she kept the garments, so we had lots to wear.'

Those who decided not to go to technical college but to stay on at school until the leaving age of fifteen, did not go straight on to the dole queue. There was a great variety of jobs awaiting the school leaver in the fifties and early sixties, as Graham Jackson remembers: 'I had a choice. It was like, what do you want to do? There was a furniture-maker's in Great Queen Street who did all the Masonic work, furniture and regalia and all that sort of thing. There was Pollard's the shopfitters, they were at Highbury. And there was France, the undertaker, and I went for that.'

At that time, France, based in Lamb's Conduit Street, Clerkenwell, had a shop just off Monmouth Street. The firm, which had been founded in the nineteenth century in St James's, was the only undertaker in the West End. Graham was trained on the job. 'I went right through it, from a boy, done all the polishing, putting the handles on, lining all the coffins, then making them, going out on funerals, conducting funerals, I done the lot. The one thing I wouldn't do was embalming.'

Graham's training on the job did not amount to an apprenticeship, but the fact that there were so many traditional crafts around meant that there were plenty of those available, too. John Carnera could not follow the family trade in terrazzo mosaic: 'I suffered from eczema and in those days people didn't use gloves or anything like that, so that would have been a real trial for me.' He fell into bespoke shoemaking – a craft he has followed for half a century – quite casually. 'The Youth Employment Officer came round to the school and asked what I wanted to do. I told him I had no idea. He says there was a job going at this shoemaker's in Duke Street, St James's. "Do you want to have a go at that?" I said "All right then," and trotted down to Poulsen Skone Ltd at 12 Duke Street, and they took me on.

'I couldn't be an apprentice straight away because you had to be sixteen, so I spent a year polishing shoes, basically. Then, on my sixteenth birthday, my father signed me up to stay for five years, and I learned the trade there. I started on £3 a week, going up by five shillings each year. I thought it was a lot of money. I'd never had my own clothes, always had my brother's hand-me-downs. The first time I ever went out to buy my own clothes, new, you can't imagine how pleased I was, how happy I was to have clothes that had never been worn by anyone else before.

'There was a lot to learn. First of all, you have to see the client, measure his foot, instep, bottom instep across the joint, instep to heel, all the appropriate measures, then use rasps to carve a wooden last. You start with a foot-shaped block of a hard wood such as beech or birch, as it has to take quite a beating, and shape it according to the measurements. You design the upper on a piece of paper, then cut the various pieces in leather, the uppers and the linings from that design. That's called clicking, because the knife you use makes a clicking sound as you cut. So that's the last-maker, and the pattern-cutter and the clicker, who's usually the same person.

'From there it goes to the closer, who stitches all the pieces together and punches out all the holes. Number five is the bottom-maker, who cuts an insole from the shape of the last, and from that cuts a toe stiffener and a heel stiffener and blocks them in. Then he lasts the shoe: you have to damp the leather, and work it when it's mellow, using pincers to pull it over the last, to get its shape. He then sews a welt, which holds the upper to the sole, and then sticks a sole on, and hand-stitches it. Then he builds a heel to make the finished shoe.

'You draw the last out when the shoe is dry, rub out the inside, fit the heel sock, then put in a pair of fitted trees, that are turned, by lathe, from the last. Then the finished shoe goes to the polisher, who polishes it up. The whole process takes three months. The person who does the bottom half of the shoe is usually known as the shoemaker, so people assume he does it all, but someone who does the whole shoe is rarely much good, so we're all specialists in different areas, although you usually learn more than one.

'I did a five-year course at the Cordwainers' Technical College in Mare Street, Hackney, two evenings a week. Poulsen & Skone paid for my tuition. On Tuesday evening I used to do clicking and on Wednesday evening pattern cutting and designing. And then I had a day release all day

Friday doing last-making and shoemaking. I passed my City & Guilds after five years, and then at twenty-one my old governor, Mr Skone, offered me a job at £6 10s. a week.

'I said I would have to talk to my dad, because in those days fathers, especially Italian fathers, ruled the roost. So I went home and told him, and my dad said, "Well, I don't think that's enough." He was a friend of the manager of Gamba, who made ballet shoes at the corner of Dean Street and Old Compton Street, next door to where we used to live. So he went to see his friend next day, and told him what I had been offered, and asked if they had a job for me, because he thought I could do better. "Oh yes," he said, "We'll give him £8 10s. a week." So my father told me to tell Mr Skone that it wasn't enough, I wanted £8 10s. a week, because I could get a job cutting shoes at Gamba's for that.

'So I did, and Mr Skone said, "No, I don't think you're worth it." That's how they used to talk to you. You were just a slave. I told him that that's what I had been offered, and he said, "You better go then."

'I thought that was it, and I wandered downstairs to our workshop in the basement, and the company secretary, a really nice man called Bannister, who was Skone's right-hand man – he ran the business for him, basically – chased me downstairs. "Don't do anything hasty," he said. "Let me talk to Mr Skone." So he did, and a few days later Skone came back to me and said he wanted to see me in his office.

'"Well, OK," he says, "Mr Bannister's told me

177

lots of things, and I'll give you £8 10s. a week, but I want you to bring your cutting board up here, I want to watch you, see that you're worth what I'm giving you." And that's what I did, for three months, did my cutting upstairs in the shop. It must have worked!'

It must have, as John now co-owns Cleverley's, a bespoke shoemaker in an arcade just off Bond Street.

John's experiences with wages were pretty typical. Apprenticeship was not an easy option. Not everyone could stick it out. His boyhood friend, John Solari, for instance, was apprenticed as a mechanic in a garage at the back of Belgrave Square, but the wages were so bad that he quit for a job in the Post Office, at Mount Pleasant.

One place where there were plenty of opportunities in the West End was the rag trade. The making of clothes incorporated even more separate crafts and specialities than shoemaking, and it made sense for all these specialist workers to be in the same area, and for the people who supplied them and sold their wares – wholesale or retail – to be there too. Berwick Street, especially the north end between Broadwick Street and Oxford Street, was the centre of the rag trade in Soho, with virtually every address housing a business related to clothing and accessories. Handbag makers, lace manufacturers, silk merchants, working tailors (men's and women's), hosiery makers, drapers, costume makers, manufacturing milliners, buttonholers, gown makers-up, trimmings dealers, belt makers (men's and women's), mantle manufacturers, embroiderers, woollen merchants, gown makers, blouse manufacturers, retail tailors, children's clothes makers, textile merchants, button manufacturers, gown sellers, blouse makers-up, uniform makers, button dyers, rayon dealers, dressmakers, and feather, flower and novelties dealers: all of them could be found in Berwick Street in the fifties. Although most worked to supply the trade, some were prepared to take on a personal commission, as Ronnie Mann remembers: 'I had my wedding suit made up in Berwick Street at a place called Paul's; most expensive suit I ever bought, that was.'

In the schmutter (from the Yiddish meaning 'clothing' or 'rag') trade, the word 'cabbage' has never had anything at all to do with mounds of greens and Sunday dinners. One of the most skilled and important people employed in the trade was the cutter, whose job it was to cut out the pieces for as many garments as possible from each bale of cloth supplied for a particular order. For example, a designer and the fashion house may have estimated that fifty garments can be cut from a bale of fabric and supply the manufacturer with the requisite amount of material for their order. However, a skilled cutter may get fifty-three garments out of a bale by clever placing of the pieces. Those extra garments have always been known, for some reason, as 'cabbage', and an illicit cabbage trade has always run parallel with the legitimate rag trade. Some dealers even specialized in cabbage. Sometimes the sweatshop/factory owner was in on the scam, and sometimes it was something that the cutters and machinists did on the side, by way of workers' perks to make up for the low wages paid by unscrupulous employers.

Naturally, cabbage was the bane of designers' and fashion houses' lives, because the garments were identical to their product but could be sold for a fraction of their retail price in markets, pubs and small provincial shops that were well away from the prying eyes of clients and the law. Cabbage was (and remains) the fashion industry's equivalent of bootleg music and films, infuriating to the legitimate side of the industry due to the loss of income and the status of their product, but very good news for the more economically challenged among the rag trade workers and their grateful punters.

This is perhaps one reason why people in Soho always seemed a little better dressed than their equivalents elsewhere. 'Several tailors came to our church, so we were all very well turned out, in suits,' Francesco Camisa remembered. The suits may not have had the cachet of a Savile Row label, but they were made up by the men and women who made suits for Savile Row, so they had the quality.

While many of the jobs available in the rag trade were basically drudge work, there was always the possibility of advancement. John Carnera remembers that his best friend, Peter Enrione, who lived in 8 Old Compton Street, 'started as an apprentice at a place called La Chasse, which was just off Berkeley Square, I think Hill Street, and went on to become the Queen's dressmaker. La Chasse was one of the London fashion houses, and he started off there as a tailor, and progressed from there to working for Norman Hartnell. Hartnell's number two was Ian Thomas, and Ian's number two was Peter Enrione.'

This time-honoured background in the rag trade helped one of Soho's streets became a national, then international byword for fashion in the sixties. The mods started frequenting clothes shops in Carnaby Street in the early sixties, but apart from a few discreet boutiques and Italian tailors, it was no different from any other street in Soho until the psychedelic fashion explosion made it *the* place to go to buy the clobber that would help you to emulate your rock 'n' roll heroes and their girlfriends. By 1962, Carnaby Street was flourishing and was a Mecca for anyone wishing to be 'with it'. As Carnaby Street shopkeeper, Peter Anderson, recalls in *Soho* by Judith Summers, 'it was a retailer's dream. The street was packed with teenagers, and all of them ready to spend. We were closing the door on them. We were coining it. We were literally standing on money because we couldn't get it in the till. And everything we sold had to have Carnaby Street written on it.'

Thanks to the likes of John Stephen, the first retailer in Carnaby Street to cater specifically to young, male fashionistas, blokes ditched the greys, blacks and browns that had long dominated their wardrobe and broke out into brilliant colour. Girls and boys alike donned the eye-swivelling, swirly patterns of psychedelia: Carnaby Street and its patrons positively reeked of patchouli oil for a decade or so, and peace and love ruled. Local florists did well too. Echoes of

181

the sixties remain in Carnaby Street, although today it is frequented by tourists rather than young people at the forefront of fashion.

Ronnie Mann's wife, Sandra, 'can remember Carnaby Street starting, because I worked in Great Marlborough Street in the offices of Warwick Woollens. My aunt was a matcher, who worked for John Kavanaugh. She used to go round with the little samples, matching up materials they needed for certain things. That was just when Carnaby Street started. I can't remember what Carnaby Street looked like before all that happened. Just can't picture it. Just like Poland Street, one of those little Georgian side streets with ordinary shopfronts.'

Ronnie agrees that there was little to distinguish it. 'When I first knew Carnaby Street, at the beginning of the fifties, it was just another side street. There was a big frame-maker's near there called Wheatley's, who were the cutting edge of technology and weird design, while we was all about tradition, so when we had a job that didn't suit us, I used to walk over there to them. It was just off Carnaby Street – Foubert's Place. Carnaby Street was an ordinary street, ordinary shops.'

Yet many of those 'ordinary' shops in the West End had extraordinary things going on in them. Mike O'Rouke's family had worked in Covent Garden market for generations, but as his father had lost his leg in a childhood accident, he could not do heavy work, and had to look further afield. 'One of his jobs,' Mike remembers, 'was up at Green Park station, working for a firm of taxidermists. He used to go in there of a Saturday morning, to open up and things like that. He quite often met the Queen and the Duke of Edinburgh; they used to go in there to look at the exhibits and all that. It was quite funny, him coming home and saying, "Oh, the Queen popped in today."'

Then there were the specialist shops selling unlikely goods, such as the tack shop in St Martin's Lane where you could buy a saddle, or Wisden's cricket shop in Great Newport Street, which sold everything to do with cricket – bats, balls, stumps, pads and scorebooks, as well as the famous yearbook – in an area far from anywhere where it was safe to ride or you could find enough greenery to make a wicket.

Pollocks Toy Museum in Monmouth Street was a lovely fantasy world that sold toys; here you could simply marvel at the collection of Victoriana, such as the toy theatres. The Old Curiosity Shop, which inspired Dickens's novel, was near Lincoln's Inn Fields. And, opposite Freemasons' Hall in Great Queen Street, Toye, Kenning & Spencer sold Freemasons' regalia.

'The oldest building in the West End was an Elizabethan house built in 1601 in Lower John Street,' Derek Hunt reminded me. 'They used to repair watches there, repair clocks.' He also remembered 'The violin Shop just by Duck Lane, at the end of Broadwick Street. You can tell from the building that before that it used to be the Butchers' Arms, a pub.' One of my own favourite shopfronts was the perruquiers (wig-makers) in lower Wardour Street, where, according to Derek again, there was an arch whose foundation stones were laid by Sarah Bernhardt and Henry Irving.

Owen Gardner, who spent his entire working life in retail, particularly remembers a specialist shop in Greek Street, Madame Cadec's. 'She was a Frenchwoman, and she had a tiny, tiny shop, a little curio shop, things hanging from the ceiling and everything else, and she specialized in copperware. She would drive to France, buy bits and pieces, and bring them back and sell them in her shop. At Page's, we used to sell exactly the same copperware, but everybody went to her; she used to sell more copperware than we did, although we had a shop five times the size, because they thought it was something different. In actual fact, the copperware came out of the same factory in Birmingham.

'But she was a lovely character, did things that we as a business couldn't do. She'd go and see the chef, and the chef would say, "I can't afford to buy any pans," and she would ask what he could afford. He might say "A bag of potatoes" or something, so she would give him the two pans, but give a bill for a sack of potatoes. She worked there right up to the day she died. She had a heart attack driving back from crossing the Channel up to London, and ran off the road.'

Owen also reminded me about the tradesmen who supported the retailers. One stuck in his mind, although not necessarily for the character of the shopfront. 'There were all kinds of people in the West End who did signs for windows, and stuff like that. I always remember as a fairly young lad, I used to go into this particular place that did all our window signs, for the sales and that, and in the back room it had pictures all over the wall of – I

184

was going to say every star you could think of, but that would be an exaggeration – all in the nude; Marilyn Monroe, Diana Dors, all these people. I don't know where they got the photographs from, but they were all stuck up on the wall there.'

I remember some wonderful tiling in the shops in Soho, in butchers' shops particularly. Hammet's had lovely tiling. And I also liked the distinctive art deco lettering that picked out the name, 'Benoit Bulke, butchers, charcutiers', at 27 Old Compton Street. The sign above Gamba was another favourite, largely because of the picture of a ballerina, but also because the lettering was so very distinctive. I always liked the huge and highly colourful harlequin suspended above the Parmigiani delicatessen, where my father had his shop. All these signs were welcome landmarks for me, telling me I was close to home in Old Compton Street. L'Escargot, the restaurant in Greek Street had a painted hanging sign outside of a man riding a snail. I loved it, because he looked so jolly and happy. Of course, the designers and craftsmen who created these, and many other, icons of my childhood were anonymous, which makes it all the sadder when their work disappears along with the shops that they adorned.

When you are young – and especially when you were young in the decades before cars widened everyone's horizons – the local shops define who you are, become part of your identity. In Soho, they gave you a sense of rich possibility, of a much wider world, full of dreams and promises. Alberto Camisa summed it up best: 'You could get absolutely everything you needed without crossing Regent Street, Shaftesbury Avenue, Charing Cross Road or Oxford Street: the candlestick maker, butcher, wig maker, everyone was there. There was a car showroom in Poland Street garage – Ford. The rich and the poor all came in together. There was a violin factory in Beak Street, and people who made gold braid for the army uniforms. Every trade had its corner, making and selling everything you can think of. I can't think of a trade that wasn't present in Soho. Except funeral directors. Soho was more for the living!'

8

Street People

Although – or perhaps because – there was far less traffic, the streets of the West End were rarely empty by night or day. As well as the crowds bustling their way from one place to another, there were people who made their living, and sometimes lived their lives, on the streets. Some relied on their talents (which could be vanishingly small) to earn a crust, others conducted retail businesses on the pavements – with or without a licence – while others relied on their wits, scamming and hustling passers-by to survive. Soho's streets, it seemed, had more than its share of all of them, adding to the unique atmosphere of the place.

There were a lot of buskers on the streets after the war. Some of them had worked in music halls before they joined the forces, and found work hard to come by once they were back on Civvy Street. Others were displaced persons, unable or unwilling to return to their old, pre-war lives, who were trying to scratch a living while they thought about what to do next. They turned up in town centres all over the country, grinding out tunes on squeeze-boxes, washboards, spoons, fiddles or trumpets. Many wound up in London's West End, where there were so many cinema and theatre queues to entertain.

A relatively common sight in those days was a one-man band, with splash cymbals tied to the inside of his knees, a drum strapped to his back and drumsticks attached to his elbows to enable a steady thumping rhythm while his hands were occupied with a guitar or banjo and his mouth with a wind instrument – a harmonica or a tin whistle – attached to a neck harness. It was a logistical challenge to see just how many instruments they could festoon themselves with and what tune they could play that would incorporate at least a bar or two from all of them. The clatter made by one-man bands as they moved from one pitch to another had to be heard to be believed. There was no mistaking one on the move.

Late on a Sunday morning, the scratchy, tinny opening bars of 'The Sheik of Araby' would announce the arrival of my favourite buskers in Old Compton Street. I believe they were called the Sons of the Desert, and if they weren't, then they should have been, on account of their fezzes.

It's only now, thinking back, that I realize the probable significance of those bright splashes of red that looked for all the world like upturned flowerpots, each with a single, natty black tassel. Before the Second World War, everyone wore a hat as a matter of course. Indeed, few would step out of their own front doors without their 'titfer': it simply wasn't done. Men could choose between the cheesecutter (or flat cap), the trilby, the Homburg, the fedora or the bowler for day-to-day wear and in summer, the Panama or a straw boater. Their choice of headgear spoke volumes as to their class, occupation and aspirations. Although the subtle nuances of headgear and class have now been lost, in the late forties and fifties they were still instantly recognized by any British man, woman or child in the street.

A fez said kasbah, Araby, Egypt, the mysterious East and the desert. My favourite buskers were boxing clever; their startling headgear told passing prospective punters that they had fought and suffered alongside Monty in his North African campaigns. A fez proclaimed that its wearer was a seasoned 'Desert Rat' – even if he wasn't – and the punters would approve, either because they'd been there, too, or had a son, a brother, a husband, a lover or a pal who had: this helped to loosen passers-by's grip on their small change.

A bright red fez also showed up well in the dim light of winter, or on a foggy day. It was exotic, and a spot of exoticism never went amiss when a body was trying to flog something that people didn't actually need, especially when times were hard and money short. People craved distraction from

188

rationing, the atom bomb, poverty and the 'make do and mend' culture that had dominated their lives for so long. The Sons of the Desert provided all that with their street-level entertainment.

To my, admittedly unsophisticated, five-year-old eyes, they were wonderful, it was as simple as that. The music issued from the flaring horn of the old-fashioned (even then) hand-cranked gramophone that played the brittle, shellac 78s of the day. The needle that ran in the record's grooves was enormous, big enough to darn fishermen's socks. The precious gramophone had its own transport, in the form of a battered, black, well-sprung perambulator, which was pushed from pitch to pitch by one of the troupe. Sometimes there were seven of them, and occasionally as many as eleven. As well as their fezzes, the buskers wore 'penguin suits', a kind of evening dress featuring a long tailcoat and pinstriped trousers.

Their act was a combination of acrobatics, silent comedy routines, and a sand dance – performed on genuine sand transported in an old fire bucket that hung from the pram handle. They kept all sorts of other props in the pram besides the gramophone, including ancient Egyptian headgear to complement what they fondly imagined to be the ancient Egyptian moves of the sand dance. They moved their heads backwards and forwards in time to the music in exactly the same way as amorous pigeons moved theirs as they strutted their stuff on our windowsill. Even today, I can't see pigeons moving that way without thinking of the Sons of the Desert and their sand dance.

The grand finale was always a human pyramid.

189

At the very end of the show, the acrobats would tumble, in turn, starting from the very apex of the pyramid down to the ground, and finish off with a neat roll or a somersault. They never, ever, crashed into their audience, however close or pressing it was. They never lost a fez either, even when they were upside down. I always wondered how they did that. My brother said they nailed them to their heads and I really believed him because, being four years older, he knew everything. Now that age has brought a little more wisdom, I reckon they must have had some sort of sticky tape.

'Meg of the Gleaming Gums' was a name I coined for a small, round woman in a headscarf and ancient winter coat who sang badly, but operatically – in a fruity soprano – to queues in Leicester Square and Piccadilly. Others I spoke to remember her being able to hit all the notes, but not necessarily in the right order. The reflection of the famous Piccadilly Circus lights would flash on and off her toothless gums as she warbled her way through 'We'll Meet Again' and 'Danny Boy'.

Sometimes Meg was accompanied by Jumping Jack, a tall, lugubrious man with grizzled locks and long, skinny arms and legs. He wore an ill-fitting harlequin suit with diamond-shaped splashes of red, blue, yellow, green and white, and would caper about, dancing, wearing a mournful look and holding out a hat in his hand. He was Meg's 'bottler', the collector of the all-important lolly.

Not all buskers were musicians or dancers. I remember an escapologist who often 'did' the

West End. He also turned up at the Tower of London, once trippers had re-established their well-worn sightseeing trails. He had a sidekick who would fasten his hefty chains with huge padlocks, tie the neck of his sack with rope, or shutter and bar a cage contraption and then start the dramatic countdown to the performer's marvellous escape.

On busy street corners in the shopping streets stood men who twisted long, sausage-shaped balloons into various animals. Although they flogged the results of their efforts, their schtick was really the making of their colourful menageries. Their hands were so deft and quick that they were almost a blur. They prided themselves on being able to make any animal that their audiences requested. Although I remember well the tortured squealing of the balloons as their hands twisted them into shape, I never remember one bursting, which was what their audiences were often waiting for. As I was afraid of sudden bangs, I watched them work with my fingers in my ears, just in case. When they had done, the results of their efforts were either sold on the spot or tied with string to float in the wind above their heads like a weird, weightless, airborne zoo.

Street vendors sold an amazing variety of things. I remember a lot of injured war veterans selling stuff from trays slung around their necks. It was not unusual to see a facially disfigured man, someone missing a limb, or a blind man, flogging boxes of matches or packets of razor blades or ballpoint pens. These were the most popular

191

lines, and may well have been supplied by a veterans' charity. They were always sold by men, presumably because women were not usually combatants in the Second World War and thus were not eligible to be licensed as street vendors or to be supplied with goods to sell.

Women did, however, sell flowers on the streets, and sometimes fruit. The flower 'girls' of Covent Garden, some of whom were quite elderly women, would pick up what was left unsold at the market in the late morning, bunch it up and hawk it on the streets, especially to the theatre and cinema crowds in the evening.

The wonderful aroma of roasting chestnuts was a familiar one during winter months of the late forties, fifties and even into the sixties. On bitter days, the hapless vendor would often find himself surrounded by a small mob warming their frozen hands and legs near his glowing brazier. Often, feelings of embarrassment for copping a swift, free warm-up led to the purchase of a newspaper cone of hot chestnuts, so the vendors only really minded if the crowd got so dense that fresh customers were kept away. Then a few choice, often witty words would send the heat-scroungers scurrying, only for them to be replaced by more frozen shoppers.

For years and years, chestnut sellers disappeared from London's streets and they were sorely missed by those who remembered the wonderful smell, the distinctive taste and, of course, the free heat. However, I've noticed that one or two have re-appeared around Christmas, as a nod to nostalgia and in response to popular demand. There's nothing quite like the smell of hot chestnuts wafting around shoppers as they schlep wearily from shop to shop, to bring a glow of festive feeling back into the commercial Christmas chore.

In Leicester Square there was a stall that sold glass animals, run by a man known, appropriately enough, as 'Harry the Glass', although he also answered to Harry Murphy. He made the animals as well, and was a fully paid up member of the Magic Circle. He was, apparently, a very good magician when he was sober, but sadly, he drank like a fish. His favoured form of transport was a black cab that he drove himself in those days before the breathalyser. There were several other glass-animal sellers in the West End. One, called Reg, had an oxygen cylinder by his pitch and would make the animals on the street – which brought in more customers, naturally.

For a long time after St Anne's Church fell victim to the Blitz, so all that was left was its tower and churchyard, the site of the missing church was a car park. There was also a bookstall there, run by a man who sold second-hand whodunnits, romances and the like from the top of his stall and kept dirty books for his more 'discerning' customers underneath. I know this because I'm pretty sure that my father, among others, supplied him with them.

An army of fly-pitching spivs toted suitcases from pitch to pitch in the post-war decades. They would rest their suitcases on a couple of upended wooden beer crates and open them with a flourish to display packets of nylon stockings, or gloves and scarves, or knickers, or men's socks, or battery-operated toys with flashing eyes and jerky movements, or tea towels, or bottles of perfume – the list went on and on. They'd usually have a lookout posted with his eyes skinned for a policeman's helmet approaching among the crowds. If a bobby hove into view, a whistle so piercing that it could slice through the sound of the bustling crowds, bus gears grinding and lorries rattling, would alert the salesman, who would slam down the lid of his case and scarper, mid-spiel sometimes, and take a turn or two round the block, or nip in for a cuppa somewhere. When the coast was clear, it was back to the same pitch and the lookout on the same corner. They must have made a living for at least two.

Buying from a spiv with a suitcase was fraught with pitfalls. Sometimes a packet of nylons would consist of just one stocking, or a mismatched pair with one long enough to fit a giraffe and the other little more than a sock. The 'French' perfume could turn out to smell like drains or lavatory cleaner, having been knocked up in somebody's bath out of God knows what. The spivs relied on the anonymity of the streets to get away with it.

Alongside the vendors, there were sharks. Many specialized in the three card trick, also known as 'Find the Lady' or 'Three Card Monte'. The trickster would set up shop on a crate and place three cards face up. One was a queen: often, but not always, the psychologically more attractive queen of hearts. Once the trickster had allowed prospective punters a good look he'd turn the cards face down. Then he would move the cards around so rapidly that onlookers would be too confused to keep track.

One of his stooges would take a punt, while at least one other kept an eagle eye out for the police. The stooge who was betting would place a sum of money on the beer crate, apparently confident that he could 'find the lady'. Naturally, he would have no problem because he and his partner had pre-arranged the 'lady's' whereabouts. The stooge would carry on 'winning' for a bit and once he had drawn in a crowd with his glad cries of triumph and joy, his performance would encourage the more naïve in the crowd to have a go. This time, however, the trickster would palm the queen, thus leaving the punter no chance of winning.

A variation on this trick was 'Find the Pea' or 'Find the Ball'. Instead of cards, the trickster would pull the same stunt using a dried pea and three walnut shells or, for the more organized, a small ball and three plastic cups. But no matter what the props, the schtick was exactly the same.

Another classic scam was 'Take a Pick'. Eager punters would shell out a few bob to pull a straw from a cup. If the straw had a 'winning' number on it they'd win a small prize, worth a tiny fraction of their original stake. The notorious Jack Spot used to boast of making £50 or more a day at this scam as early as the twenties, when he charged just sixpence a punt. The sum Spot made amounted to a small fortune in those days. I assume that the profits made in the forties and fifties were even greater.

There never seemed to be any shortage of mugs

to take on the sharks, even when the scam was obvious. 'There was a guy outside Foyles,' remembers Graham Jackson. 'He used to have a box and little envelopes. And he'd put them all in a box, and one of them contained – I think it must have been a pound note. And what he'd do, he'd shuffle them all up, and – the same old trick – he said, "Right, pick one." And one of *his* blokes, of course, would go up, and take it – "Oh, you've won a pound, mate. Well done." It was like half a crown a go, and these mugs would pay half a crown, and the bloke's got it in his hand, he's got the winning packet in his hand.'

Historically, the West End has always had a soft spot for misfits, characters and wild eccentrics, showing an easygoing acceptance, and sometimes a real affection, for the many weird and wonderful types who would not be tolerated elsewhere. Being partisan, I'd say that this is particularly true of Soho, but that could be because Soho welcomed my peculiar little family when the housing estates of suburbia had shunned us as pariahs, cursed with a virulent form of leprosy.

It is hard to understand now, in more enlightened times, just how judgmental, class-ridden and conventional post-war Britain was and just how difficult it was for people whose faces simply did not fit. Many of these West End characters would end up at the Nucleus, Gary Winkler's all night coffee bar, which stayed open until around six in the morning. A place that served hot food, cooked by someone who gloried in the name of 'Denis the Menace' or, more sinisterly for a cook,

'Dirty Dennis', the Nucleus was a godsend to musicians and actors who needed somewhere to come down from an evening performance. Insomniacs and those poor souls who slept rough were also grateful to have somewhere warm and dry to sit over a coffee or a plate of spaghetti bolognese, especially on cold, wet nights.

Gipsy Larry – a very well known West End 'face' who earned his crusts playing a tea chest wherever he went – used to hang out at the Nucleus. Tea chests were quite a common buskers' instrument in the post-war period when materials were scarce and the money to pay for them, scarcer still. The instrument was made from a tea chest with a sort of neck/fingerboard arrangement, often made out of a broomstick, jutting up in the air and with a single string strung under tension from the broomstick to the chest. It was played a bit like a double bass: the different notes depended on where along the length of the string you plucked, twanged, thumped or, sometimes, bowed. The chest itself acted as a sounding box and, occasionally, seconded as a drum.

Sometimes, if you took a stroll down Monmouth Street, you'd see a full-sized wooden cross parked against a wall outside the Nucleus. That would be a sign that King David was in and holding court. King David thought he was the son of God, but why he didn't call himself Jesus, I'm not sure. Perhaps he thought that God had two sons, the famous one and His little brother, David.

The story of Ernest the Astrologer, another regular at the Nucleus, was a sad one. He was said to be red hot at drawing up astrological charts and was always to be seen with a hefty tome on the subject. Despite being in his mid-thirties, he looked about seventy, partly because he had long, grey hair that straggled to way below his shoulder blades. This in itself was fairly unusual in the days when the short back and sides was still in favour with many men. Rumour had it that Ernest never slept and had taken a vow not to cut his hair until he found his girlfriend. He'd lost her one day in a cinema queue. She'd been there one minute, Ernest had looked away – his attention caught by buskers perhaps, possibly even Meg of the Gleaming Gums – and when he turned back, his girlfriend had vanished into thin air. Ernest haunted the West End ever after, peering at queues in vain, longing for his missing girl to reappear. The general opinion was that she'd taken the opportunity to leg it to the nearest tube, and had got away while the going was good. Ernest was found dead one day, in the graveyard of St Giles Church, sitting in a deckchair (some say an armchair), with a large book of astrology open on his lap.

Another character who lived on the streets of Covent Garden was remembered by Olga Jackson. 'Then there was old Niffy Whiskers, used to sell papers. We called him Niffy Whiskers because he had this long hair and long beard ... he was obviously a very educated man. It was very sad, really. And he would go around selling papers. We used to feed these stray cats just off of Drury Lane, we would to buy these heads and things from the fish and chip shop, stew them up, then take them out to feed to the cats, and I remember one day he really ripped me off a strip, because I was giving food to the cats, and he didn't think I should be doing that because people were hungry, etcetera. My mother said "I reckon he's been crossed in love." But to her, anybody who went off the rails was always crossed in love.'

And then there were sandwich-board men. There were loads of them. They fell into two main categories: eccentrics determined to air their views on a variety of subjects, and those who advertised on behalf of local businesses. Several of the former were convinced that the End was Nigh and were moved to tell us all so. They were not alone in their beliefs. The recent wars and the atom bomb had concentrated everyone's minds most powerfully on personal mortality, as well as on the terrifying possibility of general annihilation, so the doom-laden messages written in curly scripts, in chalk, on sandwich boards rang an uncomfortable bell with almost everyone.

There was also the flying saucer brigade. The fifties saw a positive rash of stories of abductions by aliens and sightings of flying saucers (they were nearly always saucers, rarely flying cigars or airborne spheres) and, of course, there were sandwich-board men determined to share their personal experiences of the phenomena. I remember two; one was utterly convinced he'd been abducted and the other was sure he was about to be.

The walking advertisements were almost always homeless men of one sort or another. Most were alcoholics who had lost everything and were nearing the end of that ghastly, progressive disease. Some were mentally ill, and others were simply misfits who could not manage in a more conventional, structured life. All were eking out an existence by trudging the streets with their heavy boards advertising anything from a local gentlemen's outfitters through to restaurants or even stage shows that needed to drum up more custom.

All sorts of men wound up in this unhappy band, including a High Court judge, the son of a peer of the realm, a one-time millionaire, a composer, an actor, musicians and show business people, a greengrocer, a dentist, teachers, clergymen, a doctor or two, a journalist, writers and artists. Each morning these poor souls would form a scruffy line to collect their boards from a place in Frith Street – or it may have been Dean Street. They'd then head for the main shopping areas like Oxford Street, Regent Street, Piccadilly, Leicester Square, Charing Cross Road or Shaftesbury Avenue to walk up and down, up and down until the shops closed and the shoppers headed home. Then the men would return to the yard, dump their boards and queue up again at a hatch to collect their day's pay. Sometimes, a man would be so overcome with thirst and the DTs that he'd dump his board and nip into a pub for a stiffener, but he did so at his peril, because there were inspectors who did the rounds to make sure that their men were on the job.

Some individual street people have woven their way into Soho folklore. The stories about Ironfoot Jack are legion. My own memory of him was that he was often drunk, sometimes raving and a tiny bit scary if you were knee high and very young. He wore a cloak and a large hat and had a habit of climbing up on the roofs of cars to declaim dramatically about this and that. The iron foot played hell with the car's bodywork, but, not being the owner of any of the vehicles, Jack was indifferent. Such trivialities were beneath the 'King of the Bohemians', as he dubbed himself, often from the top of a car.

'Quick, let's dive in here,' Father would say if we saw Jack coming towards us. 'What a dreadful schnorrer that bugger is!' We'd take swift and decisive evasive action to evade Jack's cadging.

Jack's iron foot fascinated me, partly because I'd never seen anything like it before – or since, for that matter – and partly because of the sparks. Being low to the ground, I got a good view of the foot in question. It was a built-up boot affair, to make up for Jack's short leg, with a typical shoe or boot arrangement in leather at the top, but the metal sole was a sort of platform with iron struts between the sole and the shoe part. When Jack was drunk, which was frequently, he'd drag the offending foot and sparks would fly, giving me an impromptu firework display.

Ironfoot Jack was mainly famous for the con tricks that he pulled. He advertised for people to send ten bob (some say it was a fiver, but that seems an awful lot for the times) to receive the secret of making money 'by return of post'. When he got an enquiry, he'd reply promptly with the advice, 'DO WHAT I DID...' Another scam was to advertise his patent fly killer. Again, on receipt of five (or ten, depending on who told the story) shillings, he'd post back two small blocks of wood, one marked 'A' and the other 'B' and instructions to 'Place the fly on block A and whack it hard with block B'.

The restaurant was one of his bolder efforts. He rented a semi-derelict building where the electricity had been cut off. Undaunted, Jack arranged to have paraffin lamps liberated from local night-watchmen, and lit the place with those. Impressive menus were provided, in French no less, to add a little class, but every item on them, bar one, was crossed out due to 'shortages' and 'rationing'. The one dish left was 'poisson et pommes frites'. When the diners duly ordered, Jack would yell the order into the non-existent kitchen and 'a lad' would sprint down to the nearest chippie, grab the requisite portions of fish and chips, sprint back, dump them on plates and then Jack, with the great dignity of a seasoned *maître d'hôtel*, would serve them. Other sources say that Jack did the sprinting himself, but if this was so, there must have been a veritable blizzard of sparks and a terrible racket from the iron foot. Needless to say, the restaurant closed after a few, short weeks.

I realize now, looking back, that there was a knife-edge quality to Jack that I found frightening, because he was unpredictable. On the other hand, Father found that he was all too predictable in his endless search for handouts. Gary Winkler thought Jack 'a great character' but Daniel Farson, in *Soho in the Fifties*, writes that 'Ironfoot Jack's determination to rise above his shortcomings was admirable, but I found him a dreadful old bore, and was far from certain that his story about the restaurant was true.' Possibly, scruffy old Jack didn't fit comfortably into Farson's rather rarefied milieu of boozy and artistic friends.

The cries of 'I gotta horse, I gotta horse!' echoed throughout the land in the fifties; or at least, those parts of the land that boasted a racecourse. Ras Prince Monolulu was a national character, by far and away the nation's best known and loved black man. His schtick was to claim that he was a tribal chief from Abyssinia or Ethiopia. Prince Monolulu was concerned less with strict adherence to the facts than with creating a mood, and to do that you have to get the imaginary landscape right. He dispensed tips on horses for a price, talked about racing end-lessly and may have taken illegal street bets.

I remember the Prince as an imposing, but friendly, figure in an ostrich feather headdress. The long feathers stood straight up from his head and waved gently in the breeze, or wildly as he declaimed his wonderful spiel. This was followed by a monologue that meandered down the fascin-ating, and sometimes surreal, highways and byways of his fertile imagination, via a gentle joke or two at the expense of the white man's imagined 'superiority'. He was the racecourse and street corner stand-up of his day.

Many a harassed mother had cause to sigh with relief when she spotted Prince Monolulu majestically holding court from his bench in Soho Square. He kept a benevolent eye on the local kids for their busy parents for free. While kids played hide-and-seek round the fake Tudor hunting lodge behind him or rolled about squealing on the sooty grass at his feet, he would be selling the names of the 'winners' at the 2.30 at Cheltenham, Epsom or Ascot.

It was an arrangement that suited everybody. Kids loved Prince Monolulu, or Peter Mackay to give the name that his parents handed down for him. His place of birth was not Abyssinia, nor indeed anywhere in Africa, but was most probably Guyana. The First World War had seen him interned in Germany, and on his release he decided that a change of country was definitely in order. He made his way across Europe, working variously as a male model, a fortune teller, a boxer and even briefly passed himself off as an opera singer.

His career as a racing tipster really took off when he won a massive £8,000 by backing Spion Kop at 100–6 in the Derby of 1920. Ever after, no race meeting of any note was complete without the sight of ostrich plumes waving in the breeze above the punters' heads and the cries of 'I gotta horse, I gotta horse...' floating across the winners' paddock. Prince Monolulu died in 1965 at the age of eighty-four.

Timothy Cotter, sometimes known as 'Phyllis', because he was quite effeminate, or 'Rosie', because he habitually wore a rose behind his ear, didn't trouble with a sandwich board. He stuck to begging and running errands for his meagre living. Rosie had a despised rival, who also wore flowers, usually carnations and chrysanthemums as I recall, although any flowers would do, tucked behind *both* of his ears. I don't know the rival's name, but people often confused the two men.

Rosie's usual haunt was Berwick Street market, where, according to Janet Vance, kindly barrow boys more or less kept him going. Some donated bits of money here and there for a night in the dosshouse, hot meals and cups of tea when the weather was cold. Mostly, though, they gave him the slightly bruised fruit and vegetables that weren't quite fit for sale, on the grounds that hard cash could be exchanged for bottles of the booze that had brought him so low, whereas an orange or an apple could not: and anyway, they were more nourishing.

Rosie, in his cups, was a terrible screecher, and I sometimes found him quite frightening, because, like Ironfoot Jack, he often seemed very close to the edge. When he died, the *Daily Mirror* reported that 'His endless kindness, especially to children, made him a very popular figure.' Personally, I don't remember him being particularly kind to children. I suppose it depended on just how drunk he was. I do know that he was barred from most of the local pubs, partly because he annoyed the customers by always being on the scrounge, even from complete strangers, and partly because he enjoyed creating a scene by screaming scurrilous comments from the doorways. These tirades would cease abruptly when he was hurled unceremoniously back out on the pavement.

Dan Farson once made the mistake of giving Rosie half a crown, although he came to regret it, because after that rash act of kindness, whenever Rosie saw him he'd shriek, 'Mr Farson, Mr

Farson, dear! Give me the price of a drink.' And when he was refused he'd add, 'Oh, well, give me the kiss of life.'

Rosie's overt campness would not have worried Sohoites at all, but it would have deeply offended the strait-laced morality of the times. In the fifties, homosexuality was most definitely illegal, and the authorities decided on a crackdown that led to many arrests and trials. Sometimes Rosie would show signs of having been quite badly beaten. Word on the street was that the beatings occurred while he was in police custody, and this may well have been true on some occasions. In those days, the police force could get away with rough treatment of troublesome prisoners. It was a standing joke that Rosie's only known fixed address was the police station. I am also sure that some beatings took place in dosshouses when his sexuality had annoyed less understanding dossers, or on the street when he was so drunk that he was reduced to sleeping rough.

Eventually, Rosie's tough life took its toll. He died with neither friends nor known relatives. This meant a pauper's funeral, something that the Berwick Street traders, for whom he had become a wildly eccentric mascot, would not countenance. They decorated their stalls with pictures of Rosie and the flowers that he so loved, and had a whip-round in order to send him off in style. They collected enough money to do just that, and on the day of the funeral in excess of two thousand people arrived to bid a final farewell. The funeral procession brought the streets of Soho to a standstill, and men removed their hats to show their respect to one of Soho's legendary, if not necessarily well-loved, characters. 'We won't see his like again,' the crowd murmured, according to Dan Farson, who added, with truthful cynicism, that the newspapers and the crowd uttered all 'the usual dishonest euphemisms when someone disconcerting dies'. It does seem that a fair few that nostalgia and recent history have deemed to be 'characters' were, in fact, tragically 'disconcerting'.

9

'No Squeezing 'til it's Yours, Missus!'

For Londoners, Up West is the place to go shopping when you really want to splurge, and it's been that way for a long time. Ever since Oxford Street was developed by the Earl of Oxford late in the nineteenth century, it has attracted a wide variety of shoppers, from the quite well off to those of much more modest means, while the elegant Georgian streets and arcades in the angle between Piccadilly and Regent Street have been the place to find shops selling the luxurious and the bespoke – jewellers and tailors, watchmakers and shoemakers.

In the years after the war, however, splurging wasn't high on most people's agenda. For most of the people who lived in the West End, shopping had little to do with ease and luxury; more often it was about looking for the necessities of life, and often not finding them. What a lot of us don't realize is that a great many people in the forties and early fifties were seriously hungry, thanks to shortages and rationing.

Sonia Boulter has never forgotten what hunger felt like. 'I remember starving, literally starving, when I was a youngster. I was grateful for anything. I remember, after the war, my mum taking me to Berwick Street, and going round the back of a bombed area to see this woman, probably a sixty-odd-year-old woman, who was selling chickens from a cardboard box on the ground. They must have been black market. I can remember Mum picking around, having a look, trying to find a chicken. That sort of thing sticks in my memory. Food was very scarce, money was very scarce, and parents did what they had to do to feed the family.'

Something that anyone wanting to buy food had to do was queue. Everybody who lived through the years of rationing remembered standing in line. Nowadays people get cross if they're delayed a few minutes at the checkout, but in the forties the restrictions of rationing made endless queuing a way of life. 'The fish queues were the longest,' Barbara Jones remembers. 'You'd queue for hours at the fishmonger's in Chandos Place. I'd do two or three hours, then my sister would do two or three, only to find out there was No Fish Today.'

Something that made the queues longer was the fact that, during the war, shoppers had to register with certain nearby shops in order to prevent fraud, and were only allowed to use their ration books and coupons at selected places. It wasn't until rationing finally came to an end in 1954 that people could shop around for the cheapest or best offers, or for the shop that had what they wanted in stock. One-stop shopping was rarely an option, either. Few grocery stores sold every rationed foodstuff. 'We had to register at more than one grocer's,' Owen Gardner remembers. 'We went to a shop in New Row, run by a Welsh milkman, but they didn't sell bacon, so we went to a wholesaler in St Martin's Lane for that. He had great big sides of it hanging up, and we used to have to go in and say, "Can I have my two rashers, please?" or whatever your ration was.'

Mike O'Rouke also remembers having to make the rounds. 'I used to do the shopping for my mum when I was old enough, using ration books. She used to tear out a little coupon, give it to me and send me to the Home & Colonial and other shops up on the Dials. She just used to point me in a direction and say, "Here's a coupon, go up there and get that."'

Sonia Boulter's family were registered with Hammet's, near the Rupert Street end of Berwick Street market. This was a provisions shop that met most needs. 'It was a grocer's, butcher's, everything, and I can remember going in there with my mum, and having the ration book, and having to tick it off for butter, or bacon – everything you bought you had to tick it off. Not far from Hammet's was the Home & Colonial, and Mum would tell us to go and get a carton of broken eggs, because broken ones were off-ration. It was a treat to have eggs.'

The deep joy of any foodstuff off-ration in those hard, hard times cannot be overestimated, as Barbara Jones recalls. 'In Great Queen Street, off Drury Lane, where the Connaught Rooms are, there was a shop called Jack's. You'd go down two steps into this shop and buy a sherbet to eat with your fingers, and sometimes they used to have little lumpy, gnarly end bits of chocolate-coated toffee. We used to go in and say, "Got any sweets off the ration?" In fact, you'd go into any shop and ask for goods off the ration.'

Cooked food bought from a shop or in a restaurant was off-ration, so pie and mash or fish and chips not only provided nourishment, but also preserved precious coupons. As an added bonus, there was probably less queuing involved and no cooking or washing up to be done.

Making a meat pie at home would involve queuing at the butcher's for meat and lard, and probably another queue at the grocer's for the flour to mix with the lard for the pastry: and there was no guarantee that there'd actually be any lard, flour or meat when you finally made it to the counter. It could literally take days to assemble the ingredients for a meal, and it would also take several people's rations or weeks of hoarded coupons.

No wonder so many opted for pie and mash from a shop or market stall or cod and three-penn'orth from the local fish and chip shop. Most people ate their fish supper straight from the newspaper it was wrapped in. There is still a school of thought that says it tasted better that way.

Another way to eat off-ration was to seek out unusual food – easier done in the cosmopolitan West End than most places in Britain. Sonia Boulter remembers a very special treat: 'Near the Bar Italia was a shop that sold just horsemeat. You'd go in there – or Mum would send us in, because they used to like children – and get a couple of steaks. And I remember seeing half-horses hanging up. I didn't think anything of it. I used to love horsemeat: I wouldn't dream of touching it now. It was lovely in those days, when you didn't have any meat, it was brilliant. It was either that or no meat.'

'Sometimes, when Mum couldn't afford any-thing else, we'd have a soup made of milk, rice and peas, and that was a meal. Milk, because it was good for you, rice, because you got plenty of it, and peas because it was vegetables.'

Vegetables were never on ration, but of course supplies of many of them, and most fruit, dried up completely in the war. Many took a while to return, especially fruit, and what there was was often too expensive for working families – which is why the newly formed NHS started doling out orange juice for children. Shortages were less marked in the West End; most of the fruit and veg in England passed through Covent Garden market, and the local retailers – provided they got up early enough – could have their pick.

Very, very few ordinary families would have owned a refrigerator in the fifties. This meant that food shopping had to be done on pretty much a daily basis – certainly for such perishables as milk, fish and meat – and generally within a few streets of home. As there were very few cars, anyone who went far afield to shop had to bear in mind that they would have to schlep it home afterwards on the bus or on foot. And once they'd walked it to the street door, they often had to heave it up several flights of stairs. There were sixty-six steps to our flat, and this was no joke with several bulging bags of shopping about one's person.

My memories of shopping for food, and those of most of the people I spoke with, revolved around the wonderful Berwick Street market, the vibrant heart of Soho, which has been weighing out produce to local people, and local businesses, for more than three hundred years. Although some local restaurants got their supplies directly from Covent Garden, most of them were supplied by the market. 'There was no ceremony about it,' Alberto Camisa recalled. 'They would come down and leave orders for the next day, ten sacks of potatoes or whatever, and the stallholders would go and buy it at the Garden next morning.'

A market is a place of wonder for children. Its many sights, colours, sounds, smells, tastes and textures make an impression that lingers for a lifetime. Many of the people I spoke to still remember their trips to Berwick Street market with their mum as an event, even if the market was on their doorstep and the trips were frequent. And when they were old enough to go on their own, there was so much activity, so much life that they just could not be bored. Owen Gardner put it best: 'That was a fascinating place. Everybody went there. Everybody knew everybody. It was Soho.'

Of all the people I spoke to, no one knew, or

loved, Berwick Street market quite as well as Alberto Camisa, who grew up in the centre of it, in the house above his family's famous delicatessen, Fratelli Camisa. 'Berwick Street market was all food all the way from Broadwick Street through the alleyway and into Rupert Street down to Shaftesbury Avenue. You couldn't get a pitch: it was packed with stalls, there was no room between. All the stalls had lots of lights on in those days, tilley lamps, lanterns, and the stalls had canopies – dark green canopies, dark blue canvases, or awnings – over the stalls. They all looked nice, made quite a picture. It was a great community; hectic, noisy, very friendly. Obviously, there were family rivalries, particularly between stallholders, pitches and stalls and so on: there were basically three or four families, cousins and that, ran the market. Some were from Soho, others from the East End.'

Sonia Boulter confirms this. 'At one stage, all the barrow boys down there, they were all connected, the brother of this one was the uncle of that one. It was very family-orientated down there. We knew a lot of the barrow boys by name and could have a chat. All it was when I was a kid was fruit and veg, and in those days it had the name of the best fruit and veg market in London.' Sonia's friend, Maria Mechele, actually lived in Berwick Street, and was the cousin of many of the stallholders there.

Many of the stallholders specialized. There was a potato stall, a stall that sold only spinach and cauliflowers, a banana man, and so on.

'I had the dubious distinction of being the

213

youngest barrow boy in Berwick Street market, twelve years of age, selling nothing but lemons on behalf of my employer, who had the stall next to mine,' Andrew Panayiotes told me. 'You could hear my call to all the prospective punters throughout Berwick Street. "C'mon girls, get your lemons here. Five for a bob."

Alberto Camisa also remembered how 'The stallholders' kids used to come out on a Saturday, and help them out with their packing, summer and winter.' The stalls and barrows were packed away overnight – and all through Sunday – on bomb sites and lock-ups all round Soho, little courtyards reached through alleyways between buildings. Previously, they had served as stables and carriage-houses, but now they generally housed the costermongers' wheelbarrows. They were locked away every night and pulled out early in the morning. 'The market traders had big heavy wooden wheelbarrows with steel-rimmed wheels,' Alberto told me. 'I remember hearing them rumbling about around five, six o'clock.'

A stallholder's day began even earlier than that, before the first sparrow had coughed. 'I had to be at Covent Garden at four in the morning and bring back produce that would not fit on the truck, piled high on a two-wheeled barrow,' Andy Pullinger recalls. 'It weighed a ton, and if I wasn't careful, it would fall to the back and I had a hell of a job to bring it back up again.'

Andy had started working in the market in 1957, when he was still a schoolboy. 'The first job was when school had finished for the day. I had to put the barrows away at night after the market was closed. They were stored in a bomb site, the entrance of which was the next street over. After a while, I graduated to working Saturdays and holidays on the fruit and veg stalls. The first couple I worked for were called Gertie and Sid Hamburger. Next I worked for Sid's brother Johnny, who was a bit of a joker. He once sent me to the chemist's for a bottle of "maid's milk". It took a while to figure out why the sales lady looked at me that way.

'My third job was for Johnny Benson: he was quite the man with the women. On Saturday mornings he had a stall on Church Street, so I looked after his stall in Berwick market on Saturdays. Opposite was a barber shop where I had my hair done every Saturday in preparation for the night out. The barber never failed to ask if I needed "Anything for the weekend?" Next to the barber was a fish and chip shop, and in front of that was Arnold the Tie Man. As the name implies, his stall sold only ties. I don't think he would make much of a living today.

'It was fun being my own boss for the day. After the bomb sites had been cleared, they built a pub right behind the stall. I was never thirsty, and usually finished the day giving the fruit and veg to customers. At day's end I would take the takings to Johnny at Edgware Road. He was usually quite happy with what I did.'

Throughout the fifties, the market was all frenetic bustle – on six days a week, at least. Raye Du-Val, who lived nearer the Oxford Street end of Berwick Street, remembers Sunday afternoons being 'weird, because you'd be looking out of

215

your flat, looking along to where the market would be, and it's all empty, everyone's gone down Brighton, somewhere like that.'

'Sunday was very different, no market, not much traffic,' Alberto Camisa's brother, Francesco recalls. 'Sunday was the only time you could have a lie-in. The only thing that used to disturb us was the Salvation Army band playing on the corner of Berwick Street and Peter Street at about nine in the morning.'

It wasn't just the stalls that drew people to Berwick Street market; the surrounding shops were full of staples and specialized foods. Andy Pullinger told me that his first memory of Soho 'was going shopping in Brewer Street with my mum, and seeing all the produce hanging in the windows of the butcher's, fish in barrels at the fishmonger's and grocery items laid out in front of the stores.'

Janet Vance also remembers there being 'a butcher's, a baker's and more in Brewer Street. In Peter Street you had a Jewish kosher shop, Jolson's, and a Jewish boot mender's – Brahms they were called – and then there was the smoked salmon shop in Brewer Street that sold the big gherkins and rollmops and things. And Grodzinski's the bakers were there. You had the Greek shops selling their sort of stuff. The shops had their own stalls outside.

'Rupert Street was classed as the posh end of the market, more expensive. Rupert Street had Hammet's. Berwick Street was cheaper. The well-known fruit and veg place was Habgood's; they had their shop and they had their stall outside, selling the same sort of thing.'

For Tricia Bryan and her mum, who lived at Tavistock Square, it was a fair haul to Berwick Street, but they made it anyway. 'It was basically fruit and veg,' remembers Tricia, 'then, as we got more sophisticated and started eating Italian food and things, we went to the delis there.' The delis helped to give Berwick Street its unique flavour, its raffish, cosmopolitan air. Fifis – the French working girls – referred to it as the *marché Français,* a welcome home away from home for girls who often must have felt lonely and isolated as they walked alien streets.

While Sohoites remained faithful to Berwick Street and would never have thought of 'playing away' at another food market, there was another option for Covent Gardeners and Bloomsbury-ites. Chapel Street market in Islington wasn't exactly local, but it was easy to get to, as Ann Lee points out: 'We used to go on the tram from Kingsway, right up Pentonville Hill to Chapel market. We'd go and pick up fruit and veg and what have you, and get the tram back home. Where we were in Drury Lane, you had the choice: jump on a bus or tram from Kingsway to Chapel Street market, or walk to Berwick Street.'

The two markets had contrasting characters. Perhaps a little larger than Berwick Street, Chapel market was more of a general market. It had a strong East End character to it, with shops selling the cockney delicacies of jellied eels and pie and mash. For some, the latter were a deciding factor in persuading them to take the tram. 'Chapel Street, that was my mum's favourite,' Mike

217

O'Rouke remembers, 'because they had a couple of pie and mash shops up there, and that was me mum's favourite.'

Some people didn't bother with going to the market at all. Peter Jenkins's mother 'never went to Berwick Street', although she sometimes sent him to Covent Garden after school, when the wholesalers were closing down, to see if they were prepared to sell something off. 'All the other food shopping was done on Drury Lane. There were some very good old grocery shops there.'

Another family drawn to Drury Lane was the Jacksons, who lived in Covent Garden until 1941, when they were bombed out to Blooms-bury. Their old stomping ground in Drury Lane drew them back, however – even Graham, who was born after they moved. 'Drury Lane was its own little village, wasn't it? There was everything there,' he remembers. 'There was the oil shop, where we used to take the accumulator in to get charged, for the radio. We used to walk from Ridgmount Mansions all the way down to Drury Lane, carrying it. There must have been some-where else we could have taken it, but we always seemed to take it there.'

His older sister, Olga, agreed. 'We used to put in the mileage. It was habit. We was born and brought up round there, and used to go back. You had the first Sainsbury's in Drury Lane. The very first one.'

John Sainsbury and his wife, the daughter of a dairyman, opened a small grocery store at 173 Drury Lane, a house with three floors and an attic, in 1869. After their initial success, John

Sainsbury planned to establish a small chain of stores, one each for his six sons to manage. It's all a far cry from today's chain of supermarkets. I have always suspected that Mrs Sainsbury's family was Welsh: the great majority of the dairies in the West End were run by Welsh men and women, so much so that even those with English proprietors were referred to as 'Welsh dairies'. This may have had something to do with Sainsbury's specializing in butter, cheese and dairy products for much of their history.

The Jacksons were registered for dairy rations with Sainsbury's in Drury Lane. Olga remembers 'the cheese, and the butter that they used to pat and pack themselves, and the big high chairs that you'd sit on while they did it'. Butter pats – wooden paddle-like things with carved surfaces used to shape and brand the butter – came in all sorts of wonderful designs. One paddle might have a design of wavy lines and the other would have a picture of a cow or something: it could be a thistle, or buttercups, it varied from dairy to dairy. Butter was stored in large ceramic bowls, often decorated with a blue and white pastoral design involving cows. The grocer cut a lump out of the butter and weighed it. Next, the paddles were used to pat the lump into shape, taking great care to centre the design properly: dairies were proud of their product. Once the butter pat was made, it was wrapped in greaseproof paper and tied with string to keep the flaps closed.

Most of the food shops in the West End were small and specialized, although there were exceptions, such as Fortnum & Mason in Piccadilly, the more modest Hammet's, and the Civil Service Stores in the Strand, which had a food hall on its ground floor. These shops were nothing like modern supermarkets: they were more like food department stores – or, in the case of the rather grand Fortnum's, a food emporium. Pepe Rush remembers Hammet's 'as like a modern supermarket, but old-fashioned', with what were effectively separate shops in the same building.

The normal practice, however, was for the butcher, the grocer, the baker, the dairyman, the greengrocer, the cheesemonger and the fish-monger to have their own specialist premises. I have vivid memories of some of these lovely small shops around Soho: a butcher with lots of game hanging from steel hooks, both inside and outside; drool-inducing displays on glass trays in the win-dows of fragrant pâtisseries; and particularly, the exotic and exciting delicatessens, festooned with hams and salamis, infused with the scents of coffee, garlic, vanilla, chocolate and dried mush-rooms, and humming with activity in a variety of languages – Italian, French, Yiddish, Greek.

These wonderful shops were Soho's pride and joy at a time when meat and two veg – and no seasoning apart from far too much salt and possibly, for the brave, some white pepper – was as adventurous as cuisine got for most people in Britain. There were so many delicatessens in Soho – over fifty, according to Alberto Camisa – that expatriates could find just about anything they might want from the 'old country', no matter which one it was.

'Where we were in Berwick Street,' Alberto

explained, 'there was a Jewish delicatessen immediately to our right, a butcher's shop next to him. In Peter Street, there were three Jewish delis and a big fish and chip shop. In Old Compton Street there were ten or twelve – a French delicatessen, three Parmigiani shops, Demonises, the Lena Stores – and everybody knew everybody's prices. If someone came in for a chorizo, we'd say, Go to Ortega – that was another one in Old Compton Street – They have it at two and sixpence a pound. And if Ortega had someone wanting Parma ham, they'd send them round to us. It was like an open-air department store.'

Soho has been associated with gourmet and foreign food in one way or another – cooking it and importing it, as well as selling it – since the French arrived in the seventeenth century, and the Italians, Chinese, Greeks, and many others have carried on this tasty tradition ever since. A description in the *London Courier* in 1955 revelled in the exotic nature of the foodstuffs available. 'Through the windows of a Soho fishmonger one can see squids and cuttlefish, crayfish, red mullet and eels, and vast sheets of dried cod. The greengrocer sells peppers of every description, artichokes, celeriac, custard apples, avocado pears and about half a dozen different kind of beans. It could not be anywhere else.' For this writer, continental food shops signify Soho as surely as the 'huge beer barrel' of St Anne's Church clock.

'There is a famous oyster bar in Old Compton Street that is quiet and English,' the writer continues. 'There is a roaring Italian café where

221

the waiters sing. You can buy really good croissants and omelettes in this street, and sandwiched between the restaurants are those gigantic Italian grocery stores, bulging with twenty different kinds of enormous cheeses with twenty different smells, and more over the counter. Racks of pasta, straw-coloured bottles of wine, rows and rows of sausage hanging in racks above your head: fat ones, red ones, black ones, white ones, brown ones. Eight different kinds of rice in bins, ten different kinds of sugar.'

In the fifties, the switch in grocery retailing from the market model – where everything was weighed out and separately bagged in front of you, according to your needs, but you had to wait to be served – to the supermarket model – where everything was pre-packed and priced and you had to wait, in theory, only for other customers' purchases to be totted up – had only just begun.

The supermarkets had their fans – they certainly made shopping quicker, once you got used to the new rules – but the shops that leave the most vivid memories are ones from the pre-pre-packed era. Graham Jenkins remembers Law's, in Drury Lane: 'All the currants and that used to be in aluminium-lined drawers. They used to tell me, Go on, help yourself. I used to go in there and get a few currants and raisins out of the drawers. Their cheese and all that was on display – you'd get that smell, when you walked in the place, with all that mixture of foods, the dried fruits and that.'

On the other side of the Strand, Barbara Jones went to Darby's in Craven Street. 'It was a general provisions shop, a grocer: they sold beer, and I also got Pepsis there. It was one of those shops with a flap in the counter, and a trapdoor down to the cellar; a real old-fashioned place, with biscuits in tin boxes with a glass lid.'

Leo Zanelli harbours fond memories of 'a great big sweet shop in Leicester Square. I remember it vividly because they would always have a giant block of honeycomb and they would chip a lump off for you.'

Pepe Rush, who lived just down the road from me in Old Compton Street, remembers the shops there very fondly. 'Pâtisserie Valerie was opposite where I lived, between the newsagent and the Vintage House. The Café Bleu was not far away, and a tobacconist in Frith Street was where my dad got his cigars.' So did mine. Father smoked big, fat, Romeo and Julietta Cuban ones that smelt wonderful. 'Pugh's dairy was round the corner, run by Pugh's daughter,' Pepe recalls, 'and on the corner of Dean Street, first there was an Algerian café or something, and later there was Anello & Davide, where my mum bought her ballet shoes.'

As well as Pugh's Welsh Dairy in Frith Street, there was another in Peter Street, in Green Court, with a really memorable feature. 'I always called it Mrs Cooper's,' remembers Janet Vance. 'It had a cow outside, a cow-sized metal cow. You put your money in a slot, used the tail as a pump, and filled your jug from that.'

Sonia Boulter remembers Slater, Bisney & Cook, along Brewer Street, for other reasons: 'It was a very high-class butcher's. My youngest brother, when he left school, went to work there for a while. Taught me all about meat, you know, the cuts. It was a lovely shop. Lots of tiles, lots of windows, very clean-looking. The counters were always spotless.'

I am delighted to say that some of these shops still flourish today, West Enders being slower than most to sacrifice quality, choice and taste on the altar of vast profits and bland uniformity. The shopkeepers, in turn, don't want to let family reputations, gained over generations of hard work, fall apart. And the work *was* hard. 'We used to open from half-past eight to six o'clock or half-past,' remembers Alberto Camisa. 'At Christmas time we opened from seven until nine or ten at night; we opened Christmas morning. Thursday afternoons we were closed. My parents never went out at night, they were knackered. The shop opened at nine but they were up at half-seven, and it shut at six, but by the time you'd closed up and cleaned up, it was seven thirty.'

Hard work was a family tradition. Ennio and Isidoro had lost their first business in the war, and had had to pull themselves up by their bootstraps, building up their business again from scratch at the shop in Berwick Street. They were helped by having family ties with other shop-keepers, particularly the Parmigianis. The three Parmigiani shops in Old Compton Street were run by cousins. Like the Camisas, they came from Tasorgno, 'in Parma ham country'.

There was never any question that Alberto and his brother Francesco would follow in their father's footsteps, 'You started working as soon as

The day after a bomb destroyed part of Newport Dwellings in April 1941, killing 48 people, including Sonia Boulter's grandmother.

Above: The Bedfordbury kids, including Ronnie Mann (*top left*), gather for an outing to Box Hill with the actress Julie Wilson (*centre right*).

Below: Girls from the Bedfordbury Estate are dressed in their best frocks for races on Coronation Day, 1953.

Above: A bunfight — or possibly muffin worry — in Bedfordbury in Coronation week. The kids wear caps in patriotic red, white and blue.

Left: After a hard day's schooling, home for tea: parents collect their children from St James's and St Peter's in 1955.

Below: Hard-boiled eggs go flying in the boys' egg and spoon race at the Bedfordbury Coronation celebrations.

Above Left: Gamba's craftsmen make ballet shoes for latter-day Pavlovas and Nijinskys in the 1960s.

Above Right: Happy to be of service: two smartly turned-out waitresses take a break in Soho in 1955.

Fruit and veg porters ply their trade in the Palladian arcades of the Covent Garden Piazza in the late 1950s

A typically shy punter, with pulled-down brim and turned-up collar, browses the shelves of what looks very like my father's shop in 1956.

Working girls pass the time between clients, watching the world go by from a first-floor window in Soho in 1956.

'Major' Knowles (*right*), a street bookie in Covent Garden, accepts a customer's bet in the street.

Chas McDevitt selects the tunes on the jukebox in his Freight Train Coffee Bar.

Dancing in the street: happy punters jive outside the Freight Train on the opening night in 1958. Note the 'Continental' moustaches and flared skirt.

The cramped cellar of this Old Compton Street coffee bar was the birthplace of British rock 'n' roll. My father's flat was above a deli next door to the right.

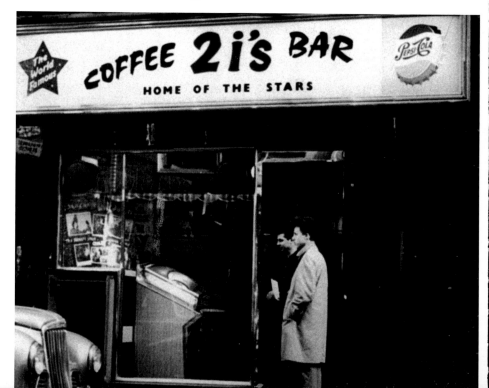

Above: George Melly sang
blues and jazz with Mick
Mulligan, but on this club date
vocalises with Russell Quaye's
City Ramblers skiffle group.

Above: A busker entertains
a queue in Soho in the 1950s.
I love the little girl dancing
along and the skinny lad with
the umbrella — were they part
of the act?

Left: Men carrying overcoats
queue to enter the Windmill
on a hot July day in 1951.

Local face and bookmaker, Albert Dimes, celebrates his acquittal on charges of wounding in 1955.

Jack Comer, aka Jack Spot, was an old-style East End villain. His knife fight with Albert Dimes — in which he acquired his scar — has become part of Soho folklore.

Former boxer, and later West End club-owner, Freddie Mills, signs an outsize book outside a Charing Cross Road bookstore in 1953.

Few West End characters were as colourful as tipster Prince Monolulu, seen here in 1956.

you started walking. As soon as you could see above the counter, you'd serve. You'd come home from school, finish your homework, if the shop was still open, you went downstairs. On Saturdays, you would help out. Go and get stuff from the cellar, put it on the shelves. We had our little chores. Like most people, we had bare wooden stairs, and we had to wash the stairs once or twice a week with a scrubbing brush.

'Kids always helped out. If their parents had restaurants, they'd help out in the kitchens, wash the dishes, help lay the table. The shop, workshop or restaurant was considered part of your house. Most people lived above it, next door to it, or not far away. It was all family-run, so you helped your dad or mum do the work. It wasn't slave labour or anything, it was just expected that you would help your parents. When the shop shut, *then* you could go out and play.

'The shop wasn't very long, about thirty feet, and sometimes there were seven of us behind the counter and we did not have time for lunch, we were that busy. There would be two people downstairs bringing stuff up from the cellar.'

Naturally, time brings changes and many shops have disappeared: Fratelli Camisa has long gone from Berwick Street, for example, and the building was demolished in 2008. Some familiar names remain. Pâtisserie Valerie has made people drool for as long as I can remember, the Algerian coffee shop still prides itself on supplying quality coffee beans and teas to a devoted clientele, Lena Stores continues to supply pasta, dried beans and much, much more from its corner of Brewer

Street, and there are several others that are still trading. Unlike Covent Garden, Berwick Street market is still there, although the barrows have fallen silent: trucks bring the produce from Nine Elms now. The faces, and the accents, of the costermongers have changed over the years but the cries of, 'No squeezing 'til it's yours, missus, surely your mother told you that,' or something similar can still be heard above the general racket. West End locals still have some of the best food shops in the country in which to forage for their three square meals – and nowadays there are no ration books or coupons to worry about.

10

Different but Equal

'Ooh, bona to vada your dolly old eek,' declaimed the distinctively nasal tones of Kenneth Williams in the justly popular sixties radio programme, *Round the Horne*. Most listeners could only have guessed what Williams was saying, but of the relative few who actually understood every word, the great majority would have been living, working or playing in London's West End. Kenneth Williams and his sidekick, Hugh Paddick, always started their sketch with the catchphrase, 'Hello, I'm Julian and this is my friend Sandy,' and then launched into Polari, the secret language adopted by some, but certainly not all, of Britain's homosexuals.

In those profoundly class-ridden days when the population was summarily consigned to 'top drawer', 'middle drawer' or 'bottom drawer', Polari was most popular with working-class gay men. Ordinary seamen (but not officers), dockers in the East End and show people in the West End used Polari extensively in the forties, fifties and sixties. 'Higher class' thespians, such as Sir John Gielgud and the bisexual Sir Laurence Olivier, probably rarely, if ever, used it, but 'chorus boys', bit part players and stagehands did. Hotels and restaurants boasted quite a large gay population and many of those working in West End establishments were fluent Polari speakers in their off-duty hours. 'Julian', his 'friend Sandy' and *Round the Horne* were a much-loved part of Sunday afternoons for a large section of the UK population and it seemed to matter not at all that most listeners didn't know what on earth the pair were talking about – which is just as well, as often what they were talking about was wildly *risqué*. How Polari speakers must have loved to have been in on the secret!

Here's an example of a Polari exchange.

Man one: 'Oh, vada the omee ajax who just trolled in – her in her cod lally-drags. Bona eke, bene corybungas but a fashioned riah if ever I clocked one. She must be on the team.' *(Translation:* 'Look at the man next to us who just walked in, him in his bad trousers. Nice face, good arse, but a wig if ever I saw one. He must be gay.')

Man Two: 'Nanti, nanti ducky, she's a charpering omee, I've seen her down the charpering carsey. Time to scarper and toot sweet.' *(Translation:* 'No, no dear, he's a policeman, I've seen him at the police station. Time to leave and fast.')

Polari had its roots as a lingua franca for the travelling peoples of sixteenth- and seventeenth-century Europe. Beggars, buskers, pedlars, tinkers (not to be confused with the Romany people, who had their own language), sailors, travelling theatrical troupes, dance troupes, rogues and prostitutes all used Parlyaree, the language that would metamorphose into Polari and become beloved of gay communities. Sailors brought the language to the East End, where it mixed with thieves' cant, back slang ('riah' is back slang for hair, while 'eke' is short for 'ecaf', back slang for face) and rhyming slang ('scarper' is rhyming slang, Scapa Flo – go). Travelling entertainers brought a slightly simpler version to the theatreland of the West End, although as gay sailors and entertainers often mixed when they hit the West End pubs, clubs and gambling joints, the two became virtually interchangeable.

In the twenties, it became the fashion among homosexuals to refer to men as 'she' and they often gave one another women's names. Quentin Crisp describes days spent with the 'girls' in the Black Cat Café in Old Compton Street, 'buying each other cups of tea, combing one another's hair and trying on each other's lipsticks while waiting for something to happen. The fashion continued well into the forties and fifties, especially, but not exclusively, among Polari speakers. Muriel

Belcher, the bisexual owner of the famous drinking club, the Colony Room, in Dean Street, always referred to her favourite male customers as her 'daughters'.

It is hard to believe in these more enlightened times that a private language was necessary, but in those post-war years homosexual acts were illegal in this country – at least for men. Lesbians were never prosecuted because when the Offences against the Person Act (1861) was followed by section 11 of the Criminal Law Amendment Act of 1885, which outlawed any kind of sexual contact between men in 'public or private', legend has it that the enthusiastically heterosexual Queen Victoria point-blank refused to believe that women were capable of such behaviour. The law had, in fact, condemned some gay sexual behaviour for centuries. At one time, the death sentence was imposed for sodomy, while in the period of this book, prosecutions for 'gross indecency' could, and did, result in terms of imprisonment for those unlucky enough to be caught and found guilty.

Even by British standards, post-war attitudes were particularly narrow and judgmental. Why this should be the case is open to interpretation – but it certainly led to increased vigilance by the police and an upsurge in the arrest and prosecution of gay men. According to court records researched by Matt Houlbrook for his book *Queer London*, the total number of recorded convictions for homosexual acts in the London area in 1937 was 251, and by 1957 that number had almost doubled to 491. Had the record of convictions at Westminster magistrates' court been available, the 1957 total would have been a good deal larger.

In his book about his involvement in the famous Lord Montagu court case, *Against the Law*, Peter Wildeblood contended that class prejudice played a part in his prosecution and that the stiff prison sentences imposed were due to the fact that the men he and Montagu were consorting with were of a lower class, and were thus perceived to present a real threat to society that had to be contained. As he pointed out, 'The very words of the law are impregnated with emotion on the subject; murder is merely murder, but homosexual acts are "the abominable crime" and "gross indecency".' And homosexuality was a crime twice over. As one of my contacts said, not only were there 'swingeing penalties' for those found out, but 'your neighbours and family would castigate you'.

Class boundaries had been broken down, or at least badly knocked about, in barracks, below decks and in mess halls during wartime, and they threatened to be further undermined during the uneasy peace of the atom bomb years immediately following the bombings of Nagasaki and Hiroshima. It became imperative to get our society back on an even, familiar keel in the doomed hope that new fears would dwindle once old certainties had been put in place once again.

As gay people were consigned to a secretive subculture, it was inevitable that the 'top drawer' elite would come into contact with subjects from the two other, lower, drawers and their many, heavily nuanced subsections that only a born and bred Brit would understand – and the one place where the classes could meet, mingle and mate with enthusiasm was the West End. Leo Zanelli witnessed an incident that illustrated this: 'I can remember once in Shaftesbury Avenue, there was a crash, a black cab side-swiped a car. I looked up and three sailors got out one side to talk to the cabby, and three gentlemen in evening dress got out the other side and walked straight away. I remember thinking, that's a bit strange...'

The three gents were far from alone in fancying sailors. Josh Avery, a sailor himself and the subject of Nigel Richardson's book, *Dog Days in Soho*, knew that certain 'posh blokes' liked consorting with 'other ranks', especially one in a sailor's uniform. Although he was straight himself, Avery thought nothing of exploiting this taste in exchange for a place to stay, endless drinks and some other necessities of life. It was after picking up Dan Farson that he was introduced to the fifties Soho bohemian society that Farson made the subject of his famous book, *Soho in the Fifties*.

It's difficult to convey the depth of the longing that the general population had 'to get back to normal' after six years of chaos. In the post-war years, having any kind of 'airs and graces', 'showing yourself up' or 'putting yourself forward' was very definitely frowned upon. Adding flamboyant homosexuality to the mix was several leaps too far. Anyone who has read *The Naked Civil Servant*, or has seen the erstwhile habitué of the West End, Quentin Crisp, interviewed, will know that then, as now, some gay men were colourfully eccentric. 'The rumours about homosexuality that

231

were now spread ... suggested it was a much larger monster than had originally been suspected,' Crisp wrote, 'devouring not only all ballet dancers and a few actors but thrusting one claw in at the door of the homes of apparently quite ordinary citizens. The cry went up that England was going to the bitches. The police, to show that they took this prognostication seriously, began to clean up the West End.'

Nigel Richardson suggests in his book that the defection to the USSR of the Communist campers, Guy Burgess and Donald Maclean, in 1951 added fuel to the systemic homophobia of the day, another reason for the continuing crackdown on 'male vice' and West End 'filth spots'. Before they defected, Burgess and Maclean had been enthusiastic members of the Gargoyle Club in Meard Street, and made no secret of being Communist spies when they were in their cups, which was often. However, the devil-may-care, anti-establishment punters at the Gargoyle were unimpressed, and either thought it was some kind of joke, or were too busy drinking, flirting and sleeping with one another to do anything about it. It certainly never occurred to anybody to report the pair to the authorities.

It was generally believed that homosexuals chose their sexual orientation simply to be different and awkward, and therefore it was possible that they could 'turn' straight young men to their wicked, deviant ways. This irrational fear underpinned both the law's and society's attitudes to gays. If they could turn our youths 'queer', the reasoning went, then conversion to Communism wasn't out of the question either. It is hard to believe just how frightened the authorities were of Communism in the fifties. In Burgess and Maclean – who were 'top drawer' defectors, homosexual and Communist sympathizers – three great bogeys of the day met. The appalled establishment thought that their chaps simply did not behave like that. It must have been because they were 'queer'; that was the obvious explanation.

Despite the various amendments to the original Act, it was never actually illegal to be gay: it was simply illegal to do anything about it. Thus gay men were theoretically condemned to a life of loveless, sexless isolation. Those who could face neither chastity nor marriage were forced to go 'underground' to seek lovers, companions and friends who, like themselves, understood the relatively few legal highs and the many dreadful lows of being gay in the mid-twentieth century.

The liveliest underground gay scene was, naturally, to be found in the tolerant, all-embracing Soho, where the unwanted, despised and marginalized from all over Europe had been welcomed for centuries. From the eighteenth century onwards, homosexual men and women had flocked to the West End, and along with them came cross-dressers, transsexuals and those who enjoyed all kinds of sexual pleasures above, below and far beyond the plain old procreative sort. As ever, Soho was way ahead of the times in its acceptance of homosexuality as simply a part of humanity's richly textured life. Quentin Crisp, for example, recalled fifties Soho with affection: 'In the Coach and Horses a man was asked to leave because he persistently made fun of me. When this happened I knew for sure that Soho had become a reservation for hooligans. We could at last walk majestically in our natural setting observed but no longer shot at by the safaris that still loved to penetrate this exotic land.'

Derek Hunt, an actor who came to London in August 1960, remembered that Sohoites in general, and theatricals in particular, had a much more relaxed view of homosexuality than their contemporaries. In an article in the *Soho Clarion*, he wrote: 'I headed straight for the Interval Club at 22 Dean Street. [It's owner] Molly Balvaird Hewitt, a strong character in her early eighties, never minded two actors sharing a room – "Why, dear, that's all right. They can't have babies."

'The chorus boys were always very gay in those days,' he told me in an interview. 'They were using Polari. I'd never heard of it before. I was in rep in Swansea once, and someone asked me, "Are you gay?" and I said, "Of course I'm happy." I didn't know it meant that, so he explained it to me. "The theatre is the only business in the world where gay and straight people mix and there's no problems." People were much more open-minded about that in the business than anywhere else. It was part of life.'

Derek also found acceptance on the streets. 'The prostitutes would say, "Would you like a nice time, dear?" and I'd say, "Oh no, I'm from the village." "Well bugger off, you little sod." [laughs] Something like that.'

One of the best known groups of gay and bisexual characters to gravitate to Soho were

234

significant members of an infamous, boozy, bohemian set who frequented the Colony Room, and were memorialized in Dan Farson's *Soho in the Fifties*. 'Muriel's place', as the Colony Room was also known, was a single, rather shabby, first-floor front room reached by climbing a dingy, narrow staircase from a nondescript entrance in Dean Street. Over the years, its reputation – and that of its owner – have reached mythic proportions, thanks to Farson and a group that included several artists, a poet or two, a film-maker, a photographer and several career boozers who appeared to do little else with their time.

Muriel herself was described as a handsome Jewish dyke, although she was, in fact, bisexual, with a long list of lovers to her name. Her best-remembered partner was a Jamaican woman. One story tells how the couple fell out and the lover returned to Jamaica, but missed Muriel and her London life so badly that she rang the club one night to tell her ex-lover that she was home-sick. With an ear-shattering bellow that stopped her customers' glasses *en route* to their lips – which was no mean feat – Muriel roared, 'But you ARE home, cunty.' Apparently, it was the final 'y' that was so telling: without it, you were one of the despised; with it, you were one of the chosen. As George Melly said, 'She was camp, and the very delivery of camp makes your sentences sound witty.'

Francis Bacon, the hugely talented, maso-chistic, visceral artist, was one of Muriel's very favourite 'daughters'. He joined the Colony's devoted clientele when he was still on his way up

235

and struggling. Muriel took to him straight away. To people she liked, she could be warm, funny, kind, loyal, incredibly generous and very thoughtful. However, the opposite was also true; if she didn't like you she could be monumentally rude and dismissive.

Muriel struck a deal with Bacon that she would pay him a modest retainer to bring customers to her club. She made it quite clear that the abstemious were not welcome, and neither were 'frugal fuckers' nor 'boring bastards'. Many of the people Bacon brought to the Colony were, if their reputations are anything to go by, neither tight nor boring. One exception was John Deakin, another, rather disgruntled, gay punter. He was notoriously mean in spirit, which was readily accepted, but was also tight with money, booze and cigarettes, which often led to unpleasantness and ostracism. Muriel Belcher couldn't stand those with long pockets and short arms, and would bellow, 'Get your bean bag out, Lottie!' at Deakin and his fellow skinflints when it was their turn to buy a round. Deakin was regularly barred from her club when he failed to comply, and simply transferred his allegiance to the Caves de France, a nearby French-run establishment that was enormously tolerant of diverse sexuality and bohemian impoverishment. Actors, painters, poets, writers, dancers, prostitutes of both sexes and all were welcome to open a tab at the Caves, where Secundo Carnera, John's father, was a barman in the evenings.

Bacon's artistic pals were a self-absorbed, hard-drinking lot who were so tight-knit that they excluded anyone who didn't amuse them, or whose faces simply did not fit. This attitude applied to more conventional gay men, who were dubbed 'suburban dentists'. Witnesses from the time say that both Bacon and Farson had a penchant for violent men. Temporary membership of the gang would be offered to anyone who would oblige with the occasional beating, but when they ceased to amuse, they were summarily ousted. Josh Avery, the subject of *Dog Days in Soho*, seems to have been one such temporary member, whose rejection, when it came, was complete.

One who was never a part of this 'in' crowd was my old friend Bill. He didn't enjoy either violence or what he saw as their particular brand of bitter and spiteful humour, so he avoided Bacon's crowd. Bill was a variety artist in his day and a gentle soul who, being a child of his times, had felt compelled by convention and the law to conform and that meant matrimony.

'When Marie left me it was a blessed relief all round,' Bill admitted ruefully over a cup of tea at his home in Neasden. 'And of course, it made everybody feel sorry for me. But the truth was, I was making her bloody miserable and the strain of keeping up appearances was driving me to drink. That's how I sometimes came to be in the same pubs, like the French, as that Farson bloke and that little shit, John Deakin. I'd drown my sorrows any chance I got, and I liked to get into Soho. I never went to the Colony though, not my kind of place at all. I did go to Gerry Campion's clubs, he was a sweet bloke and he turned a blinder to us lot as long as we kept it clean and discreet.'

I asked Bill why he married if he knew that he was gay. 'It was expected. My mum seemed to expect it and so did Marie and her mum. Then there was her brothers; big they were, all of 'em, I was scared of them.' We talked a bit about prevailing attitudes at the time, then Bill added, 'There was the law, don't forget. My mum would have had my guts for garters if I'd been up in front of the beak.'

Others, like Colin, simply resigned themselves to a lonely bachelorhood, which in his case was in Hampstead. 'I lived with Father for many, many years. This is the house I was born in,' Colin told me. 'I was too afraid to seek out men like myself until I was getting on into middle age. Even after the law changed, I was still too terrified of blackmail and of losing my job at the bank.'

When Colin's father passed away, Robert, a colleague from the bank, showed him the way. The West End was where they went to meet friends and to socialize. 'There was the Crown and Two Chairmen in Dean Street, that was a pub we liked,' Colin recalled. 'Afterwards there was an all-night coffee stand, just off Wardour Street, down an alley, we'd go there after last orders, late at night. There were clubs, but they were always moving around, you had to have radar to find them.'

We talked for a bit about how persecuted gay men were in the fifties and then got on to the happier subject of food. 'Gennaro's was one place we went, for special occasions – and Wheelers. We once saw that artist chappie there, Francis Bacon, with some cronies. Not our sort

238

at all. I was never "with it" enough for the clubs or that arty crowd. I felt out of place.' Colin talked of the need to protect his job and of how disastrous being 'found out' as gay would have been both to his prospects of advancement, and his being employed at all. 'Of course, the bank never knew. We both knew that we would have been out on our ears if they had.'

The all-night coffee stand that Colin referred to was also remembered by Leo Zanelli. 'Just off Dean Street, there is a little street there, Bourchier Street, through to Wardour Street. There used to be an all-night café, there, with a van. If you stayed there an hour you'd bump into twenty or thirty prostitutes, loads of young fellers, several gay fellers, everybody.' Leo's experiences gave the lie to the official view that gay men were predatory, out to make 'converts'. 'I was aware of queer people, as we called them then, hanging around the all-night café in Bourchier Street, but I was never bothered by them. I can remember my mate Billy, chaps coming up to him and saying, "Excuse me, my friend over there likes you." He'd say something like, "Sorry, his tits aren't big enough," and they'd walk away.'

Colin didn't mention the gents' urinal a little further up Bourchier Street, where it becomes too narrow to drive through, at the Wardour Street end. Leo Zanelli remembered that it was 'one of these big green cast iron places, and it was difficult to use because of course the gays were cottaging there all the time'. When it finally disappeared, a policeman told Leo that 'it had been purchased by a Texan who'd taken it to

America because he wanted it to remind him of the Good Old Days. Whether he meant the cottaging or just general life in Soho I don't know.'

The Sexual Offences Bill of 1967 allowed consenting males over the age of twenty-one to do as they pleased in privacy, but being outed as a gay man or a lesbian could still mean instant dismissal from a job or career. And of course, younger people were unable to follow their inclinations, even though their heterosexual peers were free to indulge as long as they had reached sixteen, the age of consent. The logic behind this discrimination was the illogical fear that older 'queers' would lead young boys astray whereas, according to the law, it was perfectly all right for their heterosexual brothers to seduce schoolgirls of sixteen.

Soho has long offered asylum to those who found the outside world a hostile place. Way back in the eighteenth century, the Frenchman Chevalier d'Eon lived happily as Mademoiselle de Beaumont in Brewer Street. Mademoiselle sought sanctuary in Soho when moves were afoot to certify her as a lunatic in France. Far from ostracizing the cross-dressing Frenchman, Soho-ites took her to their hearts, and couldn't have cared less that she was 'a confirmed bachelor' who chose to live as a woman for most of the time.

Occasionally, she reverted to her male form, and there was some confusion among the population as to her actual sex. Soho being Soho, bets were taken. Casanova declared categorically that d'Eon was a woman, on account of her shapeliness and

240

her disinclination to take female lovers. It was only when d'Eon died that the matter was cleared up once and for all. Mademoiselle had been born a man.

In the fifties, cross-dressers were known as transvestites. My Great-Uncle Norman was one. I never met him, as he died when I was a baby, but I understand from my mother that he was a lovely, gentle man and half of a devoted, heterosexual, but childless couple. Norman had his clothes and his wife, Dorothy, had hers. He had many garments made by a specialist dressmaker who worked in rooms above a shop in Berwick Street. His outsized ladies' shoes came from a shop in Walker's Court that supplied footwear to showgirls and larger sizes for pantomime dames, drag queens and other cross-dressers who, like Norman, had no connection with show business at all. He repaired radios.

Sometimes Dorothy and my mother would enjoy a day out in Soho shopping with Norman. Mother told me that the shopkeepers and the dressmaker showed no surprise at fitting a man into ladies' wear. 'The dressmaker was a real charmer called Nat and he seemed to be genuinely fond of Norman. He had been dressing him for years.' Mother thought that Nat might have been a fellow cross-dresser. 'Norman bought his wigs in Gerrard Street. I know that he used to go to dances somewhere in the West End, where there were other men dressed as women.'

I remember walking along Old Compton Street fairly early one Monday morning when I was a child. Ahead of me was a young lad in school

241

uniform, a satchel over his shoulder. There were two cross-dressers walking towards us, the seven o'clock shadows under their make-up being the only giveaway that they were men heading home after a night on the town. I noticed the schoolboy do a double-take as it dawned on him that the two ladies were, in fact, men. His shoulders began to shake with a fit of the giggles and without a word passing between them, the glamorous pair parted as they drew abreast of the boy, lifted him gently off the ground, turned him upside down, walked on a few feet, then just as gently turned him the right way up and put him down again. Then they winked at me and carried on as if nothing had happened.

Great-Uncle Norman was not the only cross-dresser that Mother knew. There was Violet as well, who had been at teachers' training college with Mother, and who lived in Baker Street and worked in the West End. I remember Mother taking me to meet her college chum for tea at the Lyons Corner House at Marble Arch.

The person who walked towards us had a very short, severe haircut. She wore a tweed three-piece trouser suit in an age when women did not wear trouser suits, as well as a shirt, a tie and, of all things, a monocle. I wasn't sure why this slender man was called 'Violet' and assumed that he was like 'Rosie', the street person who hung around Berwick Street market and wore roses tucked behind his ears. But when Violet spoke, her voice was definitely female.

It seems that, while male cross-dressers were often straight, like my Great-Uncle Norman, most women who cross-dressed in the fifties were lesbians. Many lived with their female partners as 'man and wife'. One such pair were Rene and Suzie. Rene, or Irene as she was christened, was the butch partner and Suzie the 'femme'. Rene wore man drag right down to Y-fronts, vests, Brylcreem and liberal quantities of aftershave. Suzie was never to be seen in anything but full make-up, dresses, skirts, blouses and high-heeled shoes. Suzie wouldn't have dreamt of wearing slacks, as we called them in those days, even in the privacy of her own home. The couple lived in Brewer Street, and would sometimes volunteer to take me to the park or the zoo. Suzie had been a prostitute when she and Rene had met, and gave up the game when it was obvious that their relationship was a keeper.

I remember the couple with great affection and was sure that they were happy together. It is only with adult hindsight that I realize part of the charm of looking after me was that they could pretend, for the odd afternoon at least, that they were a complete family, something I am guessing they must have longed for.

A Polari speaker would have called the operation that changed ordinary seaman and Liverpudlian, George Jamieson, into the stunningly glamorous April Ashley 'a remould'. Hers was a familiar face in the West End, even before she became one of the first transsexuals to undergo a sex realignment operation. I remember April being pointed out to my father by his friend, Campanini, although I didn't know what they were talking about at the time. All I could see was

243

a lovely-looking, smartly dressed woman sitting in the window seat of a restaurant as we passed by. As April Ashley says about herself, 'I was exquisite, darling – slim shoulders, wonderful legs, incredible skin and a 23 inch waist.'

Unwittingly, April Ashley drew the attention of the law-makers to transsexuals. Before she married the Honourable Arthur Corbett, neither the law nor the *Sunday People* newspaper had really noticed the anguished men and women who felt that they'd been born in the wrong skin. The law didn't notice, either, when April met Arthur at Le Caprice restaurant in 1960, and the couple courted and wed.

Sadly, the *Sunday People* did notice this. In 1961, an article outing April as a transsexual and, worse, a transsexual married to an aristocrat appeared. 'Lower drawer' residents were not supposed to hop into 'upper drawer' territory, as Peter Wildeblood had noted in *Against the Law*. That may well have been at least part of the essence of April and Arthur's 'transgression', because in 1963 pressure was applied to Corbett by his family to dump his wife or risk losing his inheritance. As the latter included the title of Lord, £4 million and an estate in Scotland, Arthur sought to have his marriage annulled, claiming that he had not known that April had been born a man. The court found for the not-so-honourable Arthur and the marriage was duly annulled. The shattered and traduced groom, who also enjoyed cross-dressing, was able to keep his money, his title, most of their joint possessions and several of April's beautiful frocks.

'My case unmarried all the thousands of trans-sexuals living in Britain,' April told an interviewer. Whether, at that stage, there were that many transsexuals who had had the surgery is open to debate, but there were certainly a good few living as man and wife. What London's West End had taken easily in its stride was not true of the rest of the country, and April was driven into exile. 'The government condemned me as a freak,' she said as she packed up and left for America.

A transsexual who did not feel the need to emigrate was Angel, a regular at the Nucleus. Hers was a familiar face in and around Soho for many years and as Gary said in his interview, 'Angel was about the first transvestite who'd had the operation.' I asked if Angel was good looking, as April Ashley was, and still is. 'Yeah, I suppose so,' he said. 'Dark hair. Course, we had quite a few gays at the Nucleus. We had a gay waiter who was very funny. He lived in St Giles High Street.'

I expressed my surprise that both the waiter and Angel were out in those tricky times. 'They didn't mind us knowing,' Gary explained. 'We were easygoing. We were an odd society of people, and when you say we were bohemians, in a way we were, and we were very broad-minded, so... Angel came down to my coffee bar a lot. She wasn't a poet or a musician or anything – her fame was her transsexuality.'

Several factors have led Sohoites in particular, and West Enders in general, to take a 'live and let live' attitude towards unconventional sexual tastes and orientations. For one thing, the area has a long association with theatrical, artistic and

245

bohemian types, known for their tolerance, and celebration, of difference. Most importantly, Soho's population includes the descendants of refugees from all over Europe, who, having known persecution themselves, show a marked disinclination to persecute anyone in their turn. And, of course, Britain was the only country in Europe to make a crime of homosexuality. The waves of French, Italian, German, Swiss and Greek immigrants had no history of legalized homophobia and therefore neither did their descendants.

It was 1967 before the law was finally changed in Britain, and consenting adult males were, at last, no longer committing a crime when they enjoyed sex with each other. This reform, based largely on the conclusions of the Wolfenden report into homosexuality that had been commissioned a decade earlier in the wake of the Montagu/Wildeblood case, was seen as a keynote piece of legislation in defining the liberalism and 'permissiveness' of the sixties. All it did in reality was codify a 'live and let live' philosophy current in the West End for decades – even centuries – if we remember Frenchman Chevalier d'Eon, aka Mademoiselle de Beaumont and her friends.

11

The Entertainers

In the forties, fifties and even into the sixties, almost anyone could bump into their favourite stars of stage, screen, radio, music hall and sporting arena in the West End. Star-spotters simply had to stroll around the streets, sip a pint in a pub or have a coffee in one of its many coffee bars. What's more, having spotted someone famous, you would not be blinded by flashbulbs or shouldered aside by a phalanx of men built like gorillas, but without the apes' charm or hair. In fact, you'd almost always be greeted with a smile and graciously given an autograph while the exalted one would chat amicably to you about this and that.

My father was friendly with the Goons, for example. I remember Michael Bentine vividly: he had mad hair and one of the most expressive faces I'd ever seen. He was fond of children, I believe, because he'd amuse me with his funny voices and walks while he waited for Father to finish one of his lengthy telephone calls. Spike Milligan obviously really liked children, but his moods were more unpredictable than Michael Bentine's. When he was 'up', though, his store of voices and ditties were magical. My brother and I would laugh until we cried.

My main memory of Harry Secombe is of his accent, so similar to that of one of the ladies around the corner at the Welsh Dairy. I also sensed that he was a gentle, even-tempered man who was unfailingly pleasant to children. He had a comforting presence that the other Goons – and my father – did not possess. Something about the fourth Goon, Peter Sellers, unnerved me. I think it was that he seemed utterly indifferent to children. To be honest, I don't think that he ever even noticed us.

It's extraordinary to remember how accessible stars were to their public, by today's standards. By the simple expedient of diving into a phone box, pennies at the ready, you could call the reception of any one of the West End's luxury hotels and find out if the likes of Tyrone Power, David Niven, Ingrid Bergman or Laurel and Hardy were in residence.

Owen Gardner, who lived in St Martin's Lane, was an inveterate autograph hunter. 'We used to find out where they were staying,' he remembers, 'and then you would ring them up. You see, in those days, there weren't the dozens of hotels there are now; they stayed at the Savoy, the Dorchester – maybe the Ritz, but not very often – and you could ring 'em up.

'You'd see their pictures in the evening paper, and you knew they'd be there, there or there, and you'd just ring them all up and say, "Can I speak to Mr So-and-so, please," and they'd put you through, and you could speak to them.

'They never had minders in those days. If they were going out for the theatre, you could go down to them and you could say, "Hello, how are you? Good evening" and you'd give them a piece of paper for the autograph. They were the nicest people. I saw Elizabeth Taylor every night for six weeks while she was in England making *Ivanhoe*, because she stayed at the Savoy, and she'd come in of a night-time and say, "Hello, Owen," because I was a fan of hers at the time.

'There was a Lyons Corner House opposite the Paris Cinema in Lower Regent Street, where the BBC used to record a lot of shows. Well, we were always in there, because the show business journalists were in there, as well. They'd come in and say, "Did you know so-and-so was in town?" "Oh, thanks. Do you know where they're staying?" "Not absolutely sure, but try so-and-so." You'd get tips like that.

'People I tell now won't believe how approachable the big stars were. You'd ring and say, "Are you going out tonight?" and they'd say "Yes, we're going out at about seven o'clock to the theatre." "Do you mind if we ask you for your autograph?" "No, no, of course not." You'd be there, and they'd come down and they'd come over. It was so good-humoured as well. Judy Garland, Tallulah Bankhead, Douglas Fairbanks Junior, Bob Hope, they would all come and chat to you.'

Owen is right, it does seem unreal now, but in those days the famous weren't afraid of crazed stalkers. Words like 'paparazzi' and 'stalker' hadn't even entered our vocabulary, and 'mobile' simply meant you were still on your pins or knew a bloke with a motor. The notion that, one day, anyone would be able to take candid pictures, and with a telephone of all things, was the stuff of pure fantasy.

This is not to say that it was no big deal to meet a star. Mike O'Rouke, who lived in the Seven Dials, but went to school in West London, has a vivid memory of a meeting that would have red-blooded males of all ages beside themselves with envy. 'I collected autographs when I was a boy, and one of them made me the most famous boy in the school. When I was thirteen, Brigitte Bardot came over to a première down in Charing Cross Road, the Cameo, and I went over there because, well, I was 13 and in love with Brigitte Bardot. I got her autograph and actually met her. She was sitting at a desk in a little cubicle in the cinema and the queue was all the way up the Charing Cross Road, and I queued up with the rest of them. When I took it into school the next day, and showed it to them, and said I'd actually met her, and shook hands with her, and she'd said "Hello" to me...'

Sometimes the autograph hunters had to try a little harder. Owen recalls that, 'Around the Royal Variety Performance, they used to bring in stars specially from America at the last minute, so that nobody would know they were there, and introduce them, but they would have to do some rehearsals, and they would rehearse in all kinds of theatres. Although the show was taking place at, say, the Palladium, they'd be rehearsing at the Whitehall Theatre or even the Dominion Cinema in Tottenham Court Road, or the Odeon Marble Arch, and we would shin up a drainpipe and go in through the toilet window.

'We used to chase them in taxis! We'd stand at the Savoy, and if they were in a hurry, or just didn't want to stop and sign at that particular time, three or four of us would jump into a cab at a rank in the Strand, right opposite, and say, "Follow that car!" Sometimes there would be two or three cabs chasing them.

'We would follow them to the theatre, you know, wherever they were going. I remember we chased William Holden and his wife to the St James's Theatre, but we couldn't get him before he went in, so we went off and had a cup of tea and came back, and as everybody was piling out through the exits at the end of the show, we pushed our way in and got their autograph in the front row of the stalls of the theatre.'

Almost everyone I talked to had stories of encounters with the famous in everyday situations. Some of these occurred because the children lived or played around theatres. Olga Jackson remembers that 'We used to play outside what used to be the Winter Gardens Theatre in Drury Lane, and there was a show on there called *It's Time to Dance*, I think, with Fred Emney – big chap. It was a very hot summer, and he'd come out by the stage door, because it was so hot in the theatre – you know, during the breaks. He was a lovely man, used to talk to us children very ordinary. You took it for granted. You never thought about them being stars.'

When he was a teenager, Ronnie Mann would hang around outside the Palladium and the Coliseum, on a Sunday, because that was where the girls were: 'I remember Dickie Valentine walking out and chatting to everybody and having a cigarette or something outside.'

Dickie Valentine was also a friend of my father, as were Petula Clark, Alma Cogan, Lita Roza and her sister, Alma Warren. Where Father, the most unmusical of men, with two tin ears, got to know so many singers and musicians I can only guess, and that guess would be the canteen at Broadcasting House, just across Oxford Street from Soho, and a real showbiz melting pot if ever there was one. Other probable meeting places were the late night drinking clubs that performers went to in order to come down after a show, or on the set of an international variety show called *Chelsea at Nine* (later known as *Chelsea at Eight*, for the obvious reason that its time slot changed), which he sometimes wrote for. It ran on ITV between 1957 and 1960.

Dickie Valentine was a good-looking man with, as Ronnie suggests, a charmingly easy manner, but the singer who made the deepest impression on me as a child was Lita Roza. I thought she was *so* glamorous that I was in awe of her. Also, she sang 'How Much Is That Doggy in the Window?' and being a scrap who was deeply enamoured of anything hairy with four legs, I was mightily impressed with this. One of the things that made the deepest impression on me was that she gave me some of the chocolates left for her by stage door Johnnies, a generosity I appreciated greatly – chocolates were such a wild luxury. I didn't realize then that one of the reasons she gave them away was that she was diabetic and couldn't eat them.

Another thing that stuck with me was a hairstyle

that I'm sure Lita pioneered. Years later, there was a huge fuss when Mia Farrow had her hair cut just like it by Frank Sinatra's barber, but I remember Lita doing it first. I was so impressed by her stylish cap of short, highlighted hair that when I grew old enough to decide for myself what sort of hairstyle to have, I chose to copy Lita's. In the fifties and into the early sixties, women tended to have long hair arranged in a variety of ways, or perms, but a very short, straight, boyish and layered cap was unheard of for women or, indeed, girls. Back then, when women had few choices and men virtually none, Lita's innovative hairstyle really was startling and wonderful.

Billie Holiday appeared on *Chelsea at Eight* in 1959, but I am convinced that the first time I saw her was on the stairs to our flat in Old Compton Street, some time before that. Annie Ross, the jazz singer, and her partner at the time, the drummer Tony Crombie, lived in the flat below ours, and I distinctly remember almost knocking down a slender, black woman who was staggering up the stairs as I was running down ahead of my father. I apologized, and she told me, 'That's OK, honey,' in a funny little voice laced with an American accent.

The incident impressed itself on my memory because she appeared to be almost falling-down drunk as she lurched from side to side, but there was no smell of booze coming off her. The stairway was very narrow and, had she been as drunk as she appeared, I definitely would have got a face full of fumes. I knew all about drunkards, as both of my parents were alcoholics at the time, and so were many of their friends. I simply couldn't understand why the lady was so unsteady on her feet if she hadn't been hitting the booze. She called me 'honey', too, a term of endearment I had never heard before, and she told my father that I was pretty, before carrying on her long stagger upwards. Of course, I didn't realize who she was and could kick myself now; a Billie Holiday autograph would be a real prize to be treasured.

Sometimes you bumped into a star on the street. 'When I was a small baby in my pram,' Mike O'Rouke recalls, 'my mum was pushing me around up Long Acre. She's turning the corner and more or less crashed into this bloke who's turning the corner the other way. It was Tyrone Power. This was in his heyday, and he was one of her idols. She was gob-smacked, never said a word and always regretted it.'

Casual encounters could lead to friendship. Sonia Boulter remembers Tommy Cooper. 'I had a step-uncle who used to sell newspapers – a street vendor – and he knew Tommy Cooper because when he played the Prince of Wales Theatre, he bought a paper from him. One day he introduced us and Tommy said, "Where do you work?" and I told him, "Boots in Piccadilly Circus." He said, "I'll come in and see you one day," and he did, a few times. There was a coffee bar in Piccadilly Underground station, and he would take me in there and we would sit and chat and have coffee.'

In their schooldays, Pat and Barbara Jones both did part-time jobs at a tobacconist in Denman

Street, just down the road from the Piccadilly Theatre. 'One day,' Pat remembers, 'Fenella Fielding came into buy cigarettes. Players, Capstans, Senior Service, all those were under the counter in those days – 1s. 9d. for ten, 3s. 6d. for twenty – so you helped people out. I said to her, "What a lovely perfume, don't you smell nice," and a couple of days later she came in and plonked a bottle on the counter. I think it was called Tabu. After that, she always used to come in and chat.'

Pat's jobs led to several encounters with film and theatre stars. 'Bertoni's was a hairdresser who served all the stars, in Denman Street,' she remembers. 'I started working in there on a Saturday, and the first person I met was Audrey Hepburn, who came to London. She didn't have her fringe then. Mr Bertoni did her fringe.'

It wasn't just home-grown talent that flocked to the West End. As Owen Gardner pointed out, visiting Hollywood stars only had a few first-class hotels to choose from, all in the West End. Film stars came to talk business in Soho, to play the theatres, to eat at the restaurants and to be amused in the various nightclubs, just like their British counterparts, but they also came for the shopping. Those with a taste for fine tailoring went to Savile Row to stock up on bespoke suits, shirts and hats.

Ava Gardner, Ingrid Bergman, Elizabeth Taylor and their many friends, colleagues and rivals only had to step daintily into Mayfair to buy stunning creations and the shoes and handbags to go with them. Or they could pick up a few sparklers from

Garrard, Asprey or Cartier. Of course, any film star worth her salt would send the equivalent of a stage door Johnny to collect her purchases, while she stood around looking gorgeous and signing autographs for adoring, but respectful, fans.

Celebrities came to the West End in the fifties and sixties for a whole host of reasons. Film actors came because those years were a boom time for the British film industry (it tailed off in the seventies) and the offices of all the major film companies were located in Soho, mainly in Wardour Street and Soho Square. Established stars, along with those that were rising, or hoping to rise, would make their way to those busy offices and the surrounding restaurants and bars, to discuss projects, to schmooze and be schmoozed.

'Many business deals are talked over round the little marble tables,' Penelope Seaman wrote about Maison Bertaux, in her book *Little Inns of Soho* (1948), and indeed show business deals were talked over most of the tables in the area, and from bar stools as well. Agreements were hatched that concerned all aspects of showbiz, from 'the talent' to the frocks, scenery, shoes, locations, catering, wigs, hats, makeup, suits, music, stunts, special effects and technical bods. Anyone you could possibly need for a film, a play, a variety show or even for the newfangled telly, could be found in the West End somewhere.

As there have always been far too many actors for the number of parts available, it behove agents to locate their offices in the same areas as the film companies, the better to pick up news of upcoming opportunities as quickly as possible. The plethora of fine restaurants, pubs, clubs and bars round and about played host to producers, directors and money men, and were hotbeds of rumour, hint, whisper and gossip about new films. Naturally, diligent agents would frequent the very same places, ears tuned to scoop any news that would benefit their clients and their respective bank balances.

As a result, some show people chose to make their home in Soho, as Jeff Sloneem, who grew up in Old Compton Street in the years after the war, remembers. 'My father was a variety artist. I think he fancied himself as a song and dance man, but he couldn't really sing or dance, so he ended up as a whistling ventriloquist. He did a bit of singing, and he literally travelled the country. We only saw him about three months of the year.

'He was in a show called *Soldiers in Skirts*, which, after the war, went for about eleven years. It was continuous employment; he was about the only one in show business who could say that. He was known as Fred Sloan, sometimes with an E, sometimes without, depending on who was doing the poster. He was billed sometimes as the King of the Jungle, or the Whistling Songbird. After the show, he had reasonable work I think, for a couple of years, and then it just ... petered out. Rock 'n' roll killed variety! He went and worked in insurance, but he still kept his hand in, and he was always off on the odd gig that he did.'

Generally, the stars did not live in Soho – there simply weren't enough mansions and posh flats to go round. The ones who lived in Soho were usually the minor players or those who worked behind the scenes, or in the chorus. Various small hotels and hostels catered exclusively for theatricals. 'Jobbing actor' Derek Hunt remembers one of these. 'The Interval Club at 22 Dean Street was an old Georgian building right next to the Soho Theatre. It was cheap and convenient, three guineas full board. It was set up in 1926 in Soho Square for Catholic theatricals, although I was a Protestant and nobody seemed to mind. There was a hardware shop below, a small theatre on the first floor, a long dining room with a billiard table, snack bar and TV room on the second floor. Most of the residents were on the third floor, which had the sole bathroom.'

The club was run by Molly Balvaird Hewitt, a formidable elderly lady who was the daughter of the founder. There was also a residential house for theatrical ladies in the original premises in Soho Square. In an article in the *Soho Clarion*, Derek recalled that 'Auditions were held in the theatre by repertory companies, Joan Littlewood, the Royal Shakespeare Company, etc. Tuesdays were set aside for the Tuesday girls, a mixture of actresses and chorus girls of a certain age, playing bridge, gossiping and all mad keen on tennis and Wimbledon.'

The residents also had lives typical of jobbing actors. 'We were always skint,' Derek remembers, 'but managed to make ends meet by doing odd jobs or working backstage on musicals like *Flower Drum Song* and *Sound of Music.*' The Interval Club moved to 63 Frith Street in 1962, when the

Dean Street buildings – once a coaching inn run by Thomas Gainsborough's brother – were demolished, and it closed for good in 1965.

Once an actor had got a part, the chances were that he or she would be back in the West End to be fitted for costumes, shoes and wigs. Monty Berman was the best-known film costumier of his day. Berman's father founded the business, and was initially famous for dressing stage productions, a tradition that his son was also happy to carry on, although film was his main interest. Berman's was based at 18 Irving Street, just off Leicester Square, and was a Mecca for actors. Berman took his work very seriously, and by making everyone from the star to a lowly extra feel important, he helped actors get into character and to feel more confident in their work. Sir Richard Attenborough is quoted as saying that Monty Berman 'loved our business and was an integral part of it'. In fact, Berman occasionally provided the costumes for little or nothing in order to get a production off the ground.

Pat Jones went to work at Berman's, as a theatrical milliner, when she was just fifteen. She did the ladies' hats for *Kind Hearts and Coronets* and *The Importance of Being Earnest*, among others. 'We were right on the top floor,' she remembers, 'the milliners, alongside the tailors. The showrooms, of course, were on the ground floor. Monty Berman's father took a shine to me, and got into the habit, when anyone he thought I'd be interested in was in the showroom, of ringing up and asking me to bring something down, so he could introduce me. I never knew who would be there until I got there. So I met all the stars, which was lovely, until one day I saw *Great Expectations*, where Finlay Currie [as Magwitch] comes out of the graveyard, and that petrified me. Soon after, Mr Berman invited me down. There was this great big posh chair, in leather, like a throne. So I came in, and this person in the chair turned round when I was almost on top of him, and it was Finlay Currie. I just went "Aaargh" – really screamed. Monty came running out. When I explained, Finlay Currie said, "My dear, please don't apologize. It's a very great compliment."'

While Berman specialized in movies, another firm of costumiers, B.J. Simmons in Covent Garden, supplied the local theatres. Simmons, founded in 1857, dressed well over a thousand stage productions before they closed in 1964. They were bought out in 1941 by a local costumier and perruquier, Charles H. Fox of King Street, whose business was supplying wigs and costumes for fancy dress and theatricals.

After leaving Berman's, Pat Jones went to work for Simmons. 'I met some stars there. Robert Newton rolled up; he could hardly get up the stairs. I stayed there until I had trouble with my eyes, and they advised me not to do any close work.'

As it is today, the West End was the heart and soul of London's theatreland, with Shaftesbury Avenue, Drury Lane and the Haymarket the equivalent of New York's Broadway. Stage actors came there for the same business reasons as their film colleagues – agents, networking, costumes and so on – as well as to be dressed and shod, for work and for play. Jeff Sloneem remembers that, 'My uncle had a tailor's shop in Old Compton Street until 1954, 1955. Robert Morley was one of his customers. I remember him, because he wanted me to be in a film, when I was five or so. About that time there was an Italian film, *Bicycle Thieves*, and apparently I looked exactly like the kid in that, and Robert Morley wanted me to be in a film with him, but my mother didn't want another member of the family in show business.'

Gamba and Anello & Davide were the two main theatrical shoemakers. Gamba, founded by an Italian waiter in 1894, was just down the road from where I lived, on the corner of Old Compton Street and Greek Street. I loved to press my nose to Gamba's window and dream of being a prima ballerina like my heroine, Margot Fonteyn. Seeing that I danced with all the grace of a two-legged pony, my dreams came to nothing. Gamba was particularly renowned for making pointe shoes for ballet dancers, and in their window was a display of satiny pointe shoes in various colours, although a fleshy pink appeared to predominate. I seem to remember other items of ballet costume, too, including tights, swansdown bits and bobs for the cygnets in *Swan Lake,* and fake diamond tiaras, but it is more than possible that two entirely different shops have coalesced in my memory over the intervening years. Those who danced for the Sadler's Wells company, based at the Royal Opera House in Covent Garden, wouldn't dream of getting their shoes from anywhere else. Pavlova and Nijinsky were customers in their day. Later, Robert Helpmann and Dame Margot Fonteyn made the trip across Charing Cross Road from Covent Garden to Soho, to be measured up. Later still, so did Rudolph Nureyev.

I remember Anello & Davide's shop at the Tottenham Court Road end of Oxford Street, not too far from the tube. I dreamed impossible dreams when I passed Gamba, while Anello & Davide's shop brings jewel-like colours to mind. They made street shoes as well as tap-dancing and theatrical ones.

In the fifties, most women's shoes came in one of three basic colours, black, brown or navy blue. Just occasionally, oxblood and olive green made an appearance, but they were rare finds, unless you went to Anello & Davide, where a world of colour suddenly opened up before you. I distinctly remember tap-type shoes, only without the taps, for street wear, in at least three shades of green – lime, bottle and olive. Reds came in pillar-box, flame, maroon and scarlet, and then drifted off into orange. To our colour-starved eyes, Anello & Davide was a truly wondrous Aladdin's cave. The shop's famous customers included David Niven, who liked suede shoes, and Marilyn Monroe, who had them make some of her stiletto-heeled numbers. Later, in the sixties, they made 'kinky' boots, and distinguished themselves by supplying the Beatles' ankle boots.

Fred Astaire, famed among his peers for 'having class', was often clad from balding head to twinkling toes by West End craftsmen and women. George Cleverley made Astaire's street shoes, and Gamba his taps, while Lock's fashioned his hats and Savile Row tailored his shirts and suits: in fact, there were days when only his accent was American.

When plays settled in for a long run, their stars became part of the local scene. Mike O'Rouke remembers meeting actors from the Cambridge Theatre in his local pub, the Mercer's Arms. People like Albert Finney and Tom Courtenay used to go in there for a pint. My dad told a story about Tom Courtenay. He was in *Billy Liar* over at the Cambridge, and there was a scene where he had to go upstairs and make out he had a gammy leg. My dad was in the pub one night and he pulled him over and said, "You don't go up the stairs like that," and Tom said, "How do you know?" like, and Dad knocked on his artificial leg. I think me dad gave him a couple of tips, helped him with his performance.'

The theatres provided a handy source of extra income for many who lived and worked in the West End. The firemen from the Shaftesbury Avenue station – well versed in the mysteries of ropes and ladders – would help out in the flies, and were joined by many who lived locally. 'A lot of people in the Bedfordbury used to do a second job in the theatres,' Ronnie Mann explains, 'particularly in the Coliseum, which backed on to us. You had the showmen and the daymen. The showmen were full-time theatre workers – used to do the curtains and so on – and the daymen used to shift the scenery. I worked on the flies for two years: that was dropping the curtain, going in after I finished work in Covent Garden flower market around lunchtime. I used to do matinées.

263

Sometimes you'd go to other theatres and move the store. There wasn't much you had to do, but somebody had to do it, or nothing worked!'

Some of the supporting crafts in the area were highly specialized. The scenery and backdrops moved by Ronnie Mann were almost certainly painted at Elms Lesters in Flitcroft Street, just off Tin Pan Alley. In this long, tall, thin workshop, painters, many of them just out of art school, clambered over scaffolding to work on backdrops that hung from huge rollers running along the spine of the building, just under the roof ridge.

Another very good reason for actors to haunt the West End was to play, in nightclubs or private drinking or gambling dens. Ronnie Brace remembers nights out at Winston's, his uncle's club, when he was a teenager in the fifties. 'They all came to that club. Anita Ekberg, my father said she was the most beautiful woman he'd ever seen. Elizabeth Taylor, my father always said he'd asked her for a dance, and she was the only one – because he was a very good-looking man, my father, very good-looking – who ever refused him.'

While hard-drinking artists and bohemians tended to favour Muriel Belcher's Colony Room, show business types were more likely to congregate at one of a succession of private members' clubs owned and run by the actor Gerald Campion. Campion was a local, born in Bloomsbury in 1921 to a show business family: his father was a screenwriter and his godfather, Gerald du Maurier, was a famous actor, manager and producer.

As a jobbing actor, Campion knew that actors need a place to go late in the evening in order to come down after a show or a day in front of the cameras, as well as a place to hang out in the day to make contacts and friendships. His first club, the Buckstone, opened in 1950, and was handily situated right opposite the stage door of the Theatre Royal, Haymarket. It soon became a favourite haunt of the theatrical, television, radio and film crowds. Resting actors worked behind the bar. Ronnie Corbett first met Ronnie Barker there, when he was serving and his future comedy partner was supping.

A few years after the Buckstone opened, Campion became one of the first 'superstars' of television after landing the lead in the series *Billy Bunter of Greyfriars School*. When the series began in 1952, the BBC was the sole television channel, and everyone with access to a television watched it. Campion played the portly schoolboy until 1961, when he was forty.

In 1956 he opened the Key Club, near the London Palladium, so-called because every member had a key to its door. Acting in *Bunter* and running the Key Club must have been exhausting, and rumour had it that amphetamines helped him keep pace with it all. The irony of TV's most prominent fictional glutton subsisting on diet pills was not lost on Campion.

Gerry's in Shaftesbury Avenue was the last of his clubs. Its members included Michael Caine, Keith Waterhouse and Tony Hancock. Everyone seems to have loved Campion for his generous nature. Show business types down on their luck could always count on him to provide food and drink on tick for as long as it was necessary.

Owen Gardner's job in Page's catering supply shop next to Gerry's remembers it well. 'You went downstairs in the basement there. It was there for donkey's years, a drinking club where theatrical people could go and know that they could have a drink with their own type, their own kind, and not get bothered.'

Gambling also brought stars and supporting players to Soho. Harry Fowler, a stalwart of British cinema and television who rarely starred, but turned up in virtually everything that featured a cheeky London chappie or a bit of a spiv, could usually be tracked down to a smoky spieler (illegal gambling club) or snooker hall, or to the kitchen of our flat, where he'd play cards with Father and his cronies.

Dennis Shaw, the ubiquitous heavy in any production requiring a really scary villain, was another Soho *habitué*. I remember him vividly, because he always frightened me into hiding behind my father's legs when we met in the street, although he was never, ever unkind to me – in fact, quite the opposite. I realize now that his ability to terrify small children just by standing there must have upset him, despite the fact that his looks were what earned him his living. He was a large man with dark hair swept straight back from a low, low forehead and a heavy, warty, moley, jowly face that could frighten the dead into life. Dennis was also a gambling man, who, like Father, enjoyed a punt on the gee-gees. He could often be found propping up the counter in the betting shop, once they were finally made legal, his ugly mug buried deep in the racing pages.

Soho also attracted the stars of the sporting world. Freddie Mills's distinctive, much-broken nose marked him out as a pugilist immediately. He was the light-heavyweight world boxing champ between 1948 and 1950, and this made him a darling of the media and a sporting hero to millions. He stayed in the public eye long after his boxing career was over, thanks to the newspapers, Pathé News, and small parts in several films, including two of the *Carry On* series. He was a jewel thief in *Carry On Constable* (1960), and Lefty in *Carry On Regardless* (1961). Just about everyone knew Freddie's face, whether they liked boxing or not. His ownership of Freddie Mills Chinese Restaurant, at 143 Charing Cross Road, made him a West End 'face'. Later, he turned the restaurant into a nightclub, called, with great originality, Freddie Mills Nite Spot.

Father knew him fairly well from the snooker hall and various spielers, nightclubs and drinking clubs in the area. Freddie seemed to like children. He had two daughters of his own, Susan and Amanda, and he always slipped me half a crown whenever he saw me. Freddie's life ended tragically early in Goslett Yard at the rear of his club. He was found dead in the back of his Citroën, shot in the head with a rifle. His death was ruled a suicide, although there was no note and his business partner and his family testified he had seemed fine just hours before. Nobody ever discovered any reason why he should take his own life, although there were a great many rumours at the time and more have surfaced since. His good friends, the Kray twins, always maintained that he was murdered by members of a Chinese tong who were intent on taking over his nightclub.

Another well-known sportsman and Soho *habitué* was Bert Assirati, who was very famous in his day as a British and European wrestling champion. Although he fought as a heavyweight, he was short and stocky, a professional strongman, who worked from time to time as a bouncer in Soho. He was unpredictable, and could turn from edgy affability to charging bull in the twinkling of an eye, a character trait that unnerved not only me but those he faced in the wrestling ring, as well as the local hard men. He was such a ferocious competitor that many potential opponents refused to wrestle with him.

Despite his enormous strength and frightening temper, his wife, Marjorie, a small woman, was able to keep him under control. Father reported that, on another occasion, he turned a corner just in time to see tiny Mrs Assirati, hands on hips, berating Bert. He had picked up several stone paving slabs from a pile waiting to be laid and had raised them above his head ready to crown some cowering unfortunate who had displeased him. After a choice mouthful from his spouse, he lowered the slabs sheepishly and placed them tidily back on the pile before allowing himself to be led away like a naughty schoolboy.

One day in the mid fifties, I was out walking with Father and some of his 'business associates'. One of them, Campanini, said something that hit Bert's top note, and the wrestler lifted him way above his head and tossed him over a high wall.

A crashing, tinkling sound was followed by startled shrieks, a spluttered 'I say,' and gabbled apologies in charmingly broken English. Campanini's head appeared above the wall, festooned with bits of hard-boiled egg, cress and cake. He'd landed in the middle of someone's tea party. As he jumped down into the street, apparently unharmed, pieces of shattered china rained from his ruined clothes and a pair of sugar tongs clattered to the pavement.

'Momento,' muttered Campanini, who picked up the tongs and heaved himself up the wall again. With another apology, he dropped the tongs into the garden, saying, 'I return these to you.'

By this time, the host of the party had barged through a door set in the wall ready to remonstrate with the perpetrator of this outrage, but reassessed the situation when he clapped eyes on Bert. The sight of Campanini dripping with tea had, though, done much to restore Bert's good humour, and after a hasty whip-round he paid for the breakages with a crisp white fiver and change.

Primo Carnera, who became heavyweight boxing champion of the world in 1933, was another sporting hero whose face was well known in the West End. He was not easy to overlook, as he was 6' 6" tall and muscular with it. When Primo's vast frame was spotted ambling through Soho's narrow streets he drew the local children – especially the Italians – like a magnet. After his boxing career ended, he turned to wrestling and to acting. His role as Python Macklin in the popular *A Kid For Two Farthings* in 1955 made his face familiar to many a British household. His nephew, John Carnera, distinctly remembers having an unscheduled, fascinating day off school to visit his uncle on the set.

Among the West End's Italian population and in his native Italy, Primo was revered in much the same way as top international footballers are today. He would visit Soho every year to see his brother, Secundo, and his family. John remembers his Uncle Primo as a prodigious drinker: much to John's mother's distress, he always led Secundo astray, dragging him around too many West End watering holes while he was in town. Primo died in America, aged sixty, of kidney and liver failure, although he outlived his hardworking younger brother.

12

A Matter of Tastes

You really had to be there to know just how truly dreadful food was in Britain in the late forties and fifties – and, some would say, for decades after that. Frankly, we English were the laughing stock of Europe when it came to our cuisine. We were so notorious for our lousy victuals that it is only comparatively recently that we have even begun to live it down. There was some excuse during the Second World War: times were trying, supplies were meagre and minds were very busy with other things, such as worrying about our fighting men and boys, keeping Hitler on his side of the English Channel, dodging doodlebugs and making do and mending.

'There's a war on, you know,' was the standard reply to timid complaints about the food in cafés and restaurants between 1939 and 1945. Rationing carried on being the excuse for a good while afterwards, and even after it ended, standards didn't improve much. We'd become used to eating badly – we'd all been trained up on school dinners after all, and there was no sterner test. The meals provided by all of the schools that I attended were brought by van in large metal containers and by the time they were served up were tepid and laced with congealed fat. Anything green, which usually meant cabbage, was reduced to a soggy blob on the side of the plate. Mashed potato came with hard lumps, often grey in colour: these were used as missiles to be flicked at enemies and friends alike while teacher's back was turned. Many a café, buffet and restaurant produced food to a remarkably similar standard, although the spud missiles tended not to fly in cafés quite as readily as they did at school.

J. Lyons & Co. was a rare exception, in that it provided some of the best plain food of those times. There were three basic kinds of outlets: Lyons Corner Houses, Maison Lyons and the tea shops that later became among the very first self-service cafés. They owned other enterprises as well, but the places affectionately known as 'Joe Lyons' teashops' are what they remain famous for, long after the last of their kind closed its doors for ever. The company always aimed to provide good food at reasonable prices and cooked in immaculately clean kitchens.

Most reasonably sized affluent towns with a large middle class had the boon and blessing that was a Joe Lyons Corner House. These were huge buildings with restaurants on several floors, all served by a central kitchen. The food was schlepped by 'Nippies', highly trained, silver service waitresses clad in black dresses, white aprons and caps. A national institution in their own right, Nippies were so famous, and so instantly recognizable, that their various uniforms over the years were made in children's sizes so that little girls could play 'dressing up' and aspire to becoming a Nippy themselves.

London had three Corner Houses, all in the West End. The first was in Coventry Street. Later, others opened in the Strand and Tottenham Court Road. The poshest Lyons outlets were the two Maison Lyons, one at Marble Arch and one in Shaftesbury Avenue. The musicians and Nippies were set in sumptuous surroundings: I remember loads of greenery and stylized fake palms at the Marble Arch Maison.

Meals in a Corner House or Maison Lyons were usually accompanied by live music from the sort of piano trio I always thought of as Annie Crumpet's Tea-time Three, or a small orchestra, playing light classics and the popular music of the day. Each floor of the Corner Houses had a name like 'Grill and Cheese', 'Bacon and Egg', 'Restful Tray', 'Brasserie' and 'A La Carte'.

The tea shops were much more basic, but still knocked out decent snacks, a choice of maybe two cooked meals and, of course, teas, buns, cakes, ice cream sundaes and all sorts of things on toast, including baked beans, sardines, eggs and tomatoes. At one time, there were eleven Lyons outlets in Oxford Street alone. As always with the English at the time, the difference between eateries was a class thing. Anyone in the lower middle class or a bit above could nip into a tea shop when out shopping, but the Corner Houses were a touch more genteel.

Of course, anyone with the money to pay could use them, or the Maisons, but the Corner Houses were aimed at those who considered themselves 'a cut above', being at the top of the middle-class tree. Corner Houses had a food hall on the ground floor where various Lyons products were sold, including chocolates, preserves and many more grocery items from across the Empire. But they never sold the leaf tea that they served in the cafés and restaurants, a special blend that was unique to them and which, they boasted, produced the very best cuppa to be had anywhere. Lyons also anticipated the home delivery service offered by pizza parlours today – they delivered food anywhere in the Central London area twice daily.

Sonia Boulter remembers her local Lyons Corner House fondly: 'In those days it used to be a shop, a grocer's shop, and you used to go down Sunday and buy a French cream sandwich for two and six. My dad would say, when we were a bit older, "There's some money, go and buy a cake," on Sunday. I remember there was live music; you'd go upstairs to the Brasserie I think it was, there was someone playing a piano. Now it's an amusement arcade.' The Trocadero Restaurant on the corner of Shaftesbury Avenue and Windmill Street was then a J. Lyons enterprise, although it had opened its doors in 1896 and finally closed them in 1965. The building is still there, and still called the Trocadero, but the inside has changed beyond all recognition.

I remember spending many a happy hour scoffing in Joe Lyons with my mother, my grandma and a variety of great-aunts. The demise of the Lyons empire was a real loss to us all. As it is, they are remembered with nostalgic affection by anyone who ever noshed a toasted teacake, a banana split, a boiled syrup roll, or sautéed kidneys, or who supped a reviving cuppa in any of their tea shops or Corner Houses.

'At the end of the Second World War, catering was a kind of visual and nutritional desert between the works canteen and the Ritz,' Ken and Kate Bayne noted in an article written in 1966. This was true, with the exception of Joe Lyons and their much smaller, and snootier, rival, Fuller's Tea Rooms. Things were so bad on the food front that, in 1951, the journalist, campaigner and gourmet, Raymond Postgate, launched the *Good Food Guide* in an attempt to give the long-suffering British public a definitive guide to where to find edible fare. To this end, he enlisted the aid of family, friends and the readers of his column.

He started off by writing articles inviting readers to send in their recommendations of places where eating could be classed as the pleasure it should be, rather than the endurance test it usually was. His aim was not only to help the public to find something good to eat, but also to encourage chefs and cooks to try harder. Readers responded enthusiastically, and eventually he had collected enough information to launch the first edition of the guide. A grateful public fell on the book with glad cries of joy. Postgate was neither knighted nor sainted for his efforts, but in the opinion of many he should have been because restaurateurs – posh and humble, and those between – began to strive to gain entry into the guide. Thus Britain began its slow progress towards good dining. Those restaurants, inns, hotels and cafés that achieved the status of an entry in the guides strained to stay there. This was good for business, and it was good for the taste buds and stomachs of those who cared.

There was only one place, though, where you could always find an actual selection of decent eateries, and this was Soho. Soho restaurants were famous as far back as the late eighteenth century, when the artist Sir David Wilkie sang the praises of the King's Arms in Poland Street. The food was simple, tasty, cheap, cheerful and, what is more, 'we have all the advantage of hearing all the languages of Europe talked with the greatest fluency, the place being mostly frequented by foreigners: indeed, it is a very rare thing to see an Englishman; while there are Corsicans, Italians, French, Germans, Welsh and Scotch.'

According to Richard Tames in *Soho Past*, a review of Kettner's restaurant in *The Times* towards of the end of the nineteenth century kick-started Soho's wider fame as the place to eat. Before then, its establishments had largely catered to locals. Oscar Wilde loved Kettner's, and dined there often. Kettner's *Book of the Table* became a must-have reference work for anyone interested in things culinary. The founder of the restaurant, an Austrian, had formerly been chef to Napoleon III, Emperor of France. I don't know how he wound up bringing his skills from the French court to the modest, sooty surroundings of Soho in 1868, but we can only be profoundly grateful that he did.

France also sent us Maison Bertaux, which set up shop in Greek Street in 1871, after the Franco-Prussian war deposed Napoleon III. It is believed to be the very first French pâtisserie in London, and is still providing gorgeous cakes and strong, French coffee almost 140 years on. Sonia Boulter remembers that 'They used to serve the most beautiful coffee cake, luxury, really nice.' I'll second that.

The 1886 *Baedeker's Guide to London* recommended ten 'cheap and good foreign restaurants in Soho', and more were to follow. Georges Gaudin opened L'Escargot around 1900, and this, too, survives into the twenty-first century. Around the same time as Gaudin was introducing the joys of snails in garlic to the English, there was a rash of theatre-building in the West End. The theatre crowd – audiences, players and the supporting cast of dressers, lighting bods, scenery shifters, stage managers, prompts and all – opened up a whole new trade to the enterprising restaurateurs in the area. Then, as now, audiences tended to eat before the show, while the players and the rest came after it, exiting the stage door looking for food, good company and a place to unwind.

Gennaro's is thought to have been the first Italian restaurant in Soho. It opened its doors in Old Compton Street in 1909, but was bombed out in 1940, and moved round the corner to 44/45 Dean Street, where the Groucho Club is now. John Carnera was bought up in the flat above the restaurant, where his father, Secundo, was employed.

Many Italians love their opera, and the Royal Opera House is close by in Covent Garden, so, naturally, once Gennaro's had settled in, Italian singers and patrons, looking for a taste of home, soon found the restaurant and passed the good news on to their friends, colleagues and relatives. Both Caruso and Gigli ate there in their day, along with many another famous, and less famous, face.

Penelope Seaman wrote in *Little Inns of Soho* that 160,000 people had dined at Gennaro's in the previous year, suggesting that the English appreciated decent food, just as much as the visitors to our capital. 'In the forties and fifties,' John Carnera told me, 'it was one of the most famous restaurants in Soho. If you wanted Italian food, that was the place to go.' Mr Gennaro was a man who simply loved to serve his patrons, taking real pleasure from ensuring that people were both well fed, and served with courtesy, knowledge and charm. John Carnera described him as a 'wonderful old Neapolitan, with a handlebar moustache. There was a rose in his lapel and he used

277

to greet the ladies, "Ah, signora," he would say and kiss their hands. He was a real old smoothie.'

'Our aim is not to make money and get out – our business is to look after our customers,' John Koiza is quoted as saying in 1988 about Jimmy's, a Greek restaurant that was opened by his cousin, Jimmy Christodolus, in August 1949. It's a theme that keeps cropping up in reference works and in the interviews I conducted. Providing the very best in food and service really was a labour of love for Soho restaurateurs, and in many places it remains that way to this day.

Peppino Leoni opened the Quo Vadis restaurant in Dean Street in 1926 with just seven tables. By working hard and, most importantly, providing food of a consistently high standard, impeccably served, he saw his enterprise grow. He always felt that it was important to make a customer who wanted beans on toast and a glass of water as welcome as the customer who wanted a three course meal and a bottle of wine. This philosophy helped him build the place up until it was serving more than 450 meals a day in the tourist season, and a little over half that number in winter. He took pride in keeping up exacting standards, and employed seventy people to make sure that they did not slip. 'My kitchen is not as clean as the Savoy's ... the Savoy's is as clean as mine,' he assured Jeffrey Bernard when he was interviewed by him in the mid sixties.

Wheelers, in Old Compton Street, was one of my father's favourite haunts. During his time in Soho, it was a hangout for an arty, bohemian crowd. Francis Bacon, Lucian Freud, John

Deakin, Colin MacInnes and Daniel Farson were just a small handful of the regulars who could be found knocking back white wine and oysters throughout the fifties. In the same period, Wheelers was offering more than thirty different recipes for lobster and the same again for sole, which illustrated that English fare didn't have to be dreary, and that inventiveness was alive and well in Old Compton Street.

Most of Wheelers's cooks at the time were Chinese – which may explain the diversity of the menu – but the boss was a Whitstable man, Bernard Walsh. He originally took the Soho property to sort his Whitstable oysters for the kitchens of the big London hotels, but as soon as he opened, he found that the local people kept dropping into sample his shellfish. Oysters were thought to be an ace cure for a hangover, so eager local tipplers were often the first through the doors in the morning. Walsh decided to make his informal customers more comfortable, and built a bar for them to sit at. It wasn't long before he was running a full-blown fish restaurant and, over time, a modest chain of restaurants that were to become nationally – and indeed, internationally – famous.

In complete contrast, Pitta's, at 10 Old Compton Street, was a relatively cheap and cheerful place run by a reticent, retiring Greek Cypriot called George Pitta, who was rarely seen out of his kitchen. His fellow countrymen, Andy and Nick, waited tables, along with a red-headed waitress called Ruth. She was Irish, and had a prodigious memory, which made the service both efficient and friendly. Like all successful restaurants, they knew that good service always adds to the charm of a place. It is such a pleasure to be recognized, to have your favourite order memorized and to be made much of. Of course, such treatment brings patrons back time and again.

I am pretty sure that Andy and Nick went on to found the Star, just a few doors down from Pitta's. Pitta's was the favourite haunt of theatrical people and artists of all kinds, whereas the Star catered for many musicians and, like Pitta's, also provided basic English food at reasonable prices. By the late fifties, diners had grown a tad more adventurous, so that the Star also offered a variety of Greek dishes.

Most of the places I have mentioned so far started life in Old Compton Street. If one street could boast so many good eating places, it isn't hard to imagine just how many there were spread around and about Soho as a whole. *Little Inns of Soho* lists twenty-six places that its author, Penelope Seaman, thought had something special to offer: they included representatives of France, Italy, Yugoslavia, Hungary, Greece, Cyprus, Spain, Russia and Austria, all of them cooking away and enriching the gastronomic lives of Englishmen and women, as well as children like me and a good few of my interviewees.

Soho was also virtually the only place, apart from the docks, where you could find Indian and Chinese food in the decades after the war. Sonia Boulter grew up in Newport Dwellings, in what is now Chinatown, right beside where the pagoda stands today. Opposite her flat was the Canton - it is there to this day. 'It was the second Chinese restaurant or café in the area that I can recall. That's going back to the forties.'

Maxim's, at the Wardour Street end of Gerrard Street, was the first Chinese restaurant in the area. It boasted a small band, complete with a bandleader, and there was music and dancing to accompany the food. 'It was quite posh in those days,' Sonia Boulter recalls. 'I knew Maxim's Chinese Restaurant very, very well, because my dad worked there. He was a barman. After school, I used to go down to the staff entrance, a long way downstairs, and I'd be fed by the Chinese people with noodles and that. It was the first place I ever had a lychee. I was eating Chinese food from about the age of eight [in 1948]. We didn't say no to any food in those days.'

At the time Sonia remembers, the area between Shaftesbury Avenue and Leicester Square was on the cusp of a massive change. It was about to metamorphose from a typically multicultural, working-class district of Soho, into the China-town we know today. Property was old and cheap, and was offered on short leases only, which made it cheaper still. The landlords were hoping to make a post-war killing on the land for redevelopment. Before the war, England's Chinese population of around two thousand souls had been concentrated in the docklands areas of Liverpool and in London's Limehouse. These areas had been battered by bombs, and after the war were flattened by the bulldozers that came to finish off the job that Hitler had begun. As well as losing their homes, the Chinese lost their jobs, as the authorities made it difficult for non-British nationals to sign on as merchant seamen. To top it off, much to the delight of British housewives, the twin-tub washing machine had been invented, and was soon making its appearance in our homes: launderettes began to flourish, too. This was not good news for the traditional Chinese laundries that had flourished for decades, but now began to disappear.

Something had to be done, and, in the late fifties, Chinese businessmen and entrepreneurs began to move Up West and open restaurants. Earlier Chinese restaurants had catered mainly for their own people, but the war changed all that. Servicemen who'd been stationed in the Far East came back home with a taste for Chinese cuisine, and soon the restaurants began to flourish. Farm workers displaced by changes in the world rice markets flooded in from the Hong Kong Territories to staff the new restaurants. Not long afterwards, Chinese food outlets of one sort or another had spread beyond London, to towns and villages everywhere.

Indian food has had a place in our hearts since the sahibs and memsahibs who served in the British Raj brought a taste for its spices back with them on retirement to Blighty. Then, of course, there were the lascars, or Indian sailors, who had to eat when they arrived in our ports. Once again, military service in India during the war brought back men who loved the food, and they, in turn, introduced it to a wider range of appreciative stomachs. As a 1956 food guide, which lists four Chinese restaurants and two Indian in Soho alone, suggests, many Londoners liked to embrace cuisines very different from our own.

Italians returning to post-war London from the Isle of Man and Canada, where they had been interned for the war years, were joined by a new wave of Italian migrants fleeing an economically depressed, war-battered Italy. With them, they brought trattorias. These were considered by Italian restaurateurs, such as Peppino Leoni of Quo Vadis, as cafés rather than restaurants. They were less formal for one thing, dispensing with crisp, linen napkins, heavy cutlery, sparkling glassware and courtly service in favour of brightly coloured Formica tables and counters, mirrors, mosaics, frescos and potted plants. They brought a little of the colourful Mediterranean to grimy old London and drew even more people into Soho – especially the young.

The coffee bar and espresso culture of the fifties also began in Soho, partly because of the large Italian community and partly because Gaggia had their first British premises in Dean Street. Achille Gaggia invented the espresso machine that bears his name in Milan in 1946. Pino Riservato, an Italian dental technician, set up Riservato and Partners to import the machines to England, and in 1953 got Gina Lollobrigida to open the Moka Bar at 29 Frith Street, England's first coffee bar, to show off his wares. The Moka claimed to be 'patronised by over fifty nationalities', a claim to fame that typified Soho's pride in its traditionally multicultural appeal.

The advent of espresso was the beginning of the end for milk bar culture, which lasted well into the sixties, and even the seventies, in provincial towns. Mr Gaggia's shining machines transformed many traditional 'caffs' and Italian 'greasy spoons', which cut the grease and stodge from their menus and acquired a set of toughened glass cups and saucers (which not only looked modern, but also made sure that drinks soon got cold, discouraging those who wanted to linger all night over a single cup).

The colourful informality of trattorias and the all-important coffee bars made Soho the Mecca of the newly discovered teenager. Before the fifties, those who had reached their teens were just young replicas of their parents, on the cusp of joining Mum and Dad in adulthood – teenagers as a separate, distinct group with their own tastes and cultural influences, entirely different from the stifling conformity and rigid class structure of their parents and grandparents, were unknown.

The older generation had had their crack at running things their way, and two devastating world wars had been the outcome. It was time for change. It was time for the young to make their own, distinct mark on society. Teenagers began to create their own music and their own fashions and they were as radically different from what had gone before as it was possible to be. Many of them made the pilgrimage Up West to buy their new fashions and to hang out in the coffee bars, to socialize and set the world to rights.

The time young people could spend in a tea room was severely limited. Once you'd finished your cuppa and bun it was time to pay up and vacate the table. Fuller's Tea Rooms were the worst, apparently, because they were 'very posh'.

The waitresses were snooty, and the punter had to 'drink their tea and bugger off': there was no question of being allowed to hang about with your mates, eyeing the girls.

Coffee bars were different. Old fogeys tended to steer clear of them, and the owners didn't mind their young customers hanging around for hours chatting up the talent. In Italy and other parts of continental Europe, there was a tradition of using trattorias, coffee houses and pâtisseries as places to meet and talk, or simply to watch the world go by, and that notion arrived in England along with Gaggia and the drink that is so popular now in the twenty-first century, the cappuccino.

Individual coffee bars soon became associated with different factions. The 2I's in Old Compton Street was for rock 'n' roll and skiffle fans. Old Compton Street also boasted the Prego Bar Restaurant, Heaven & Hell, and Act One Scene One, a theatrical dive. Bunjies, in Lichfield Street, catered for the beatnik and folk music crowd. Le Macabre in Meard Street, with its eccentric decor – coffin-lid table tops and menus printed on 'tombstones' – was also more of beatnik kind of a place, while Les Enfants Terribles in Dean Street attracted beatniks and bohemians with a serious turn of mind and a small pile of Jean Paul Sartre, Françoise Sagan and Jean Genet tucked under their arm for all to see.

It wasn't only teenagers. Bohemians of all descriptions enjoyed the ambience. The Nucleus, in Monmouth Street, was a basement coffee bar that stayed open until five or six in the morning and attracted all sorts of night owls – 'Jazz Men,

Painters, Writers, Sculptors, Poets (and Lay-abouts)' as its ads proudly proclaimed – while the Gyre & Gimble in John Adam Street also nurtured folkies and skifflers. Carlisle Street offered the Partisan, a hang-out for left-wing political types, while an arty crowd swarmed into Trattoria Terrazza in Romilly Street from the moment it threw open its doors. According to Jeffrey Barnard, the place attracted 'writers and painters, film directors and extras, and also a great cross-section of businessmen and lovers'.

Not all of the coffee bars were welcoming. When I became interested in coffee bar culture, I went to the Macabre, Les Enfants Terribles and, of course, Bunjies, but I never entered the Bar Italia in Greek Street because it seemed to be the sole preserve of Italian men and was more than a little intimidating to a young girl. It still is, even to an old girl – I wandered in there a few years back by mistake, but the very male, vaguely hostile atmosphere soon had me back through the door, looking for somewhere more welcoming.

Sonia Boulter, though, had an 'in' at the Bar Italia because she had a relative on the inside. 'My cousin, the one with the ponytail who looks like he's in the Mafia now, he's Italian, he always used to be in there with his dad and my other cousin. You rarely saw anyone but Italian men there; it was like a clique. But I was fortunate because my cousins were there. You would be allowed in, but because I had a connection with the Italians I was made welcome.'

The new coffee bars brought in a new range of taste experiences; along with the impossibly exotic frothy coffee came continental pastries and other delights. Gary Winkler, who took over the Nucleus in the mid fifties, remembers, 'We were very famous for our spaghetti bolognese, because then it was unusual. I'd been in the army in France before I was demobbed, so I brought in some unusual ideas from France. We used to have milk with grenadine, which was a French drink, like a milkshake but with pomegranate juice, and we had yoghurts, which were virtually unknown then. You know, musicians who used to come in and play, we'd always give them a bowl of spaghetti, keep them going.'

Father moved out of his flat in Old Compton Street in 1960. Although I no longer had a home there, I was continually drawn back, as a teenager and a young woman, to its coffee bars and music venues, but also to its cheap and cheerful restaurants and, if I was in funds, its more expensive ones as well. My taste buds had been fine-tuned by the things I found there, and there was nowhere else to get the fine nosh I was used to. I had grown accustomed to the fact that Soho was always ahead of its time. It took the quality and cultural diversity of food seriously decades before the rest of the country and, of course, there was the pull of the music. Postwar Soho always seemed to be in the vanguard of any new trends, and slowly, very slowly, the rest of the country would eventually follow.

13

Making Music

I believe that the social freedoms and cultural innovations that swept Britain in the sixties had their roots in Soho in earlier decades, and nowhere is this more obvious than in the field of music. I'm not talking about the music made in the area's opera houses, concert halls and ballet companies – even though these had plenty of aficionados, including my own family – nor the dance band stylings, light crooning and up-tempo novelty songs that were the staple of broadcast music at the time. I'm referring to what was then considered underground music, produced by and for young enthusiasts coming up from the streets. Modern and traditional jazz, folk, blues, skiffle and, later, rock 'n' roll all found a home and a place to grow in Soho.

The lines that link the jazz music of the twenties with the Beatles-led 'Beat Boom' of the sixties are unbroken, and in the post-war years they form a knot around Soho, where the music's freedom of spirit was valued as much as any other freedom.

Musicians naturally gravitated to the West End. There were more jobs to be had there than any-where else in the country, for a start. There was work to be found in the pit orchestras of theatre-

288

land, while big bands still played in dance halls such as the Lyceum, at the bottom of Drury Lane. Small groups worked the nightclubs, changing personnel as the job demanded. Some clubs had a resident band, while others hired musicians on short-term contracts.

A few clubs opened that were entirely devoted to a particular form of music, such as jazz, folk or blues. Before long, they were packing in punters six nights a week. Later, there were jobs for young performers in the coffee bars, while piano trios could find employment providing background music for diners in the larger Joe Lyons or the 'Palm Court' room of fashionable hotels. Even the strip clubs and the clip joints provided work for a pianist and a drummer, who would hit rimshots as another piece of costume floated to the floor. Pubs provided work for semi-pro pianists, while guitarists, accordionists and one-man bands could always take to the streets and 'bottle' for tips while busking the cinema and theatre queues.

Musicians also congregated in Soho because the national headquarters of the Musicians' Union was in Archer Street, hard by St James's and St Peter's School, and just around the corner from the Windmill Theatre. On Monday mornings, throughout the forties and fifties, musicians (and, as the old joke goes, drummers – easily picked out as they wore sticks poking out of their pocket as a badge of their trade) would gather outside the offices with the words ORCHESTRAL ASSO-CIATION picked out in relief above the door. As Ronnie Mann recalls, 'Archer Street was full of these strange blokes, all trying to get a job: we're not talking about a dozen, it seemed at the time to be hundreds of them.'

Sonia Boulter remembers them well: 'Archer Street was notorious, because on the way to school and on the way out you'd see them all queuing up waiting to see if there were any jobs. That was all they used to do, hang around there, so we met quite a few. They used to say hello, because they knew we went to school there.'

These shifting knots of people came to Archer Street to check out the Union's noticeboards, to gossip and to look for a gig. Anyone who already had an engagement for the coming week would go there to hire other musicians, usually looking for faces they knew. Mondays in Archer Street were often as much about putting old bands back together as they were about creating new alliances. At that time, the average jobbing musician would not have had a phone, nor, most likely, a permanent home to put one in.

As jazz drummer Laurie Morgan remembers, 'Musicians from every part of the musical profession would meet here, but they would only meet at specific places, where they'd arranged to meet each other. Because people were so jammed together, they might have to strike deals across, as it were, a crowded room, so instead of being able to speak properly, they would have a private way, hand signals, of letting each other know how much the money was.'

Another attraction of Archer Street for the average musician was that the Windmill was just around the corner. The theatre's glamorous dancers, as well as those whose job it was to stand both naked and perfectly still on the stage, would frequent nearby pubs and cafés in their downtime, which tended to coincide with the musicians' hanging-about-near-the-Union-having-a-desultory-chat times.

Another focal point for musicians was the north-east corner of Soho, on the far side of Charing Cross Road. Denmark Street, popularly known as Tin Pan Alley, was jam-packed with the offices of song publishers and writers and music biz agents, above shops selling instruments and sheet music. It was a place for star-spotting. Graham Jackson remembers 'going down there with Mum, and she'd say, "Look who's over there," and there's Alma Cogan just come out of one of the places'. There was another attraction for fans and musicians alike at 77 Charing Cross Road: Dobell's record shop was the only place in the country where imported American jazz, blues and folk records could be found in the fifties.

And, of course, all the clubs and cafés, theatres and cinemas – not to mention the opera houses, dance halls and concert halls – made the West End a Mecca for music lovers as well as musicians. They came from all over London, and further afield, to dance barefoot in a smoky dive, or more formally at the Lyceum, to tap their toes or do the hand jive in the 2I's basement, join in with the folkies at the Gyre & Gimble or Bunjies Folk Cellar, jive in a jazz club, or simply bop away to records played on jukeboxes or gramophones in club and restaurant basements. Often, the locals joined in.

The West End's reputation as the home for British jazz dates from 1942, when the Feldman Swing Club, London's first jazz club with live acts, opened in the basement at 100 Oxford Street. On Sunday nights, the jazzier dance-band musicians would sit in with semi-pro players, such as the young Ronnie Scott and John Dankworth, as well as the owner's young son, Victor Feldman, a drum prodigy. Feldman's became a refuge for English jazzers who had fallen under the spell of American beboppers, such as Charlie Parker and Dizzy Gillespie. Bebop, with its radically new approach to harmony and melody, and intricate rhythmic patterns, laid the ground for modern jazz.

The Fullado Club at 6 New Compton Street attracted black US servicemen, and jam sessions developed there in the post-war years. Swing musicians – many moonlighting from regular gigs with 'squarer' bands – played with young beboppers from 3 p.m. until midnight. Drummer Laurie Morgan was a dance band musician whose head was turned by hearing Charlie Parker. 'I used to go to the Fullado Club,' he remembers. 'Black American servicemen would come, and they would bring in records. It just blew our minds. The Fullado was really the first place where English bebop musicians got together as groups and played. Bebop was like a clarion call. This new world was going to come.'

In the summer of 1948, 6 New Compton Street housed the Metropolitan Bopera House. Ten of the young musicians who played there, along with the manager Harry Morris, founded Club Eleven in December that year. Club Eleven began at Mac's Rehearsal Rooms, at 41 Great Windmill Street – literally around the corner from Archer Street. The jazzmen arranged themselves into a quartet (later a quintet) led by Johnny Dankworth, and a six-piece band led by Ronnie Scott.

The growing reputations of Dankworth and Scott brought in the crowds, and radio broadcasts, record releases and concerts in larger venues saw the British – or at least the West End – public embrace modern jazz. Soon the club was packed out. It took on new premises in Carnaby Street, where it opened six nights a week. The crowds continued to grow, attracted by the atmosphere of excitement and transgression. Then, as musicians do, the founders began to squabble about money. Dankworth left to form his Seven, and things started to drift. On 15 April 1950, the club was raided by the police. Several musicians and customers were arrested and later convicted for possessing drugs or deserting from the army. Although the notoriety of what was the first drugs bust in Britain brought the club a brief resurgence in popularity, it folded before the end of the year.

In the meantime, another group of young musicians had revived earlier styles of jazz. Traditional jazz, or Trad as it came to be known, looked for inspiration to the Dixieland of New Orleans in the early decades of the century, the speakeasy styles of Prohibition-era Chicago and the bluesy, sexually charged sounds of singers such as Bessie Smith. Bessie was the particular inspiration for the singer George Melly, who, as the vocalist with Mick Mulligan's band, was at the centre of things.

While there was a certain amount of chin-stroking seriousness about modernist jazz fans – studied 'cool' was a large part of what the new sounds were about – Trad was all heat and hedonism. The grey years of rationing (which continued until 1954) were, in Chas McDevitt's words, 'coloured by the music and a liberal consumption of Merrydown cider'. Dancing – even jiving, which had been banned in many dance halls – was encouraged in the Trad clubs, while the modernists tended to sit down and nod along to the music, which might have had something to do with the apparently ready availability of dope in the jazz clubs.

They could party hard when the mood took them, but beboppers and other modernists tended to be serious about their craft; however with a Trad band though, the odd bum note went unnoticed in the joyous, boozy riot. Many of the Trad jazzers added other types of American 'Roots' music, such as folk and blues, to their repertoire, as well as the odd pop tune or calypso: the latter was enjoying a new popularity in Britain as the West Indian population slowly grew.

These differences created an intense rivalry. Although George Melly visited Club Eleven and Ronnie Scott's first club in Gerrard Street, because Scott had a policy of inviting over great American soloists, he remembers that there was little love lost between musicians of his persuasion and the modernists, who called the Trad aficionados 'mouldy figs'. Leo Zanelli remembers the schism well, from the other side. 'I grew up in an atmosphere of modern jazz and bebop, so I went to Club Eleven in a basement in Gerrard Street, and 100 Oxford Street on special nights. In those days, if it wasn't beboppish, well... And as for Dixieland, pffft. Even if you liked it secretly, you couldn't say so.'

Not everyone bought into the rivalry between the two forms. 'I started going to jazz clubs in 1952, 1953,' Chas McDevitt told me. 'There was the Ken Colyer Club, one in Frith Street and one in Great Newport Street, and then the Cy Laurie club in Windmill Street – all night Trad sessions. I also used to go to the Flamingo, in Lower Wardour Street, which was modern. You'd hear Tubby Hayes, Ronnie Scott, the Bill Le Sage trio.'

The rivalry was not just a matter of musical styles. The beboppers prided themselves on being sharp dressers, wearing slick suits. Laurie Morgan's wife, Betty, remembers that, at Club Eleven, 'We were all wearing black, sunglasses in the pitch dark, and tight trousers, the bebop look.' Trad fans, on the other hand, were more likely to sport sandals (sadly, often worn with socks) and duffel coats made of fabric so thick they could stand up on their own. Apart from that, they tended to dress casually; there was no point in wearing tight clothes if you wanted to dance.

Chas McDevitt, with a foot in both camps, remembers that, 'When I went to the Flamingo, I used to wear a really good suit, although my dad [who was a tailor] refused to narrow the trousers less than 16 inches. My girlfriend at the time had a pebble-dash two-piece suit with a velvet collar. That was Edwardian. That was the style of the time, everywhere except the jazz clubs, where a lot of the guys were wearing American-style zoot suits from Cecil Gee's, with really wide trousers – especially the coloured guys, American servicemen and a few West Indians who came over in 1948.'

In the early fifties, Wardour Street and Old Compton Street were at the centre of an ever-growing nexus of jazz venues, with clubs – usually basement joints – such as the Jamboree in Wardour Street, the Mandrake in Meard Street, the Bag o' Nails in Kingly Street, a whole succession of clubs where the Fullado had been, and the Flamingo in Wardour Street.

In the middle of the decade, the clubs were joined by a new type of venue for playing and enjoying music, the coffee bar. Places such as the 2I's and Heaven & Hell in Old Compton Street attracted an increasingly youthful and cosmopolitan crowd. Teenagers much preferred them to pubs – which at that time had restrictive opening hours and stricter policies than prevail today about letting anyone under eighteen over the threshold – as a place to meet up and hang out.

In the mid fifties, young people had more disposable income than they had ever had before, while the education reforms of the post-war Labour government had made universities and colleges more accessible to the middle classes, and even a few working-class children. The rapidly growing number of students in London provided a ready-made audience for modern and Trad jazz, for folk and for blues – and Soho was the natural place to go to look for all of them. With St

Martin's School of Art in Charing Cross Road, Soho had a constantly renewing supply of youthful bohemians on tap.

The chance to sit into the early hours over a couple of cups of rapidly cooling frothy coffee while setting the world to rights made coffee bars particularly attractive to those in their late teens. The end of the dreaded call-up in 1957 swelled their numbers even more. Coffee bar owners began to compete for their custom by providing some sort of musical accompaniment. At first, they employed young Latin guitarists to serenade the customers. Chas McDevitt remembers how, 'in 1954, on a Friday night, me and my mates would make the rounds of the coffee bars in the West End. In Hanway Street, there was the Moulin Rouge on the corner, with a Spanish singer with a guitar – well he was probably Cypriot, but pretended he was Spanish. Then there was the Acapulco next door, and one other, and they all had people sitting in, playing music. They were too small for groups to play, but duos could, which is one of the ways skiffle got started.'

The skiffle music that grew slowly in popularity through 1955 was very much a home-made affair. There were no professional skifflers – most played for free coffee or a bowl of spaghetti – although some professional musicians dabbled. Chris Barber's Jazz Band, for example, contained its own skiffle group, with Barber swapping his usual trombone for a double bass, banjoist Lonnie Donegan on guitar and vocals, and jazz and blues singer Beryl Bryden on washboard. In January 1956, 'Rock Island Line', a song recorded by this line-up but released under Donegan's name, became a huge hit. Towards the end of 1955, the bluesman Cyril Davies and Bob Watson had opened a club called the London Skiffle Centre above the Roundhouse, a pub on the corner of Brewer Street and Wardour Street. Its early sessions were sparsely attended, usually by other skifflers hoping to learn a new song, but after 'Rock Island Line' became a hit, skiffle became, virtually overnight, Britain's very first teenage music craze, and the Skiffle Centre was packed out.

The impact of skiffle is obscured to modern eyes by being viewed through the Beat Boom of the sixties. Although it spawned just a handful of hit singles, skiffle encouraged so many teenagers to take up guitars that the instrument shops and makers found it difficult to cope with the demand. By 1957, there were an estimated 30–50,000 skiffle groups in Britain. Adam Faith, who came from skiffle and went through rock 'n' roll to an acting career, remembered that 'Skiffle hit Britain with all the fury of Asian flu. Everyone went down with it. Anyone who could afford to buy a guitar and learn three chords was in business as a skiffler. It grew in cellars, nice dark cellars, and it shot up like mushrooms.'

Many of those cellars were in Soho. The one Faith was referring to was almost certainly beneath the 2I's coffee bar at 59 Old Compton Street, named for the (two) Irani brothers, who owned the building. The 2I's was managed by a pair of professional wrestlers, Ray Hunter and Paul Lincoln, who fought as Dr Death. It became a music venue almost by accident. The Vipers Skiffle Group, formed by Wally Whyton, were at the Soho Fair on 14 July 1956 when it started to rain. They sought shelter in the 2I's, and started to play. The crowd they drew led Paul Lincoln to offer them a job. Others soon followed, as Lincoln realized he had stumbled on a way to pull in many more customers for a minimal outlay. 'At first,' wrote Chas McDevitt, whose skiffle group played the 2I's in September 1956, 'the groups would play for Cokes and spaghetti, but with their increasing popularity they were allowed to bottle for tips.'

Although some skifflers performed actually in the coffee bar, in the boulevardier tradition, the action at the 2I's soon moved down into the basement. This had been decorated by Lionel Bart, a former student at St Martin's School of Art, who had once been in a band called the Cavemen with Whyton and Tommy Steele. He went for a black ceiling and stylized eyes on the wall that added to the cramped, oppressive feel. The basement could hold seventy or eighty people at most, and that gave the bands hardly any room to set up and play. Those actually in the cellar weren't the only audience. Raye Du-Val, a Sohoite and professional drummer, remembers that 'on the pavement were doors that pulled upwards. You could go in or crowd around outside and watch from there. It was a small place, small stage, just full of people.'

Other West End coffee bars began to feature skiffle. The Cat's Whiskers in Kingly Street was big enough to accommodate a stage, but elsewhere the musicians stood or sat among the customers, or were jammed against a wall at one end of the room. Owen Gardner went to Heaven & Hell, next door to the 2I's. 'It was a very tiny coffee shop. Upstairs was decorated like Heaven, with angels and everything else, very light and bright and down in the basement, down this very rickety staircase, was Hell, with very dim lighting and all these masks of devils, and flaming torches painted on the wall.' Needless to say, the musicians who played at Heaven & Hell did so among the licking flames.

Specialist skiffle clubs followed the lead of the London Skiffle Centre, including the Skiffle Cellar in Greek Street, the Princess Louise in Holborn and the 44 Club in Gerrard Street. Other impromptu venues sprang up as skifflemania took hold. Orlando's Delicatessen in Old Compton Street would regularly clear away the charcuterie in the evening and open its doors to whoever turned up. At the other end of the scale, there were skiffle concerts at the Royal Albert Hall. Chas McDevitt, with 'Freight Train', and the Vipers, with 'Don't you Rock me, Daddy-O' were both in the hit parade just a year after the Vipers had come in from the rain.

And yet, despite all this activity, all this fervour, by the beginning of 1958 it was all over. There were no more skiffle hits, and some of the new clubs closed, while others changed their name and style: the Skiffle Cellar became the folk club, Les Cousins, for example. The musicians moved on, too. Skifflers such as Martin Carthy, Dave Swarbrick, the Watersons, Ralph McTell, Davey

Graham, Cyril Davies and Alexis Korner would kick-start the British folk and blues scenes, as well as the rhythm and blues boom of the sixties. Hank Marvin, Jet Harris and Tony Meehan of the Vipers supported Cliff Richard, first as the Drifters, then the Shadows. Many more young skifflers switched to electric guitars and rock 'n' roll.

The 2I's also made the switch, and has been fêted as the birthplace of British rock 'n' roll. It was at least partly responsible for launching the careers of Cliff Richard, Adam Faith, Billy Fury, Marty Wilde, Terry Dene and Joe Brown, as well as less celebrated, but no less colourful, rockers such as Wee Willie Harris, Rick Hardy, Vince Taylor and Tony Sheridan.

Ann Lee was an enthusiastic visitor to the 2I's as a young teen. 'It was exciting. There were loads of them in there, you know, young boys with attitude. I met Joe Brown. He actually worked with my mum: she was a tea lady with a company on the corner of Drury Lane. I met Adam Faith. I couldn't afford much, so it was ideal to go there and sit yourself down with a couple of cups of coffee all night and watch people.'

Andy Pullinger also has fond memories of the place. 'In 1958, I discovered the 2I's. Tom the doorman sold tickets to the basement where we listened to rock 'n' roll music and tried to dance in the tiny space. There were several singers who made it big in the British rock music scene. Others made a living at entertainment, such as Screamin' Lord Sutch and Wee Willie Harris. One evening I met Jet Harris of the Shadows

301

outside the 2I's. He lent me half a crown, which I still owe him... Half of the entrance ticket to the basement was kept for a raffle which I seemed to win quite often – maybe because my first girlfriend was the one who drew the tickets.'

Although I lived virtually above the 2I's, I really can't remember too much about 'the scene' as such. I was just a touch too young, and didn't start swooning over pop stars until a couple of years after we left Soho. Of course, I could kick myself now, because I saw the likes of Tommy Steele, Adam Faith and Cliff Richard all the time, but as far as I was concerned, they were always cluttering up the pavement outside, and made a bloody row in the summer when we had our windows open. Sad really, and distinctly uncool. By the time I'd caught on, that particular moment had passed, and anyway, I was more of a Bunjies kind of a gal, being something of a folkie and a beatnik once I was out of jodhpurs and pretty shirtwaisters.

The reputation of the 2I's – a sign in the window called its tiny basement 'The World Famous Home of the Stars' – was out of all proportion to its size. On the Classic Cafes website, Adam Faith recalled 'a ground floor café, with linoleum floors and Formica tables. Downstairs, at night, under the street, the real action took place. Everyone expected it to be a nine-day wonder. The old-timer agents would sit around in their old-timer agent restaurants, shaking their heads, muttering "It'll all be over in a week or two."

It took a little longer than that, but by the early sixties the craze for coffee bars featuring live rock 'n' roll had largely run its course, and attention shifted to larger clubs that featured popular music, sometimes with live bands, sometimes not. Victor Caplin's aunt, Betty Passes, who ran Les Enfants Terribles coffee bar in Dean Street, was a pioneer of the disco. 'She introduced dancing to records in the afternoons and evening in about 1957. She had the basement painted black, and put in a bar – just soft drinks. Behind the bar was a record player. You paid a shilling upstairs for a token that would get you into the basement and buy your first Coke or whatever.'

Most coffee bars and cafés had a jukebox, but dancing was difficult, even impossible, because of the space, while the economics were different. People might put a few coins in the jukebox while they were sitting with their coffee, but those who came to dance to records not only paid the price of admission, but also tended to stay longer and drink more. 'In the early sixties, Soho was the hub of the discotheques,' remembers Jeff Sloneem. 'Just a few doors away from the Marquee, you had something actually called La Discotheque. There were loads of clubs where people danced to records; each one had their angle, and they all had their moments of popularity. There was one where the first hundred or so people that got in were given a single record, a 45. Another, at the top of Wardour Street, was called the Bastille, with a coffee bar above and a discotheque, built like a stone dungeon, underneath.'

John Carnera remembers one of these clubs with great affection. 'You know St Anne's Church in Wardour Street? In Shaftesbury Avenue there was an arch and wrought iron gates, and you went through, turned right and went downstairs, into what used to be a crypt or something. That got turned into a club. I used to go there regular, although I'd moved out of Soho by then. It was my favourite – it's where I met my wife, actually. It was called St Anne's, and it was owned by a Moroccan and his wife. We used to spend Friday and Saturday night there and have a good time, what you would call a disco now, drinking and music, yeah. We soon got to know everybody there, so it became a bit of a home away from home.'

There was still a lively live music scene, of course: as the sixties progressed, larger clubs such as the Marquee and the Flamingo became more and more influential. The Flamingo had begun life in 1952 as a 'luxury' modern jazz club at the Mapleton Restaurant or Hotel at the corner of Coventry Street and Wardour Street, and was aimed at a sophisticated, supper-club audience. 'It was great, the Flamingo,' Ronnie Brace remembers. 'A big club. Top club, nice surroundings. It wasn't cheap. Done with taste. They had good jazz.'

The Flamingo moved across Shaftesbury Avenue to new premises further up Wardour Street in 1957, and slowly switched from a jazz club to one featuring mainly rhythm and blues. By the time the sixties dawned, it was a favourite haunt of American servicemen and Caribbean immigrants. It had moved right away from its supper-club roots, and by the early sixties was famous for its blues all-nighters. The club's owners, Rick and Johnny Gunnell, were widely believed to have paid off the police so they could stay open until 6 a.m.

Paul C made regular trips into Soho to sample these riotous times. 'Once you got in,' he remembers, 'it was almost impossible to get out. The place you found early on in a club more or less determined where you stayed. Claustrophobic is not the word: you could hardly turn round. You could get a drink, but to leave, you had to make a really determined effort. And these were all-nighters. I remember coming out of the club and going on to the streets, just to get some fresh air, and on several occasions the contrast between the heat of the club and the coldness of the pavements made my nose bleed. It was that intense.'

In the meantime, the people of the West End got on with the timeless business of making their own music. 'My dad was a good pub pianist,' Mike O'Rouke remembers. 'He worked next door at the Mercer's Arms on and off, and he worked up in Highbury for a while, a big pub up there called the Cock, at Highbury Corner. He worked up in Islington, and he worked in Theobald's Road, a pub called the Queen's, and one called the Griffin, just off the Theobald's Road. He got around a little bit, you know. He played the piano accordion, as well. He'd take his accordion and play that one night, and the piano the next.'

Mike's dad was never famous, but at least one of my other interviewees remembers him. When I mentioned his name to Ronnie Mann, he was

305

delighted. 'I'd forgotten all about old Mickey O'Rouke! I've got a recording of him playing. Him and my old man were great mates. My old man played the piano as well as the accordion, and Mickey O'Rouke was a great pianist, as well as playing the accordion. Mickey used to play at a pub down in Theobald's Road, and my old man used to go up there, singing and playing together.'

Virtually everyone interviewed for this book had some memory of the music scene in the West End, while some of them were professionally involved. Gary Winkler, for example, had a long career as a percussionist in his own bands and various skiffle aggregations, and also ran the Nucleus coffee bar in Monmouth Street in the fifties. 'The Nucleus was just a big basement, with low ceilings and a concrete floor. At the bottom of the stairs was an alcove, and then a bigger alcove with seats all the way round, bench seats, some tables, and then you had the back room, a through room with a low stage at the far end and seats. There was dancing at the Nucleus before I put the seats in. It was all panelled with wood up to the dado rail, with murals by Diz Disley, the guitarist and cartoonist, above that.'

The Nucleus attracted a wide range of punters, from English and American writers – Jack Kerouac and Allen Ginsberg both popped in on their way through London, while Colin Wilson was a regular – to chancers, street people and members of the aristocracy. 'Lord Moynihan used to come down,' Gary told me. 'He lived on the edge of the law, always had people after him.

Married a West Indian girl purporting to be Princess Almina, and moved to Thailand, I think. Princess Almina was a waitress at Lyons coffee house when I met her, before she came up with her title. I never knew what she was Princess of.

'The club was more of a social thing for me. I really wasn't into business at that age. I was at the age of getting drunk and falling about, falling into bed with ladies who came down. I was too young to ... well, I was *too young*, and I wasn't business-minded. I think I did it more for the enjoyment than anything.'

There was plenty of fun to be had. 'We were, I would have said, the second best known coffee bar in London, behind the 2I's. A lot of jazzmen used to come down: the coffee bar was packed with musicians in general. We used to employ groups or other acts up to midnight, and after that just had a resident piano player. There was a drum kit there, and people would just pop in and sit in.

'After they finished working in the early hours, the musicians in the nightclubs loved to blow jazz or whatever. They would come down to the Nucleus, and basically jam until morning. You'd have Spike Mackintosh, a Dixieland trumpeter, sitting in with a modern-day alto player like Joe Harriott. And there were folk singers, skifflers; we had Jack Elliott and Derroll Adams, famous folk singers of the times. It was a complete mixture. When he was in England, Big Bill Broonzy used to come down the coffee bar because it was open all night and he loved to play and drink. He'd bring his own Scotch.'

Musicians would always congregate in places that opened late or offered some kind of deal on the necessities of life. 'All the jazzers used to go to the Star Café down under where I used to live at the Cambridge Circus end of Old Compton Street,' Chas McDevitt recalls. 'It was Greek-owned. You could get a meal for half a crown, lovely chops with chopped cabbage. The jazz and skiffle groups loved cheap food!' The Star was still going strong as a musicians' resort in the early sixties. At that time I was hanging out with the folk crowd, and after a gig at Les Cousins in Greek Street the performers and the audience would pop round the corner to meet up again at the Star, the inspiration for the café that features in my novels about Soho.

Although Gary Winkler claimed to have no business sense, I got the distinct impression he was exaggerating. 'Before Ronnie Scott opened his first jazz club, him and the Jazz Couriers used to rehearse in the Nucleus during the day, when it was closed. We used to lend it out for rehearsals for free. One day Ronnie took me for a cup of tea in the Rex café in Soho, told me he wanted to open a club, and asked my advice.'

John Carnera remembers the club that resulted from this chat. 'I was a great jazz fan. I remember going down to Ronnie Scott's when it was in Gerrard Street, a couple of doors along from the post office, down in the basement. There was Phil Seamen on drums, Johnny Hawksworth on bass, and Tubby Hayes and Ronnie Scott on tenor saxes. Still remember them now. I can still see Phil Seamen totally stoned out of his brain. Great nights.

Smoky atmosphere, a really dissolute kind of world.'

One of the last coffee bars on the scene was the Freight Train at 44 Berwick Street, opened by Chas McDevitt and named after his hit single, which effectively financed the purchase. Because, like the Nucleus, the Freight Train stayed open into the early hours, working musicians would go there to wind down and gossip after gigs. 'With my coffee bar being open so late, and being a pick-up and drop-off point for bands,' Chas remembers, 'the groups used to sit there at two in the morning. A lot of their girlfriends worked in Murray's Cabaret Club, along in Oxford Street somewhere, as dancers. Hank Marvin met his wife in my coffee bar.

'Johnny Kidd wrote "Shakin' All Over" in the basement. Brian Gregg and Johnny came in one night. They had a recording session next day and realized they didn't have a B-side, so they asked if they could go downstairs into the basement – because there was a jukebox upstairs – and, without an instrument apparently, they wrote the song. The next day, they recorded it: Joe Moretti and Alan Caddy put the guitar sounds on it, and it became the A-side and a big hit.' 'Shakin' All Over' – which is, according to my husband, who knows about these things, the best British rock 'n' roll single – reached number one in August 1960.

Right next door to the Freight Train, at 42 Berwick Street, another interviewee, Pepe Rush, had his own recording studio. Pepe came from a musical family: 'My mum, Pat Hyde, was a big jazz singing star before the Second World War.

After it, she went back into variety. She recorded on Parlophone, four titles a month, did thousands of broadcasts. She also recorded with other bands under assumed names, to get round her contract. She worked all over the world.

'My dad was a session musician, a violinist, and led many bands in the West End. He did a lot of sessions with the BBC, because all the studios were around the West End and he could be there in a few minutes' notice. He also had a music publishers in the basement of our flat at 33 Old Compton Street. It had originally been in Denmark Street, and he'd bought it off Victor Silvester's pianist. One of the blokes they published was Ralph Butler, who wrote "Run Rabbit Run", a nice old bloke. My dad used to go to the BBC to get things played. They did a lot of light orchestral music.'

Pepe's own talents lay more in electronics than in music. After he left school at fifteen, 'I worked in a studio in Denmark Street, and was at the very first recording that Johnny Kidd ever did. This bloke called Guy Tynegate-Smith – he wore one of those overcoats with a velvet collar – brought in this guy with a guitar and he was rank. He was the worst singer/guitarist I ever heard.

'By that time Dad was conducting the Talk of the Town cabaret, he led the dance band, so we had a good bit of money, and we built this little studio, in Berwick Street. This bloke came down to make a recording, and he was fantastic. He said, "Don't you remember me, mate?" and reminded me of the session a year before. I said, "But you were absolute crap, you were the worst

I ever heard." "Yeah," he replied, "I've improved." It was as if he'd sold his soul to the devil.'

Johnny Kidd was not the only famous name to pass through young Pepe's studio. 'The Shadows came down to play backing tracks for this bird. At the end they said, "We're recording a song called 'Apache'. Any chance we can do a demo?" I said yeah – it was all set up. They were pleased with it; I often saw them around Berwick Street and they would say they thought it was so much better than the version the label released, it was earthier and stronger.'

Pepe also installed sound equipment in clubs. 'This bloke Raymond Nash was the owner of La Discotheque in Wardour Street, the first one to be called that. I did these discos for him, and he suggested we started up a factory to build amplifiers. In this factory in Portland Mews, which was bordered by D'Arblay Street, Poland Street, Berwick Street and Broadwick Street, I built mixers for the London Palladium, as well as most of the equipment for the discotheques in Soho and other parts of England, Europe, the West Indies and the USA.'

Just across the road from Pepe's studio was the Top Ten Club, a haunt of drummer Raye Du-Val, who, in his own words, was 'never famous, but well known'. Raye was born in Soho to French parents in 1932. Inspired by the great jazz drummer, Gene Krupa, he turned professional when he was fifteen, and still plays today. His closest brush with fame came when he lied about his age to get a job with the Checkmates, the backing group of Emile Ford, who had just had a number one hit with 'What Do You Want to Make Those Eyes at Me For?' 'On Saturday night,' he remembers, 'Emile came to see me, offered me the job, and on Sunday night we played the Palladium, on TV with Norman Vaughan. I was on a tall plinth, and I could see it was in two parts, and it was moving. I thought. I was going to dive off any minute.'

The Top Ten club was in the basement below the House of Sam Widges coffee bar on the corner of Berwick Street and D'Arblay Street. It was opened by the rocker Vince Taylor, who later sold it to Raye and Mick Pastalopoulos, who also managed the Freight Train for Chas McDevitt. 'Sometimes I'd have a heavy night in the Top Ten,' Raye remembers, 'and I'd come out about seven or eight in the morning, to stagger to my flat across the road, and when you'd come out, it was like an episode from *Breakfast at Tiffany's*. A dark blue sky, the streetlights were still on, the street cleaners were going up and down and the people were just coming into work, you know, the office workers, it used to be a fantastic feeling, that time in the morning, not quite breaking, no sun yet, a wonderful experience.'

It was at the Top Ten that Raye found a place in the *Guinness Book of Records* with a succession of drum marathons. 'In 1959, I played for 30 hours, 3 minutes, 15 seconds, then the same year I played for 82 hours, 35 minutes, 14 seconds, then in 1960 I played for 100 hours, 1 minute and 15 seconds.' The records were all the more remarkable because Raye did not realize he was allowed a five-minute break every hour, and would take

312

his bathroom breaks still banging out a rhythm on a drum he carried with him. When I asked Raye how he had managed it, he replied lugubriously that 'I 'ad 'elp', in the form of amphetamines.

One of the many ways that post-war Soho anticipated the sixties was in the ready availability of drugs. It was the modern jazzers who started it, as Laurie Morgan's wife, Betty, explains. 'They thought because this was going on in America, and a lot of American musicians were taking heroin, that if they took heroin, they'd be able to play like that.'

Raye confirmed this. 'I done a bit of this and a bit of that, you know, got into a lot of bad ways, got on the dope scene, basically because Gene Krupa was supposed to have taken the gear, and I was such a disciple of his, that what he did was not wrong. There was four of us that hung about, me, Ginger Baker, Phil Seamen and Dicky deVere.' Raye and Ginger eventually got off junk, but the laconic Seamen, widely regarded as the finest drummer Britain ever produced, didn't. His addictions to narcotics and booze hastened his death, aged forty-six, in 1972. Seamen's long demise affected all who witnessed it. Gary Winkler, who described Seamen as 'a good friend when he wasn't out of it,' also knew Dicky deVere. 'He was another fabulous drummer, bless his heart, but was on heroin. Eventually, he had an operation and then became like a child, you know, he couldn't play.'

Although heroin was a problem with some jazz musicians, its use was not widespread, whereas 'speed' was everywhere. Musicians and punters

313

alike took Dexedrine and 'blues' (aka purple hearts) or chewed the wads from Benzedrine inhalers (prescribed for asthmatics), washed down with Coca-Cola. They did it not so much to get high as to stay alert, and not to miss any excitement. 'After the music in the 2I's basement stopped for the night,' Andy Pullinger remembers, 'we would go to all-night coffee bars. We took purple hearts to stay awake. We went to the Macabre, in an alleyway off Wardour Street. It was done up with coffins, skeletons, spiders' webs and other witches' accessories. Not much to do there except talk and snog. Another one was at the end of a lane between Berwick and Wardour Streets, which had jukebox music till dawn. We would stay there until six in the morning, then go to a second-floor coffee bar near Charing Cross Road for breakfast.'

The blues and R&B 'all-nighters' of the late fifties and early sixties were also sustained by pills. 'The Flamingo all-nighter was paradise for me on a Saturday night,' remembers Victor Caplin. 'We would be turfed out at about eleven-thirty only to line up and pay again to get back in for the late night session, blocked on a handful of purple hearts and dressed up to the nines in the current "stylist" fashion to listen to R&B. Black American airmen stationed at Lakenheath or Mildenhall would frequent the place, and it was our first real live exposure to the culture that these bands emulated and we aspired to.'

Drugs were available in the clubs or, if you had the contacts, at doctors' surgeries across Oxford Street and around Harley Street. Failing that, there was the street. As Raye Du-Val points out, 'On every corner you had a bunch of guys, talking, doing something shady. We had Soho Sid, the PersianYid, a right character, fag hanging out of his mouth...'

Some of the musicians were not averse to moving things on themselves. Raye tells how he came out of his flat one day and saw a poster on a news-stand saying, SOHO DOPE PEDDLER CONFESSES ALL. "I wonder who that is?" I thought. I bought the paper, and it was me!' Raye had been injudicious when talking to a young lady who, unknown to him, was a reporter.

If supplies of amphetamines failed, there was always Preludin, Raye believed that baking Valium tablets changed their nature from a tranquillizer to a stimulant. And, of course, there was marijuana, the archetypal drug of the sixties. When the police raided Club Eleven in 1950, that was what they were looking for. 'I can remember going down to Club Eleven to smoke,' Leo Zanelli remembers, 'and it sometimes made me feel a bit sick, and sometimes mildly happy. Virtually all the weed – marijuana they called it then – came wrapped up in dark green greaseproof paper. To get it, you had to know someone. You had to ask someone, and it would come to you. A feller called Lefty used to flog a lot of it.

'All the musicians were on it. As far as I know, there wasn't any of them who weren't. I stopped smoking in 1953, because two of my mates from Elephant & Castle died of ODs of something and that scared everyone off everything.'

For most people, though, youthful excitement

315

was all it took. 'I loved it in Soho,' remembers Ronnie Mann. 'I was down Ken Colyer's club – traditional jazz, down in Little Newport Street – when I was still at school in 1956. I started going when I was fourteen, well below age. My brother and sister used to go; my sister was in her twenties, and I'd go with them. I went to the 2I's coffee bar, Le Macabre, Heaven & Hell; if you were having difficulty with money, they were the places you went to when you were trying to meet girls. I also went to the 2I's Jazz Club in Gerrard Street, on the corner. That was a proper Trad jazz club, came before the coffee bar. Yeah, I bloody lived in Soho. I was there about six nights a week, I suppose. I loved the jazz clubs. I loved it all.'

14

Out on the Town

If people from other parts of London treated the West End as a kind of playground, coming Up West to shop and to visit the theatres, restaurants, cinemas, nightclubs and opera houses, most of the native Covent Gardeners and Sohoites tended to look elsewhere for their entertainment.

Certainly the spicier aspects of the West End's nightlife seemed to have little interest for the locals, as Alberto Camisa remembered. 'There were two sides. There were the residents, who were law-abiding and well behaved, and then there was the nightlife, the strip clubs, Revuebar, Sunset Strip, all of that. In the evening, my parents stayed at home. If it was still sunny, June or July, you might pop out for a walk, but if you had kids with you, you didn't go for a drink. I wasn't allowed out on my own in the evening. It was a traditional continental sort of thing; the evenings were for family. At a certain time you ate, did your homework, and then you went to bed. We didn't even have a TV until just before they landed on the moon.'

For some, it wasn't simply a question of coming up with the cash for a night out. Olga Jackson was forbidden various clubs and dance halls by her father because it would be embarrassing for him, as a policeman, if she were picked up there in a raid, while for the teenage Ann Lee, nightlife in general was off-limits. 'I used to have to be in at half-past nine during the week. Even when I was engaged, at eighteen, I still had to be in at eleven during the week. If my fiancé got me in late, he used to get into trouble.'

Ann's solution was to call on the help of her grandmother, Cissie Glover, who lived downstairs. 'She was a real character, my nan. She was handy to have around, because as well as not being allowed into certain places, I wasn't allowed to wear certain things, so I used to stash my winkle-picker shoes down my nanny's flat, along with my make-up. I'd say to Mum, "See you later," and go to Nanny's and get my shoes on, put my bit of make-up on. When I used to get in at night, I had to run into Nanny's first, change my shoes and wash the make-up off.'

317

This ruse served Ann very well for a while. 'Then, one day, my mum cleaned out Nanny's tallboy, found the shoes, found a pencil skirt, found the make-up. When I got in, she had them all on the kitchen table so I could see 'em, and said, "Don't say a word. They're all going in the bin." And they did. So I went and got more, and said to Nanny, "Don't let her find them again!" The skirt used to get rolled and put in a shoebox with the shoes and make-up and laid in the bottom of the wardrobe. Mum didn't find them again.'

The boys had it easier than the girls, of course, although Owen Gardner's mother had one strict rule: 'She told me I wasn't allowed to go to the pictures on Sunday. She used to say you've got six other days of the week to go to the cinema. Of course, I did go sometimes. "Where have you been, Owen?" "Well, I've been around..."'

For young men, the West End held dizzying possibilities. John Carnera remembers a typical weekend in his late teens and early twenties. 'Six of us used to run together: me, Peter Enrione, Henry Camisa and John Solari were Italian, or of Italian extraction, Percy Christopher – a nephew of Danny La Rue, Danny Carroll that was – was of Irish extraction, and the other one was Hans Dieter Maurer, and he was German. His aunt ran Maurer's Restaurant in Greek Street, which had a big spotted cow in the window – I'll never forget it. Apparently it was quite a top-class German restaurant, which is kind of surprising after the war.

'On Friday night, we would start in the Helvetia, next door to Kettners, the restaurant, in Old

Compton Street. We used to have a drink there, meet all our mates, then go on down the club, have a few hours down there, [wryly] see if we could pull any birds. And then about midnight or one o'clock, somebody would say there was a party going on, and we'd all troop off down to Eel Pie Island, on the Thames at Twickenham, down Streatham way, up to Hampstead, wherever there was a party. My mother wouldn't see me back again until probably Sunday. God knows what happened in between. I can't remember.'

To some extent, John's 'lost weekends' followed a family tradition. He tells me that his Uncle Primo used to tour the world as a wrestler after the Second World War. 'One of the stops was always England, and he'd always stay in London at the Regent's Palace Hotel or the Strand Palace Hotel. He used to come and see us once a year, every year, in Soho. My mother used to hate it: her head would go in her hands and she'd start crying when she heard he was arriving. My uncle was very strong on the drink, so he'd take my dad out and we wouldn't see him for two or three days. By the time my dad came back, he looked about ten years older, 'cause my uncle was a fearsome drinker. He used to take my dad out on the piss for a couple of days on the spin, and my mum knew she'd have to pick up the pieces when he got back.'

Although, as Alberto Camisa pointed out, the great majority of the residents rarely frequented drinking clubs, strip clubs or nightclubs, pubs were a different matter. There were plenty of street-corner pubs in the West End, more than there are now. Some of the local hostelries catered mainly for the theatre crowd, gay men or other visitors, but there were others, tucked away in side streets or on street corners, that the residents could more or less call their own. 'We used to go to the Mercer's Arms, next door,' Mike O'Rouke remembers. 'Everyone knew everyone in there. It was like the Rovers in *Coronation Street*. We used to play darts and that. It was very much a local: you used to get a few of the stars from the Cambridge Theatre go in there, but mostly it was people from the surrounding streets.'

'My father was a great pub man,' remembers Owen Gardner. 'He went to the pub next door, the Cranbourn. My mother knew that as soon as he said he was going next door for a drink, she wouldn't see him again until closing time. He didn't drink a lot, but he was a good conversationalist. He'd go there, and he'd meet people – one regular, Ulrica Forbes, did the drawings of Charles and Anne when they appeared on National Savings stamps when they were children. She was always in there.'

Ann Lee's father was a regular, but not frequent, pub-goer. 'Dad used to go for a drink on a Sunday lunchtime, because he worked six days a week. He'd go up the pub about half-past twelve, and he'd be in at two for his dinner. Sometimes, if the family came down, they'd all go up the pub together. They used to drink in the Prince of Wales.'

The Prince of Wales was the local not only for the Lee family, but also for the Freemasons at the nearby Masonic hall. Cultural clashes between the Masons and the less inhibited locals occasionally caused problems. 'I must have been sixteen or seventeen,' Ann remembers. 'I used to call in on Nan every morning before I went to work, just to give her a kiss and say, "See you later," and she said "You'll never guess what happened to me – but don't tell your mother. Last night I had a couple of Guinnesses and I was singing, and those bloody Freemasons got me slung out."

'I was fuming all day, so on the way home from work, I went into the pub, and said to the land-lord, "How dare you?" "What are you talking about?" he said. "How dare you chuck my nan out of this pub that she's been drinking in for years because of those weirdoes?" I really had a go. "She won't be drinking in here any more. She don't need your bloody pub," I said.

'I told Nan to go to the Sugar Loaf, said they would be all right in there, and she never went to the Prince of Wales again. My mum found out about a year later. She went in the Prince of Wales, and the landlord said, "Cor, your daughter's a fine mare, ain't she, coming in here wiping the floor with me?" and my mum said, "What? My Ann? My angel?" So she asked him what it was about, and he told her. She said to me, "How dare you show me up?" and I said, "What do you mean, show you up? You didn't even know." Mum really had a go at my nan, though.'

Like many women of her generation, Cissie Glover was fond of a fortifying bottle of stout or two. 'At six o'clock,' remembers Ann, 'you'd see Nanny go out with her little hat on and her little

321

coat, tripping out the gates and going up the road for her Guinness. Because she'd lived there so long, people would see her and say, "Hello Ciss, how are you? Have a drink, love." Sometimes on a Sunday – not evening time – after people had been buying her drinks, she'd walk into the gate of the flats and all of a sudden you'd hear her singing "Knees up Mother Brown", and then she'd shout out, "Kitteee!" and my mother would say to me, "Oh my gawd. Get down those stairs quick and get her indoors." So I had to run down the stairs and say, "Come on, Nan, let's get inside." I had to sing "Knees up Mother Brown" with her all the way across the grounds to get her indoors, otherwise she wouldn't move.

'In the end, my mum used to tell people, "If you see my mum, don't give her a drink. I don't want you to be horrible to her, but she's getting on, she can't take it." She was harmless, though. It was only because Mum would get embarrassed 'cause she used to sing at the top of her voice.'

As in any other working class district of London, Sohoites and Covent Gardeners knew how to organize a knees-up, and the Coronation in June 1953 provided a splendid excuse for a party or several. Mike O'Rouke went to a street party in Betterton Street, between Endell Street and Drury Lane. 'I remember we had quite a big party at home, too. My dad painted the outside of the house, decorated it up a bit, and we put some photos indoors, pictures of the Queen in the window.'

The large estates had their own outdoor parties, as Ann Lee remembers. 'They laid on a spread in the grounds at Wild Street, big tables and chairs, they put up a stage, there was all these benches with trestle tables. You had clowns and … there was so much excitement, and we had all these fancy cakes. We were all at this fantastic big party, all our mums were there with hats on, and our dads. Well, my dad wasn't there, because he was an unsociable sod. He probably said "Good evening", and went upstairs. He was a lovely man, but it was "Mornin", or "After-noon", and that was it.'

Peter Jenkins went to the same party. 'I remem-ber my mother coming in that morning and telling me that they'd climbed Everest. That was announced on the morning of the Coronation. That was incredible. Then the whole day was built around the Coronation. There was an enormous street party – an estate party! – and I won first prize in the fancy dress. I went as Watney's wall – Mr Chad – and the prize was presented to me by Mary Martin, who was in *South Pacific* at the Theatre Royal, I still remember that.'

Unusually, Peter also remembers the solemn events that preceded the Coronation, and gives an insight into a lost world. 'I remember coming home from school, and my mother telling me the King was dead. A great black feeling coming over me. I can't imagine that registering the same with a seven, eight-year-old today. When the funeral came, we went to see it on my aunt's television in Croydon, as we didn't have one: everybody dressed up – I wore my Cub uniform – and wore black armbands, and stood to attention as the cortege was going along Whitehall.'

A whole new perspective on the Coronation was provided by Charles Hasler, for whom it was another, very fraught, working day. 'Don't talk to me about the Coronation! I was a sergeant at West End Central, and I got put on night duty the night before the Coronation. I had a little squad of police and a bigger squad of military police and within the Mayfair area there were car parks allotted for people with blue tickets, red tickets, and our job was to keep these clear and make sure only authorized people parked in them, and we were to stay there until relieved in the morning. The day shift came out just after six and I went home on my bike and went to bed.

'I had to be back at three in the afternoon for more traffic duties. Of course it peed with rain. The uniform got me through the cordons. And then, when all the processions were over, I had the job, with all my merry men, of going out to control crowds and traffic. There were routes set up to get people in and out. One bloody idiot had produced a map showing a car route going down Lower Regent Street into Waterloo Place, but what he'd forgotten was that there wasn't a straight exit into the Mall, you had to go down the Duke of York's steps. We had to redirect all these cars all around Pall Mall, Mall Gardens: in the end we were telling people "Look mate, if you can find a place to get out, take it", because all these careful arrangements had broken down. So I had a miserable cold night before and an even more miserable evening afterwards in the rain. The only good thing, because of the weather, was that everyone went home early, because we were on a twelve-hour shift. I was happy to go off duty at one in the morning.'

I was surprised to find how few West Enders actually watched the Coronation procession – which was, after all, happening practically on their doorstep, just a short walk away – in person. Instead, like the rest of the country, they huddled around tiny black and white TV sets in their homes or at a neighbour's; many of the sets were bought specially for the occasion. This may have been because access was restricted: each school in Westminster was allocated so many places to line the route, and names were drawn out of a hat. Ronnie Mann was one of the lucky – he would say unlucky – ones: 'My lasting memory of the poxy Coronation is being soaking wet and freezing cold from start to finish. It was a crappy day; it rained. It seems to me it rained for forty days and forty nights, because I had to wear my Cubs uniform, the 12th Westminster – bleeding shorts, black shoes, cap. You had to be there hours and hours before, and take whatever sandwiches you had. Of course, there was nowhere to sit but the kerb, because we was right at the front. I can remember being excited a bit, but mostly I can remember being bored and wet.'

John Carnera was another who was successful in the lottery, and his memories are happier than Ronnie's. 'I think it was six boys and six girls from St Patrick's School were chosen, and I was one of those. I'll always remember watching the coach go by from a place on the Embankment, facing the river.'

For Ronnie, there was a consolation however.

'The following day, June 3rd, was my eleventh birthday, and it was still raining. My brother Eddie took me to the Dominion or the Paramount up towards Warren Street, and we saw *Genevieve* and *Doctor in the House*, a double bill. That was my birthday treat, and I remember that more than the bloody Coronation.'

For most people in the late forties and early fifties, going to the pictures was the basic night out. Everyone I spoke to had memories of trips to the cinema. People used to flock into the West End to see first run or art-house movies. Paul C was one of them. 'I used to go to see two or three movies in the West End every Saturday, then go down to the British Airways West London Terminal, and get the Sunday papers on the Saturday evening. This was very daring [laughs]. I had a fondness for all-night cinema. In the sixties, I went to see a whole night of Laurel and Hardy, twenty to thirty shorts, or several B sci-fi films, Bogart films, B gangster films, and the audiences – it reminds me of Thomas Pynchon's phrase, "the whole sick crew" was in there [laughs]. The snoring started during the first movie. Others were sitting there with flasks, or, like myself, trying to pinch themselves awake at four o'clock in the morning. Movie number 26 comes on. I'm going to see this one through. Whooh, it's six o'clock. It was a dosshouse, really.'

For the locals, the West End cinema map was very different, as Olga Jackson remembers. 'Our entertainment in the evenings, we had three cinemas. There was the Dominion, the Astoria, and the Paramount in Tottenham Court Road, at the Warren Street end.'

These three cinemas, as Jeff Sloneem remembers, 'weren't like a West End cinema, they were the local cinema; and the films changed every week. My mother would say, "Which one should we go to?" and I remember once she just couldn't decide, so we went to the Dominion first, and then on to the Paramount, so we went twice on the same day.'

A trip to the pictures was a weekly treat for Mike O'Rouke. 'My mother used to take me to the pictures a lot when I was a boy, on Tuesday nights, to fit in with my mum's mum, who lived down in Neal Street. She used to babysit my sister, who's three years younger than me, so that Mum and me could go to the pictures.' Mike's mother chose from one of the three local cinemas, but if there was something specific she wanted to see, there were dozens of others a bus ride away.

Pat Jones was sometimes grateful for a bit of distance from anywhere people were likely to recognize her: 'Our mother used to knit all the time, in the pictures, wherever – she didn't have to look. We went to see *Sentimental Journey* at the Edgware Road. In those days you queued for the pictures, and normally they took you in different stages, so we had to be split up. Anyway, Mother was sitting a little way away, and her ball of wool rolled away down the slope to the front, and people were moving about and started to get tangled up in it. I was very shy and introverted in those days. I just curled up and wanted to die with embarrassment. Nothing embarrassed my mother.'

Living in Bedfordbury, Ronnie Mann had a rich selection of local cinemas to choose from. As well as the three already mentioned, there was 'A little cartoon cinema where St Martin's School of Art is, the Tatler. The Cameo was a news theatre down opposite Cecil Court. In Agar Street, you had another little cartoon theatre. Then there was the Tivoli, a big cinema in the Strand, and another small cartoon cinema on the left-hand side as you come out of Charing Cross station, and there was one in Piccadilly, a small cartoon cinema. There was always an organ playing at the Tivoli on a Sunday. They used to let you in at four, and you start queuing at about three if it was a good film, like *Rebel without a Cause*. You had the B film and the main film, but basically we used to get in early and the organ used to play. The Tivoli had a really good organ.' The Tivoli had, in fact, been built as a music hall in the late 1880s, but through the war and afterwards it was a cinema.

Saturday morning pictures was a ritual enjoyed by children all over the land and the West Enders were no different. Tricia Bryan recalls that she and her friends, who all lived in Bloomsbury, were quite prepared to travel some distance for their weekly cinematic treat. 'The Granada on the Euston Road was one place where we went and the Gaumont up by King's Cross was another.' The long-suffering Paramount in Tottenham Court Road was regularly filled with hordes of children who hissed, jeered, cheered, laughed, screamed and threw things at the villain of the piece every Saturday without fail. The din was incredible: looking back, my heart bleeds for the usherettes 'armed with nothing but a torch and a face like a sackful of spanners,' as one erstwhile young punter recalls.

The Saturday morning programmes would include cartoons, some vintage comedy shorts – sometimes silent – starring Laurel and Hardy, the Three Stooges, Abbott and Costello, or Charlie Chaplin, and last, but certainly not least, serials. Some cinemas would have as many as three serials on the go at one time, all ending in a weekly cliff-hanger to bring the young punters back for more. The idea of having more than one serial (each episode lasted about ten minutes) was to stagger them, so that if one week a serial ended, the children would have to come back the next Satur-day to see how the cliffhangers in the others were resolved. Of course, the one that had ended would be replaced with the start of another. The serials, many of them from the thirties and forties, fell into roughly three categories; westerns, sci-fi and what might loosely be called historical adventures. Favourites included the Lone Ranger, Hopalong Cassidy, the Cisco Kid, Roy Rogers, Batman, Jet Morgan, Flash Gordon, Tarzan, Robin Hood, William Tell, Zorro and the Scarlet Pimpernel.

The news and cartoon cinemas were less riotous. I remember many happy hours spent at the Cameo in Windmill Street. It was my local, and like other local children, I was devoted to the antics of Donald Duck, Mickey Mouse, Road Runner, Bugs Bunny and Pluto. The Cameo was also the cinema of choice for Graham and Olga Jackson. 'We went every Friday to see news and cartoons,' remembers Olga, 'and then we used to go into Fortes for ice cream and stuff.'

'I would have a milkshake, a hamburger, a knickerbocker glory,' Graham chimed in. 'Could never eat it all.'

Pat Jones went to the Cameo in Charing Cross Road opposite the Wyndhams Theatre. 'It was an hour's cartoons that repeated itself. I liked it so much I would sit there three times round for a shilling.'

The rolling programmes and cheap admission made the cartoon cinemas a great refuge: sometimes you didn't even need a shilling. 'If the weather wasn't so good,' remembers Tricia Bryan, 'we used to go in the Tatler in Charing Cross Road, bunk in through the back door and watch the cartoons two or three times over.' The back door of the Tatler, in Greek Street, also provided a way in for Janet Vance and her friends. One would pay admission and go and open the door for the others.

John Carnera did not let lack of funds stop him from going to the first-run cinemas in Leicester Square either. 'We'd pay for one to go in, and he'd go round and open the doors, so five or six would get in for the price of one. We'd do that at the Dominion, Leicester Square, the Odeon, the Warner, and of course the Empire. We used to bunk in all of them. It was a dare as much as anything; you know what kids are like.'

If you could not rustle up enough money to send in a Trojan horse, you had to find a more ingenious method. The 'Bury kids were past masters at this, according to Ronnie Mann: 'We would bunk in everywhere. When we were kids, and I'm talking about young, we used to go down the side street next to the Astoria, leading to Soho Square. Well, there was a window to the ladies' lavatory, and I don't know how high up it was, but as kids it seemed high. One of the iron bars was loose, so a small kid could squeeze through the one that was missing and drop in, down into the ladies' lavatory, and then come out, open the push bars, and you'd all go in. We would make a sort of human pyramid, and as I was one of the younger ones, and my older brother was the leader of the local gang, I was always nominated to go in, whether I wanted to or not, and I was petrified.

'I remember the last time I did it: I was getting older and fatter, and they were pushing me through, and unfortunately for me there was some poor woman on the bog, and she hears this noise, and I don't know whether she realizes it's a kid, eight or nine, but all she can see is a face looking down on her having a pee or a poop or whatever she was doing, and this scream rent the air, and all I can remember is everybody trying to pull me down, and I'm stuck between the bars. That route was never used again.

'The London Pavilion you could go in through the cleaners' entrance, if you knew it. It was like offices, but you knew the doors to go in, and you'd bunk in there. I remember there was at least a dozen of us. When the film was on, and it was dark, we all used to crawl in on our hands and knees. If anybody come, you'd be like frozen

331

statues. And I can recall a guy coming up, a workman obviously coming up to get something walking up the side [of the auditorium], and of course he's hit something, and he's said "What the bleeding hell's that?" and he's struck a match or something to see what he's hit, and he probably wouldn't have done nothing, but we all run. And of course the poor sods in the pictures must have wondered what was happening, with a dozen kids running backwards and forwards, everybody screaming, usherettes chasing us.'

Pat and Barbara Jones enjoyed free cinema, too, although they did not have to sneak in. 'In two of our bedrooms,' Barbara explained, 'if you put your ear to the wall, you could actually hear the dialogue, let alone the music, from the Tivoli, and the organ. So, for that reason, we had two free tickets to every new film that came on.'

They had similar access to the Adelphi Theatre. 'We met Tommy Handley and the *ITMA* crew because they were right next to the Adelphi,' Barbara remembers, 'and people such as Dick Bentley and Jimmy Edwards – who later became one of my father's drinking friends, along with Tony Hancock, in the Coal Hole pub near the Savoy. We practically lived in the Adelphi Theatre.' Both sisters had fond memories of the 'Green Room Rag' at the Adelphi, a regular Sunday afternoon fund-raising event where they met the stars, who played a revue featuring excerpts from the main shows in town.

Even if you didn't get a complimentary ticket, going to the theatre could be cheaper than the cinema. 'If you wanted to see a show,' Barbara

Jones remembers, 'you would go in the morning and pay sixpence for a sort of raffle ticket that would be put on these little wooden folding stools lined up outside the theatre, and that would be your place in the queue to come and get up in the gods.'

Ronnie Mann was another regular theatre-goer as a boy. 'My mum's brother, Uncle Alf, was assistant stage manager at the Hippodrome. We used to get lots of complimentary tickets, so as a kid I went to see things at nearly every theatre in the West End. I remember seeing *The Blue Lamp* at the Hippodrome. We were sitting there watching it, when they were supposed to be searching for the bloke who killed Dixon of Dock Green and that, and they had actors, dressed up in modern copper's uniforms walking up and down the aisles looking for this guy, so he jumps up out of the audience and runs up, a gun comes out, Bang, and it was terrific at the time. Today you'd think it was corny, but I loved it.'

Ronnie's social life also included dancing at the Lyceum. 'It was a ballroom. Proper ballroom dancing, no jiving. It was big bands. In the late fifties, there was a crucial change, with the different music coming in. First you had jazz, then you had rock 'n' roll, and the Lyceum gradually changed, because of the demand. They started doing rock 'n' roll music with a DJ on a Monday, and then they did it every lunchtime, from twelve to two, and I used to go there after work in the market, from twelve to two, to have a dance. 'By the time I finished, the Lyceum had maybe two nights of ballroom dancing a week and the rest was just jiving – and it was absolutely packed, jammed solid. Girls came from everywhere because it was the West End, they used to come from miles around to go to the Lyceum, it was incredible. It was central, it was inexpensive to get in, and it was the place to be. Every era has its place to be, right for the time, then gone. I had my teeth knocked out down there with a knuckleduster when I was nineteen: I was dancing with the wrong girl.'

Anne Payne also liked to dance. After she met her future husband, 'We used to go to jazz clubs at 100 Oxford Street and went to the Cy Laurie club in Ham Yard. We enjoyed Trad jazz. We went to the Lyceum, sometimes, for the dancing, and there was a youth club down Pavilion Road, a side road opposite the side of Peter Jones, that was connected to Holy Trinity Church at Sloane Square. We had dances there. It wasn't particularly cool, but it was good just to get out.'

Ronnie Brace never actually lived in the West End, but his father's brother, Bruce Brace, owned a couple of nightclubs, Winston's and Churchill's, in Bond Street. 'When I was sixteen, we used to go down to my uncle's club quite regularly. Of course it was amazing for me, being down there, listening to what was going on in that club, seeing the women. We used to take friends down there. Not my mates, my parents' mates. The club was incredible, who they had in the cabaret: Marty Wilde, when he first started; Eartha Kitt – she'd just won over Paris, apparently, and came over here, they gave her her first job [in Britain] and she was a sensation; Barbara Windsor – she was only seventeen or eighteen then, in the cabaret; Danny La Rue; Carl Barriteau – a Jamaican clarinettist, and a great character. He led the combo, the orchestra in the club, or was part of it, you know. All the starlets used to come in, and top people.

'As my dad was the owner's brother, whenever we went in there a bottle of champagne went on the counter. I'd most probably get a light drink of some sort, you know – I was too young to drink – and then everyone would have a free breakfast about one in the morning, which is like a huge mixed grill, sausages, eggs – all on the house. There was money in the club. Champagne was expensive, you know, and specialist foods – steaks obviously and that sort of thing. Whether they had membership or not I don't know, but that would have been another way of getting cash.'

Two of Ann Lee's uncles worked on the night-club scene. 'They were a couple of characters,' she remembers. 'Uncle Tom was a glorified doorman, but Uncle Jim – he had a signed photograph from Frank Sinatra, he wanted him to go over to America to work with him, but my Auntie Else wouldn't go, and he never forgave her for it. They'd finish in the early hours, and if they'd had a drink at the clubs, they'd go to a pub in Covent Garden at like, five in the morning. At half-past seven they'd be rolling drunk, and with a big bunch of flowers for my nan, and she'd open the door and there they were, kaylied, saying "Here you are, Mother." She hadn't seen them for a fortnight... She'd come out and shout up to my mum, "Kitty!" and my mum would hear and come out and Nan would say "Tommy and Jimmy are in there." So my poor old mum would have to go down there and say, "You two. Cab. Home. You're not sitting there annoying her."

'How my Uncle Tom never killed himself or anybody else I'll never know. He used to arrive at our house early in the morning – I'd be up getting ready for school, or work, or whatever – knock on the door and you'd hear Mum go, "Oh, good God. Get in here." And he'd be like that [bent virtually double] and she'd scurf him in, sit him down and take his car keys. Because if you drank and drove in those days, nobody said a word unless you had an accident, then you got the book thrown at you. She used to pour coffee down him, and he'd say, "I'm going,", and she'd say, "You're not driving, Tommy." "Yes I am!" And he'd get the keys and go. My mum was very family, she worried for all of them, and she'd phone Auntie Doll: "Doll, he's just left me. I've tried to stop him getting into the car." Within fifteen minutes he'd phone to say he's home, all the way to Shepherd's Bush. How he got there, we don't know, and he never had one accident.'

In the same way as the great majority of West Enders never ventured into a nightclub – or if they did, it was to work behind the bar or on the bandstand – they lived among culture, but weren't necessarily fans. My father was a big ballet fan, however, and a trip to the ballet with him was always tarted up as a treat – which it was, in a way, but I was always tense in case he found something to complain about. I was taken to Covent Garden as a birthday gift when I was very young – we had a box and everything – and as Father behaved himself, it was pure joy. I loved the glittering glass and gold of the theatre, the music, the wonderful costumes and, of course, the dancing.

However, my half-sister wasn't as lucky when her turn came. They had seats in the front stalls to watch the Russian Ballet perform *Swan Lake*. All went swimmingly until the corps embarked on the dance of the cygnets. Father, who was a man of strong views and even stronger language, was underwhelmed by their technique. He remarked in loud tones that the 'Fucking corps are ragged, look at 'em, all over the fucking place, like a bunch of fucking cart-horses.' Sadly, the dancers heard him, and even if they didn't actually understand what he was saying, they grasped his sentiments and were a little thrown. The corps became more ragged: some stopped dead in their tracks, and Father's comments grew even louder.

At this point, an elderly gentleman, who was beautifully turned out in evening dress, leaned over to remonstrate with Father. Not only was his language 'deplorable', the gentleman said, but he was also ruining the performance for the less exacting members of the audience, and would he 'Please be quiet or leave.' Father took exception, and offered to give the old boy a whack. The gentleman became flustered. 'You can't hit me, I'm dying of cancer,' he said.

'Good!' roared Father, and got to his feet. He pointed to the exit. 'Outside, and I'll give you such a smack you won't live long enough to die of fucking cancer.' Luckily, Father was escorted from the premises by several ushers, the corps pulled itself together and the performance continued.

Covent Garden was the centre of British opera, yet few, if any, locals took the opportunity to go, although I heard my fair share of arias as a little girl thanks to the great tenor, Gigli. He was a little round man in his sixties and when he was shopping in my dad's 'bookshop', he used to sing as he browsed. He would sit me on his lap sometimes and sing in Parmigiani's, when I was having cassata ice cream. I never really liked cassata, because of the bits, so I used to pick the bits out, because I was – am – a chocolate ice cream kind of gal.

While I could find no interviewees who had actually attended the opera, Graham Jackson revealed that he'd 'trod the boards at Covent Garden. It was through the school, because they wanted chorus boys, and I was in the school choir at St Martin's. We went there, did all the training for Tchaikovsky's *Queen of Spades*, and *A Midsummer Night's Dream*. We could never go on stage after ten o'clock, so we could never see the end of it ... there were certain restrictions on us. I quite enjoyed the experience, because we were allowed to go in there early, we went in their canteen. The best place, though, was the engineers' shop. [Laughter] They had some wonderful pictures on the walls in there.'

For most West Enders, a trip to the pub or cinema was all they could afford, especially if they were

338

bringing up children. It was only once their kids had grown up, and could contribute to the family purse, that they could spread their wings a little. 'They used to have tea dances at the Waldorf,' Ann Lee remembers, 'and anyone could go to those. The ladies in the flats, the ones that were close and that had stayed friends for many years, they used to have a day out, or an evening out, and would go somewhere that they couldn't afford when they were younger, and now they could.'

Ann remembers one particular night when her mother and some friends from the estate went for a game of bingo at the Lyceum in the early sixties. 'There was about six of them. They had a win, so they shared it between them, and they'd all had a couple of drinks, and none of them were real drinkers. My mum had the filthiest laugh ever, and all of a sudden you could hear this laughing, and my dad said, "That sounds like your mum." Well, I looked out the window, and they were all linked arms walking down Drury Lane, laughing their heads off. They'd all had a few. They weren't really drunk, but for them, they were drunk. You could hear her laughing all the way down to the block – you could hear them all laughing, but her laugh was really, really loud. And she walked in the door and said, "Hello love, I've had a win." And he said, "Yeah, you was also laughing a bit loud." She went, "Ah shut up, you miserable sod. You're not spoiling my evening. I've had a lovely time."

'My parents never had the money when we were kids to do things like that, and as we were growing up and putting our bit back into the home, they could afford to go out and do things. And it was nice to see my mum get all dolled up. "Where you going this time?" "Oh, we're going down the Waldorf to a tea dance." And they'd all get up and have a waltz together. It was nice for them, but it took a while for them to be able to do it. It's like that for all of us, though, when you've got growing-up kids, you go without for a while, then all of a sudden, it's Whoopee!'

And after all, if the residents of England's premier playground couldn't make a little whoopee after a lifetime of hard work and watching outsiders at their revels, what a dreary old life it would have been. And one thing that all my contributors have in common is the sure knowledge that life in the West End was rarely, if ever, dreary; there was simply too much going on for that.

15

Working Girls

Smell evokes memories better than any other sense. Coal smoke always reminds me of steam trains, and of London in the dark, cold days of a fifties winter. If you add to the smoking coal any one or, better still, several of the following – a blast of roasting coffee beans, a whiff of garlic cooking in butter or exotic spices sizzling in oil, perhaps a hint of the distinctive odour of old books, and the heady floral notes of cheap perfumes – I am a toddler again, back in the Soho of my childhood, watching the passing scene with wide-eyed wonder.

The sources of the perfume – Evening in Paris or Carnation – were the 'Ladies of the Night', who were often on the streets in broad daylight. They fascinated me then, and have lingered long in my memory. In those days, many a doorway and most of the street corners of Soho had their complement of 'tarts', as they were often known. While my father was exchanging ideas, inform-ation, insults and drinks with his cronies, or erotic literature for hard cash with his customers, I was free to watch the people loitering, hurrying, strolling or, occasionally, running along Soho's streets, darting through courts and alleyways. From late in the afternoon, it was the smartly dressed and fragrant working girls who attracted my attention.

Along with the show people, they brightened up the dinginess of austerity-bound Britain in the years immediately after the war. Resources rarely ran to snazzy paint for street doors, cheerful curtains or jaunty awnings for shops. Contrary to popular belief, wartime and post-war women's clothing could be bright and cheery – it is the black and white films and photographs of the time that have led us to believe that fashions were dreary. Londoners, however, often chose to wear more sober hues because smoke from open fires blackened not only old buildings, but also collars and cuffs. The famous pea-soupers, the stinking sulphur-yellow smogs that were so much a part of London life in the early fifties, left everything smothered in layers of soot and grey, surprisingly greasy, smudges and blobs. As soap was precious and the supply of hot water was grudging – a bath was limited to a few measly inches and couples and siblings were encouraged to share their weekly dip – it made sense to choose dark colours that didn't show the grime and thus cut down on washing. Successful prostitutes, on the other hand, could afford both black market soap and to send their clothes to dry cleaners or laundries: such extravagance was considered a legitimate expense as being well turned out was good for business.

The bright red lips and nails of the working girls also provided more splashes of colour in the general dinginess, and their clothes added a much-needed touch of glamour. When everyone was allocated a mere forty-eight clothing coupons a year, and a coat would take sixteen, a costume twelve and then there were underwear, blouses, skirts and footwear to gobble up the rest of the measly allowance, it was no wonder that most people's garments looked distinctly frayed and tatty. 'Make do and mend' became the order of the day. In contrast, the working girls had an everyday chic that was the street-level equivalent of the stars of Hollywood. Second-hand glamour was an effective antidote to the relentless insecurity, squalor, misery and poverty that went with the war and its aftermath – it is no wonder that so many girls had their heads turned by it.

'Coming to London was like one possibly going

over to America,' remembered Clare, who fell into prostitution as a teenager soon after the Second World War. 'The women I was introduced to were like film stars to me.'

Prostitution and the West End have gone together since before Nell Gwyn was plucked from the streets of Covent Garden by Charles II. The heart of the vice trade drifted slowly west, along with that of the entertainment industry, in the nineteenth and early twentieth centuries. Piccadilly, the Haymarket and the streets of Soho grew in importance as streetwalkers' beats, while Fleet Street, the Strand and Covent Garden went into a slow decline. West End girls were seen as a cut above the poor wretches who would do anything and anyone for gin money in the mean streets of the East End. The victims of Jack the Ripper were all miserably poor, while the brothels and seraglios Up West were patronized by the aristocracy.

The First World War brought hundreds of thousands of young men to London on their way to the front line, or back for a few days' precious leave. This created an enormous rise in demand for sex workers in the capital, and particularly the West End, where so many other entertainments were on offer. The supply of willing women rose to meet the demand, creating a public scandal.

After the war, a sexual revolution swept through London. Those who had survived or avoided the trenches, and the Spanish flu pandemic that followed, flung themselves into a world of dance crazes, jazz, booze, drugs – cocaine was a particular favourite – and scandalous behaviour. The 'fast set' based many of their activities in West End clubs, where 'hostesses' blurred the line between show business and prostitution. Soho and Shepherd Market became famous – or notorious, depending on your point of view – red light districts. The money to be made meant there was no shortage of recruits. Even in the Depression of the thirties, working girls could earn £15–20 in a four-hour shift, at a time when a shopgirl was lucky to get more than £2 a week.

In the Second World War, history repeated itself. Camps in the Home Counties filled with young servicemen, most of whom headed straight for London when at liberty, packing the West End streets with young men who were in their prime and far from home. Essentially anonymous, they were free to seek out sexual adventures they'd never find in their own communities, where they were bound by strict social mores that demanded that a wedding came before a leg-over, and there was often hell to pay if it didn't. Reliable birth control was not always readily available and the stigma of being an unmarried mother was something no 'respectable' girl would willingly face. The tarts cajoling them from dark doorways provided many young men with their first opportunity for sexual adventuring, and the very real possibility that they might die tomorrow emboldened them to seize the chance.

The boom time for West End prostitutes really got under way when America entered the war. The vast numbers of GIs – 'over-paid, over-sexed and over here' – who came to London were even further from home and the disapproving, prying eyes of those who knew them. Better still, as far as the vice trade was concerned, they brought with them lively libidos, large pay packets and no inhibitions about spending their money on a good time.

The extra money to be earned brought more women into the streets, parks and nightclubs of the West End. In 1931, there were around 3,000 prostitutes in London, but by the end of the war this number had risen, at a very conservative estimate, to 6,700. This did not include what I think of as part-time or casual sex workers. Some were married to servicemen who were away in the forces, and saw prostitution as a way to earn extra money to buy expensive luxuries like black market goods, and to pay for nights on the town. Others were single mothers desperate for money to support their children, or war widows who also had offspring to keep. Opportunistic single women, often teenagers, were sometimes prepared to go with men for a bit of excitement, money, glamour and such elusive luxuries of life as nylons, chocolates, cigarettes – things that the American troops, in particular, had in abundance. These part-timers dropped in and out of the trade; some only hit the streets at weekends, having worked as factory hands, shop assistants or land girls during the week.

One interviewee, who was just fourteen at the time, remembers it all vividly. 'My first sexual encounter was in Green Park with one of the girls. I can't remember exactly what tree it was – it was just one or two back, because in the blackout you couldn't see very far – but it was ten shillings, which was a lot of money then. She was fair-haired and – we used to sit on the bench talking afterwards – apparently her husband was away at war, and she was a clippie. And that was a – well, I won't say it was a regular thing, but after that, if I had ten bob, I'd go down there.'

In the war (and, in fact, right up to the Street Offences Act of 1959), there were broadly two main classes of prostitute: those who worked as 'hostesses' in clubs, and streetwalkers. There were, in turn, two types of streetwalker, those who took their clients to nearby flats and those who did the deed outside – what my mother used to call the 'ten bob and find your own railings' sort of girl, like the clippie mentioned by our previous punter above. Hyde Park was a popular place for the latter, although the blackout provided many more nooks and crannies for such brief assignations. Those who were organized enough to take their clients indoors found that more and better flats to rent came on the market as wealthy people left the city to escape the bombing. As a precaution, streetwalkers rarely lived in the flats where they did business, which is why the abundance of rentable property was such a bonus.

There were so many women on the streets at times that they found themselves competing, sometimes literally fighting, for space. Newcomers had either to find new pitches or to buy out someone who was retiring. The buyer would pay a proportion of her earnings for an agreed amount of time, and the seller made sure the girls who had beats nearby were no trouble.

In the main, hostesses took their clients to a hotel or, more dangerously, to their own homes. Writing about nightclub hostesses in *Madness after Midnight*, jazz musician Jack Glicco states baldly that 'It was the girls that brought the trade. It was the girls who boosted the sales of drink. It was the girls who, when the night was done, took their chosen clients home.' During his long career as a musician in the West End's many nightclubs, he met literally thousands of such women. 'They parade through my memory in an endless stream: tall and short, dark and fair, old and young, wicked and (reasonably) good.'

After the end of the war, the GIs left and many of the 'casuals' gradually drifted off, clearing the way for a more organized trade. There was still money to be made, as men had got into the habit of using prostitutes in the war, and the fall in prices immediately after the Americans left was steadied by an increasing demand for the services of women still on the game. There was so much money in vice that the authorities feared – with good reason, as it turned out – that the police would be corrupted. When the end of the blackout made the extent of prostitution more obvious, they instituted a crackdown. Arrests for prostitution rose from 1,983 in 1945 to 4,289 in 1946 and 5,363 in 1948.

This wave of arrests did not greatly affect the number of girls on the streets, who treated the inevitable fine as a business expense. In the post-war years, Owen Gardner worked in Page's on Shaftesbury Avenue. The company's offices looked out on Romilly Street. 'We had big long windows at the time, and you could look out and see two or three of them walking up and down there – and you could see the police pick them up, too.

'The girls seem to regard it as "Oh well, Thursday's my day to be collected," sort of thing, and go to court. In those days, in the *Evening Standard* – or maybe the *News* – they used to have Courts Day by Day, and they would get fined thirty shillings or so. This was her 105th conviction, that kind of nonsense. It was just, like, in their costs, a sort of tax.' Owen was not exaggerating. Lots of the girls could have taken out a season ticket at Marlborough Street court, racking up literally hundreds of convictions.

Some of the girls were independent, while others would turn over their earnings to pimps and ponces. The difference between ponces and pimps is that a pimp has a 'stable' of girls, and actively promotes them, while a ponce lives off the earnings of one or two women with whom he has some kind of relationship. Sometimes the line between being a ponce and a lover was blurred. Leo Zanelli remembers a working girl called Rita, who lived across the road from him in Romilly Street. 'She was living with a black guy there, who was a very nice chap. You used to see him in the street, and she was always hanging out the window.

'You know, a lot is made of pimps, and there are, if you like, pimps who have groups of girls and that sort of thing, but your average prostitute was basically working on her own. She's hardly going to strike a meaningful relationship with someone working in an office somewhere. It's got to be one of the lads from the streets or round about, and they really were girlfriend and boyfriend, that sort of relationship. Sometimes they would have a row and just split up. I can't really remember anybody being terrified or saying, "If I walk away, he's going to come round and beat me up," although I have no doubt it happened.'

Leo was right. There were vicious, violent pimps in the West End. In *Madness after Midnight*, Jack Glicco makes it clear that he knew many a nightclub hostess with loose knicker elastic and a greedy ponce in the background. He writes about Therese, who 'genuinely hated the game' and 'confessed to me that she was going to chuck it. She was going to go respectable.' Therese planned to break the news to her ponce the very night she confessed her longing for a normal life, but, knowing the man in question had a reputation for vicious and ruthless behaviour, Glicco warned her to be careful. She simply nodded and smiled.

'I can see her yet,' Glicco writes, 'her eyes glowing with pride in herself at taking the decision; her soft skin clear and lovely.' Six months after this conversation, Glicco saw her again. 'She was soliciting at the corner of Bond Street and Piccadilly. Her face was partly in shadow, and when I went up to her and spoke I saw why. Down that once-lovely face ran a long and still livid scar. She did not tell me how she got it, and I did not ask. I could guess.'

In the mid twentieth century, the premier pimps in London were the Messina brothers. Usually described as Maltese, they were the sons of a Sicilian, Giuseppe Messina, who set himself up as a brothel-keeper, first in Malta – where a large concentration of British troops provided plenty of custom – and then in Egypt. His five sons all went into the family business. In 1934, Eugenio – known as Gino – came to England, and his brothers Carmelo, Alfredo, Salvatore and Attilio soon followed. Before long, they were dominating the West End's vice trade, building an empire that lasted well into the fifties. They made several thousand pounds a week from their girls, whom they paid £50 a week.

The girls controlled by the Messinas were put to work from four o'clock on weekday afternoons to as late – or early – as six in the morning. The brothers, or their henchmen, checked to make sure that they were on their beat and working the hours dictated by Gino, who appears to have been the dominant brother. They ran their girls from a bewildering number of addresses throughout the West End, and kept them on the move. They took these flats in a variety of false names, and retained the services of a solicitor to pay the rates, so neither their real names nor their favourite aliases ever appeared on official documents.

To maximize their profits, the brothers introduced the 'short-time' or 'ten-minute rule'. This meant that a client had to be in and out, as it were, in ten minutes or less. If they strayed over this time limit, then someone, usually the prostitute's 'maid', would bang on the door to remind them to get their trousers on or to cough up more money for extra time.

The rule was unpopular with punters, and its

enforcement sometimes led to violence, but it soon became the norm. Quentin Crisp, in *The Naked Civil Servant*, recounts how, when he was working in Wardour Street in the fifties, he and his colleagues would watch the girls leaning against the wall across the way from the office window. 'We measured the amount of time they were out of sight with the men they had picked up. Including getting into her flat and returning from it to the street, one woman was sometimes away for only seven minutes.'

The rule meant each girl could turn over many more punters in a working night. They could service as many as five or six men an hour, at as much as £5 a time. Girls regularly made £100 a night, a truly enormous sum when you consider that the average weekly wage was £8. Marthe Watts, who wrote of her life as a Messina girl in her memoir, *The Men in My Life*, reported servicing forty-nine men in a fourteen-hour shift on VE night: she was going for a round fifty, but she either ran out of time or stamina.

As well as making economic sense, the rule also meant that the girls had no chance to get to know their clients, or to socialize with the locals. This suited the Messinas, as isolated girls were more vulnerable and easier to control. Nearly all their girls were recruited from overseas. Even before the brothers' reign was established, the young women walking the dim, sooty streets of Soho came to be known collectively as 'Fifis', as so many of them came from France.

The British had long been of the opinion that the French were an unusually sexy and uninhibited race, with little, if any, of the tortured hypocrisy that we have historically displayed towards our 'baser' instincts. In the forties and fifties, a French girl was considered the epitome of sexual adventurousness, thanks in part to the pornographic films, books and pictures smuggled in from 'the Continent' by men like my father. The French 'sex kitten' (why a kitten should be considered sexy, only the lords of the tabloids and fifties boys of all ages knew) Brigitte Bardot's pout and figure featured large in many an Englishman's fantasies and because she was out of their reach, her compatriots on Old Compton Street had to substitute.

Later, pornography flooded in from Scandinavia, and Swedish girls took up the rather dubious mantle of fantasy nation – hence the cards festooning street doors and newsagents' windows advertising the services of French and Swedish models. Of course, not all of the women were foreign. Some hailed from no further away than Wapping, Slough or Pease Pottage, but they knew that a little creative advertising could be very good for business.

There was another advantage for the Messinas in employing foreign girls. As they often had a rudimentary grasp of English, the pimps could keep them isolated from everyone except each other. Those who joined the Messina family had their activities closely supervised by their maids, and by the brothers themselves. They encouraged their girls to spy on one another and to report any misdemeanours. Transgressions were punished with violence. Gino Messina favoured using an electric flex, ripped from a standard lamp, to beat his women into submission.

Because foreign nationals involved in prostitution could be deported, the Messina brothers developed a lively side trade in providing the girls with English husbands. Duncan Webb, a campaigning journalist on the *People* newspaper, made it his mission to bring down the Messina brothers. He was particularly scandalized by the way they traded in national allegiances: 'By bribery and corruption they organised marriages of convenience both in Britain and abroad to enable their harlots to assume British nationality.'

They were not alone in doing that, although they were probably the first to set up an organized trade. For a fee, a broker would arrange a marriage between an Englishman in need of money and a continental – usually, but by no means always, French – woman to provide her with British nationality and a British passport. Once the ceremony was over, man and wife usually didn't need to meet again. Marthe Huebourg, a young Frenchwoman, and Arthur Watts, a semi-derelict drunk, went through just such an arranged marriage in November 1937. They met briefly before they were married, and afterwards only once, when a magistrate demanded reassurance that Marthe was entitled to live in England, Gino Messina managed to prise Arthur loose from his bar stool long enough for him to appear in court to vouch for his own existence, and assure the magistrate that Marthe was indeed a citizen and thus could not be deported. Marthe never saw her husband again.

Once a young recruit had been married off, she would be brought to London and set up to work in a flat – usually, but not exclusively, in Soho or Mayfair – along with a maid. Maids performed several vital functions. They were literally maids in that they kept the place of business clean and tidy, and shopped and cooked for any girls working from that address. Other duties went beyond the usual job description for domestic service. They had to keep a weather eye on the customers, make sure that business was conducted in an orderly fashion and call for help from the pimp or even the police if things became disorderly.

After the Street Offences Act drove the girls off the streets, the maids took care of the waiting punters, collecting the money, and so on, but the practice of having maids came into being long before the Act, and there are maids shopping in Berwick Street for their ladies to this day.

Once the Messina brothers had been brought down – largely because of their exposure by the efforts of the indefatigable Duncan Webb – a Maltese-born East End gangster, Frank Mifsud, became the dominant figure in the vice trade. Mifsud and his partner, Bernie Silver, had a new angle. They also owned many of the flats rented out to prostitutes, and ran drinkers and spielers, but 'Big Frank' took in even more money by telling pimps and ponces that if they drank or gambled anywhere other than in his establishments, their girls would lose their flats.

Men who lived off immoral earnings were despised, and often victimized by 'honest villains' and other criminals. Thugs like Tommy Smithson would 'shake down' these men for easy money, knowing they would not go to the police. There was a racial overtone to some of this violence. Many pimps and ponces were overseas nationals – in the fifties, a quarter of the men charged with living off immoral earnings in London were Maltese.

It's hard for people today to realize just how many girls there were on the streets in the fifties. They were a tourist attraction in themselves, and not just for prospective clients. Paul C, who lived in Crawley, remembers taking the train to London after school with friends to soak up the sights, sounds and smells of Soho: 'It was twilight time. Winter late afternoons. Not nights. The girls being on the street was a revelation to me, really, because there were so many of them. Whatever direction you went, they were there, and it just seemed to be very busy from that point of view, but also busy from the point of view of life going on, different nationalities working and enjoying themselves.

'We had great fun observing the way the girls proceeded, which was to sort of talk guys in off the street, and then we would see them, even follow them in our imaginations going up the stairs to the room, and we'd see the light go on, and we would think, from a young male's point of view, oh yes, someone else has scored here!

'The girls seemed extraordinarily attractive and well made up, and had very attractive, very sexy clothes. They handled themselves almost like a dance routine. They'd come up, sashay up to someone, move over to the side, go round them. They could tell immediately if people were interested or not, and they seemed to gravitate back if someone was umm-ing and aah-ing, for instance. It wasn't just a case of standing there waiting for guys to come up to them, they seemed to be more pro-active – to coin a phrase. It was almost as though they were sweeping. Figuratively speaking.

'They seemed to be very practised in everything they did, obviously. They seemed to be very efficient. And what was intriguing, and sexual, and mysterious to us was that it seemed matter-of-fact to them, a job, and that was one of the most remarkable things about it. You have a job selling your body. This is amazing to a fourteen-year-old. It was X-rated.

'Once or twice, I remember getting into conversations with the girls, who were very good-humoured about it. They tolerated me and my friends, and answered our questions, more or less. How much business do you do in a day? All that sort of thing.

'If you asked them if they'd do business, they'd say, no, not you love. [laughs] Come back in ten years. And of course we didn't have any crisp notes, those great big notes they were interested in.'

Ann Lee, who lived in Covent Garden, was told 'we mustn't go to Soho. Good girls didn't go to Soho, that's where only the prostitutes were', but she found the entertainment in the street scene irresistible. 'We used to walk down Soho, we used to love it, we used to watch the girls plying their trade. We thought it was brilliant. We wouldn't have done it, we'd have been too scared, but to actually watch them, it was like "Oh my Gawd, look." And it was literally every other doorway.'

On Sunday afternoons after the war, Old Compton Street was thick with the girls, their poodles and their prospective punters. They discussed terms as the local people passed by on their way to or from church, or simply strolled in the sunshine on their precious day off. Jeff Sloneem, who lived at the Wardour Street end of Old Compton Street until 1953, remembers that 'I asked my mother, "Who are those women?" and she said, "Oh, they're looking for their husbands." But they used to take over Old Compton Street on a Sunday; on a Sunday afternoon the road was full of these women – and men.'

It was the sheer visibility of prostitution that prompted the Street Offences Act of 1959, which made it illegal for the first time to 'solicit for the purposes of prostitution'. This meant that the girls could be charged simply for being on the street; prior to this, money had to have changed hands, or a deal had to have been struck, before the woman could be arrested. The Act also reinstated prison sentences.

It did not attempt to end prostitution, just make it less visible – something that was no great problem for Sohoites, who were, in the main, a broad-minded, tolerant bunch. It achieved that, but it also made prostitutes far more vulnerable to acts of violence from punters. In the past, someone would have noticed if a girl was not back on her beat in a reasonable time, but shutting the girls

357

away in flats meant that this simple protection was removed. Having a maid, or having more than one girl working from the same address, provided a measure of security, but making the penalties for running a disorderly house much more severe effectively stripped the working girl of even that safeguard.

Despite the risks, the girls' response to the new Act was to retreat to flats and advertise for clients, although this was not possible for them all, as Chas McDevitt recalls. 'My dad ran the coffee bar for me when I wasn't there. He used to be there all night, until five in the morning. He used to talk about these two girls who'd come in in the last throes for coffees. They would help him clean the place out, sweep it up and everything. They actually worked Hyde Park. One of them came from Cardiff. She was married, and came up from Cardiff on the train, worked late evenings and went back first thing in the morning.

'They were moaning because they were being forced out of the park into premises, and they said the cheapest place they could get was seventy-five quid a week, and she was only earning ten shillings a trick in the park, so, you know, although her prices would go up if she had a house, she couldn't see the logic of it.'

Because they could not parade their wares in the street, the girls had to find other media. Some windows were full of cards advertising their services. 'That thing about "large chests",' remembers Ronnie Mann, 'That's what people used to put in the newsagents' windows, and I used to think, Why have these women got so many large chests to sell? Why are they offering French polishing?'

Others simply put a sign on the street door leading to their flat. 'I always remember we used to see the doors with "Model" advertised outside,' said Graham Jackson. "Ring bell and walk up." We would dare each other to ring the bell. One day, a big Greek-looking guy came down the stairs and chased us; we ran all the way home. It was just a thing to do, you know. We just hung around, did things. We never thought we was in any danger.'

Some girls continued to chance their arm on the streets, and take clients into alleys or other out-of-the-way places, as Graham Jackson recalls: 'In Sandringham Buildings, in the Charing Cross Road, they used to have wash houses, and all the prostitutes used to use the wash houses, and we'd be like, "Look at what I found," and they would be condoms. Of course, we didn't know what it was all about, but they'd use all that, all round there, the prostitutes, all round them back streets.'

The landings of the various blocks of flats were a refuge for girls without a flat to take their clients to. 'There were no prostitutes in our flats [New-port Dwellings],' remembers Sonia Boulter, 'but they were around, you know, and late at night you'd get the ones who weren't the regulars come in, and sometimes you might find them on the stairs. My dad used to throw them out when he came home from work in the middle of the night.'

As I seemed to spend an awful lot of time watching street scenes, I soon came to recognize the regular working girls and they recognized me. You could always tell them from the rest of the female population, because they were much better dressed. What's more, they – or, more than likely, their pimps – had the kind of money and contacts that allowed them to circumnavigate the rigid restrictions of rationing by buying from expensive black market traders. Some girls would carry a bunch of keys that they would rattle to attract the attention of passing men. Others would simply offer to 'do business' in quiet voices heavy with a variety of accents.

For me and for others, the girls on the street were a reassuring presence. They seemed to love kids, as did many Sohoites, and I made quite a profit out of my platinum blond curls, big blue eyes and, later, a passing resemblance to the infant Princess Anne. The working girls would take me for ice cream and slip me the odd threepenny bit, silver sixpence or shilling, or sometimes as much as a florin, or even half a crown. How much depended on what they had handy in their purses and how good business had been, I suppose.

I wasn't the only one to profit. 'The girls used to stand in Newport Court,' remembers Ronnie Mann, 'and as a kid I went swimming up on Marshall Street and I walked through there, and because I had long, curly hair, one of them used to give me thruppence a week. I don't know why.'

Raye Du-Val, whose parents spent the war years in France working for the Resistance, lived much of his childhood on the Soho streets, and was befriended by several of the girls during the war. 'They used to buy me things, buy me sweets, and I would keep a look-out for them, I was doing that. Running round the corner for them. Would you get me some fags round the corner, things like that. They adopted me, really. I was like a little errand boy, and they loved me for it.

'You did things for them and... You know, I made quite a bit of cash. In those days, it was like a threepenny old joe or a silver tanner. Go and fetch the paper for them, something like that. I was busier then than I ever was. I was like a bit of an urchin, really. I got on well with the girls, you know, although I got a few cuffs here and there. Especially when she had a client or something, and I put my head round the door, I got a cuff round the earhole!'

I realize now that some of the women must have had children of their own. Janet Vance grew up in rooms in a top floor flat on the corner of Frith Street and Bateman Street, across from the Dog and Duck pub, which is still there today, and a cigarette factory, which isn't. 'We had one of the flats on the second floor and the other one, it was girls, prostitutes. They didn't work from there, but different girls did in the two flats on the first floor. There were two maids, Mina and Tina, they were twins, Italians. 'One of the girls was called Mitzi and she always used to say that she worked as a prostitute to keep her daughter at a private school, and that was where the money was going.'

The women that I came to think of as 'casuals' would come to London from other places, work the streets for a few days, then go home to their

361

children with enough money to tide them over until the next working visit. Others had had children that they'd been forced, by their pimps and circumstances, to have adopted. Some girls from the country and overseas had children left in the care of relatives back home, and they only got to see them when their pimps allowed them short holidays.

The one thing all these mothers had in common was that they missed their children dreadfully. They longed to be 'ordinary' wives and mothers, and snatched any spare moments with local children they'd taken a shine to – like me.

'They used to take me out,' Jeff Sloneem remembers. 'Quite a few of them had cars, and they used to park their cars in the car park [on a bomb site in Dean Street] and then do whatever they were going to do. Quite a lot of them took me out to tea at Lyons Corner House, and sometimes in the country, for rides in their cars. I suppose I was the little boy they never had.'

The girls also made it their business to protect the local children. My father was in the habit of abandoning my mother for various periods of time to take up with other women and I remember cowering in my bed when Father was terribly drunk and engaged in a furious and violent row with his latest mistress. They were going at it hammer and tongs and the altercation culminated in my father throwing her down the stairs. The fall broke several of her ribs, or so she claimed; it had certainly been a very violent row. I was so frightened that I ran into the street in my nightie looking for help. The local prostitutes rescued me,

362

calmed me down, organized a taxi to take the woman to hospital, forcibly relieved Father of the money to pay for it and, when he looked as if he was coming up for round two, slung him down the stairs for good measure. Then they took it in turns to sit with me until Father had sobered up enough to be thoroughly chastened and, more importantly, safe to resume his childcare duties.

'They were very good, actually, to us kids,' remembers Sonia Boulter. 'They knew us, a lot of us, by name. If anybody spoke to you – and you did get that, in those days, like a dirty old man – they would say, "Leave them alone." They would, you know, protect us.

'I was going down Gerrard Street to school, and there was a tramp sitting outside the post office there. She had everything around her, and a cup of tea in her hand, and as we walked past her, she started swearing and saying things, and she threw the tea over us. One of the prostitutes saw it and she came down and she really tore her off a strip for doing it, you know, "Leave those kids alone!" because she wasn't a regular, the tramp.'

Janet Vance agrees. 'They were always nice to us kids. If they were working and anyone came up to them when the kids were there, they'd just tell the blokes to move off. They were great. We never had any arguments with them and they always kept an eye out, and your parents, my mum, when she used to go shopping, used to ask them to keep an eye on me, and they'd keep an eye, as simple as that. They were great. No hassle what-soever. Nobody interfered with them, and they didn't interfere with us.

'The decent ones didn't come out 'til seven or eight at night, when they knew near enough that the kids were on their way indoors. On winter nights, obviously, the kids went in early, but they were out – they didn't work while the kids were around that little bit.'

The working girls were not only protective of us little girls. 'They used to be on the corners, and they used to know us,' John Carnera recalls. 'Because we lived there, they'd see us every day. And sometimes, when I was a bit older, and got a little bit tipsy, they'd take me home. "You live at number 45. This is where you belong." They were very good. Lovely ladies.'

Mel Edwards, whose father was landlord of a Covent Garden pub, had cause to be grateful to a prostitute. Apparently, there was a vicious knife fight going on in an alley that he was about to use as a short cut. A woman stepped out of a door-way and barred his way, recommending as she did so that he take the longer route. 'If I'd walked into that lot, I could have wound up dead, and she knew it,' he told me.

One or two of the girls did very well for them-selves. Raye Du-Val remembers 'a little one called Fifi – it really was her name – a little French girl, she was beautiful. She would come up to my flat, I would go up to hers. No monkey business, like – I didn't want to know. She used to come down to my place, the nights she wasn't working, and she told me a wonderful story.

'This guy would come up once a fortnight, a very wealthy guy, and he'd give her 300 in readies, didn't want to know about sex, didn't want anything. In fact he tried to wean her off. The story goes, lovely man, his wife was a cripple; he'd tell Fifi straight, "I'm not here for sex, or anything like that, I just want to talk. I go home, she doesn't even know who I am." He was a businessman, and do you know, he left her two million pounds. She got one of her kids educated at Roedean, and she had another girl at another posh school.'

Jack Glicco remembers a French girl called Jeanette, in *Madness after Midnight*, who had a 'fascinating accent and a body that was sheer perfection'. She stood out because of her charm and loveliness, but also because she escaped what he considered to be a virtually inevitable end. She kept her career brief, 'about a year, during which time she must have made a small fortune, then she left to marry a wealthy and respectable stockbroker. Wise girl. She made sure that she didn't go the same way as many of her friends: to drink or drugs and a poverty-stricken old age when her looks had gone.'

Fifi and Jeanette were very much the exceptions, though. Marthe Watts was originally drawn into prostitution by the promise of jewels, furs, fine food, good wine and expensive holidays. Although there was an element of this in her life, there was also plenty of squalor, drudgery and misery. The passages in her book, *The Men in my Life*, that cover the Messina years give a flavour of just how uncertain the times were. She estimates that she earned in excess of £150,000 for Gino Messina in an association that lasted more than

365

fifteen years, yet finished her working life with little more than she had begun it with: the clothes she stood up in and maybe a suitcase or two. Certainly, Gino kept the flat she'd paid for, and everything in it.

If Marthe Watts typified the life of the 'Fifi', Clare's story, told in the BBC series *Underworld* (first broadcast in 1994), represents the more conventional life of the 'home-grown' prostitute. Clare came to London as a wide-eyed sixteen-year-old at the end of the Second World War, and soon met her nemesis. 'He was a very good-looking man: beautiful teeth, gorgeous eyes. He was everything that I dreamed of... He asked me would I like a drink. He did, in fact, use the word "ponce", but I'd never heard it. I was in love, and the material things were very important to me, so I didn't really need much persuading.'

Clare's ponce soon set her up in a flat on the corner of Frith Street and Old Compton Street. On her first day she made about £8. Her ponce called it chicken feed, and lit a cigar with a pleated £1 note. 'I was broken-hearted. My father at that time was probably earning only eight to ten pounds a week... It was a lot of money to me. I wanted to make more. I wanted to prove I was better than other ladies. The more I made, the happier he was, and the happier he was, the happier I was. Stupid.'

Clare worked the short-time rule. The number of clients she had in a day 'varied: sometimes twenty, it could be thirty. It could even be more. He was a mad gambler, and I would say without a doubt that most of his money would go, in fact, on gambling.'

Her ponce demanded total obedience as well as all the cash, and was jealous of Clare. 'I wasn't allowed to speak to any of the other girls at that time. He didn't want me to go with the Americans or young men. They had to be, as he called them, like middle-aged and older.' By the time she quit prostitution she was thoroughly disillusioned. 'It's a dangerous life, it's a dirty life, and above all you become cold towards men. It spoils you for later on in life, when you could be giving and receiving love.

'I've seen so many women die in that life – actually murdered – and the girls that I've known to be murdered, up to this present time, I've never ever heard that they've found the person or persons that murdered them. So you're a nothing. You're a nobody.'

In the morally hidebound Britain of the fifties and sixties, when having a baby out of wedlock made a woman a moral defective in the eyes of many, it was often seen as a waste of police time to spend it investigating the deaths of women who were 'asking for it' by selling sex for money. There would be no public outcry or pressure from the powers that be if the killer was never brought to book. To many of the punters and the pimps, as well as a lot of policemen, the girls were not really human, simply 'items on the club owners' list of equipment,' commodities to be bought and sold in the marketplace. If they perished, they received about as much attention as the bruised fruit mouldering in the gutters of Berwick Street. Their bodies were simply something to be cleaned up and forgotten about.

A woman I befriended in the seventies told a similar story. 'I knew a girl, beaten to death she was, and dumped like a sack of rubbish on a bomb site. Everyone knew she was one of Big Frank's girls, but nobody said nothing. Well, you couldn't, could you? I mean, we all thought that Big Frank had done her, or one of his blokes, and nobody wanted to be on the wrong side of them. Not even the police. But then, Big Frank was paying them a bloody fortune to keep their noses out of his business. Everyone knew that.'

My friend had got out of prostitution by the time I got to know her. 'I wanted to get out of the game for years before I was able to do it. I felt dirty in the end, you know, sort of rotten on the inside. I was only able to get out when I did because my looks had long gone, and I wasn't making enough money to suit my bloke. He traded me in for a younger girl in the end, and let me go.'

Although it's usual for the girls to regret the life they lived, and most of them have horror stories to tell, literally everybody I talked to who spent their early years in the West End had their own memories of the girls on the streets, and none of them were negative. Some, such as John Carnera, empathized, 'It was seedy in a way, but yet inno-cent in many other ways. The girls that I particu-larly remember were on the corner of Dean Street and Bateman Street. There was a couple there that I knew – I mean, I saw one of them grow old. It was a terrible life. I don't know how many punters they used to see a day, but you could see them visibly age.'

Like me, Janet Vance remembers just how glamorous the working girls seemed to us little girls. 'They were really well dressed, especially the French girls, and they had little French poodles, loads of them, going up and down, especially in Old Compton Street.' When Janet got older she sometimes took one or other of the girls' poodles to Hampstead Heath, 'to give it a run round'. I suppose that the poodles were gentle, uncritical and much-needed companions with uncomplicated requirements that didn't involve removing any clothing.

To Sonia Boulter, they were part of the local scene. 'There were girls everywhere. The regular ones, I knew a few of them by name or face. They were nice. One of them – I seem to remember she was called Fay – you knew straight away she was a prostitute, she looked like a prostitute. She would stand outside of a hairdresser's in Gerrard Street. She had masses of jet black hair, and she was a bit coarse; she was mouthy, but she was good to us.'

And to Leo Zanelli, they were people, neighbours. 'They were quite a happy bunch. Always moaning about being on the game. Never stopped. But always willing to help out. They were some of the nicest people I've known, without a shadow of doubt.'

16

Glamour and Sleaze

Attitudes towards sexuality were incredibly repressive in the forties or fifties, even into the sixties. A flick through the women's magazines of the period clearly shows that sexual hypocrisy had remained virtuously intact since the Victorian era: most consenting adults were at it, but few owned up to enjoying it. Women, in particular, were expected to have a very tucked-up attitude to all things sexual. Their job was to breed, but they were not expected, and certainly not encouraged, to like the act of procreation.

As a result, titillation by photograph, book, film, dance or magazine was much sought after by frustrated men, and Soho's 'faces', well-known characters who lived at the edges of the law, were the very boys to supply it for them. Naturally, it did not cross anybody's mind to aim porno-graphic material at women. Even if it had, the men behind the trade wouldn't have considered producing it. To them, women were wives, mothers, sisters or daughters whose purity could not be impugned, or a commodity to be ex-ploited, not indulged.

The glamour and sleaze industry – the two were practically synonymous in Soho – was already flourishing in the late forties and early fifties, but was given a tremendous boost by the passing of the Street Offences Act, which revised the Victorian statutes on prostitution and drove the working girls off the streets. Now that it was no longer as easy for men to find a willing girl, the demand increased for other forms of sexual excitement, while the men – and some women – who had been behind organized prostitution turned their attention to other lucrative areas that were either borderline legal – strip clubs and clip joints – or were protected by the corruption of police, such as pornography.

The new, improved and better organized trade in porn encompassed a multitude of sins, from erotic writing to blatantly pornographic photographs and everything in between. Of course, there had been a thriving trade in nude studies and erotic art long before the camera was invented, but paintings weren't normally within the reach of your average wallet. Photography changed all that. The dirty postcards beloved of Edwardian roués were often of photos taken in Parisian brothels, and the passing of the Street Offences Act, which drove many working girls to seek alternative sources of income, led to an ever-increasing amount of ever more explicit material coming on to the market. The kind of image that is readily available nowadays in newspapers was considered grossly indecent in the fifties. The antiquated Obscene Publications Act of 1857 meant that it was also highly illegal. Its very illegality is what made it such an attractive proposition to gangsters. Where the law plants its big boots, profit margins are usually enticingly large. Street corner spivs did a lively trade in traditional 'dirty' pictures and their more organized criminal brethren dealt with out and out pornography.

Many of those involved in the porn industry also worked in the club scene, where exotic dancers, striptease artistes and nightclub hostesses plied their various trades. Many of its workers were young women who had come to the West End to pursue their dreams of becoming dancers, singers and actresses but found that there were hundreds of girls lining up for every legitimate, glitzy, showbiz job on offer. Becoming a club hostess or a stripper was as near as they were ever going to get to realizing their rhinestone-studded girlhood ambitions. The criminal element also had business interests in the industry, and the law turned a blind eye while holding its hand out for cash, expensive holidays, suits, watches and cases of black market hooch. 'Malts' – Maltese men who had previously had stables of working girls in their thrall – featured large in clubland in the late fifties and early sixties.

Musician Jack Glicco tells us, in *Madness after Midnight,* that 'Girls and drink were the only indispensable items on the club owner's list of equipment. It was the girls who brought the trade. It was the girls who boosted the sales of drink. It was the girls who, when the night was done, took their chosen clients home.' To the last of these claims, he should, perhaps, have added a 'sometimes'. Not all hostesses were ladies of easy virtue, free or purchased. The girls may have promised much, but some did not deliver. Or so

Sylvia (not her real name), who was a hostess in the fifties, assures me. While Glicco paints a picture of a voracious bunch of women who were quite prepared to draw one another's blood to get at the available men who walked into a club, this was undoubtedly true of some, but not of others.

Some hostesses actually had a life plan of sorts – 'to snare a rich husband,' as Sylvia and Glicco both suggested, or to make a pile as soon as possible in order to fund a respectable trade, such as opening up a florist shop, or owning a seaside boarding-house. Sylvia knew two women. who had done just those things. 'They had their heads screwed on, unlike the rest of us who sort of drifted into it, with no clear idea what we planned to do once our looks went.'

It is not surprising that competition between hostesses could be fierce, because the more booze they shifted and the more clients they entertained, the more money they made. Drinks in clubs were always much more expensive than elsewhere. Sometimes they were the real thing. Often, however, the punters spent very large sums on lemonade masquerading as champagne for the hostesses and something known as 'near-beer' for themselves. Near-beer may have looked like beer, it may even have tasted a bit like it, but it bore little or no relation to the genuine article. It was a term used to cover a whole range of weird concoctions that were cheap to produce but had little or no alcoholic content. The club owner scored on two fronts: he made a huge profit per drink, and he didn't wind up with overly troublesome drunks to deal with when they discovered they'd been well and truly fleeced.

As Sylvia says, 'It was all a con. Men are so easy to lead, they want to impress you by throwing their money about. All you have to do is turn on the charm, be a bit suggestive, you know, hint they may be lucky if they're generous, show them some cleavage, indicate that you find them absolutely fascinating, and there you are. It worked very well in the fifties when I was young and beautiful and it is certainly still working to this day. When it comes to feminine wiles, men never seem to learn – thank goodness.'

Like many others, Sylvia became a hostess virtually by accident. 'I was stage-struck, and by the time it dawned on me that the stage wasn't nearly as struck with me, it seemed an easier way to earn my living than spending hours and hours on my feet, day in and day out, selling cosmetics in Selfridges or running about with trays of food in a restaurant. I spent a lot of my time in night-clubs, anyway, and I knew my way around.

'I danced with the men, made conversation, that kind of thing – roughly what I'd been doing all along since I'd been in the West End. The only difference was that before, all I was after was a good time, free drinks and a meal. Sometimes, if the man was really smitten, I'd get some jewellery. Once I was a hostess, I had to charm them into the frame of mind to buy plenty of drink and to be generous with their tips. That's where the money came from. If they wanted more than my company, I'd tell them that the manager was strict about the girls mixing socially with customers, and that was that. If they tried to insist, I'd call for help and they'd be thrown out on their ears. Of course, I worked in relatively respectable places. Many of the clubs weren't like that at all.'

Some hostesses were basically prostitutes who were allowed, even encouraged, to work from a club. For the women, the attraction of being club-based was that they were off the streets and so less likely to be arrested and prosecuted. What's more, there was an endless stream of possible punters on hand, and no need to freeze on cold, wet street corners. What the women did with the customers once they'd left the premises was their own concern, although some club managers took a cut.

A few clubs were, in fact, little more than fronts for brothels, and had rooms set aside where the real business of the night could be conducted. According to one interviewee, both Christine Keeler and Mandy Rice-Davies worked the clubs before they embarked on their infamous liaisons. Frankie Fraser also asserts in his book, *Mad Frank's London*, that Mandy managed a night-club before she was caught up in the very public Profumo scandal.

Sylvia describes a common scam – one she assured me she never employed herself. 'Some girls would arrange to meet a man somewhere well away from the club, such as the bar of a hotel if he looked smart and well-off enough, or Tottenham Court Road tube station if he didn't. Of course, it was the girl's job to fix the price and get it from the man before anything else happened. I was always surprised how easy it was to get men to part with their money, but they did. The girl would leave the club first, and either go home and leave the man hanging around at the agreed rendezvous, or, if the night was young, she would nip round the all night café for a coffee and a chat, then go back and start all over again with another customer if she thought the coast was clear.

'If the bloke came back, or cut up rough, well, that was what the bouncers were for. They were ex-wrestlers or boxers, mainly. Every club had its toughs to keep troublemakers out, or toss them into the street if they somehow managed to get in. I heard that some clubs used to pay genuine gangsters to sit around looking menacing, so no ordinary punter tried anything unpleasant or violent.'

In *Mad Frank's London*, Frankie Fraser confirms this: 'The first club I ever owned was in 1955 in Old Compton Street and I had a Malt front it for me... I didn't have to put a penny in it; they was just happy to have me on the payroll.' Later on, he worked the same scheme with Albert Dimes, a notorious Soho-based gangster. 'Again, I didn't have to do anything, just show up of an evening so people could see who owned it, and so they weren't going to cause no trouble.' Frankie remembers the place with pride. 'It was a classy joint, the Bonsoir in Gerrard Street, just about where the Le Ho Fook is today. It had a little band, food, everything.' Including hostesses, no doubt. 'The thing with Albert and me was we was well known.'

I can certainly vouch for that. Even I, a mere

ankle-biter at the time, knew them both by sight and knew that I had to keep out of their way. Not that they were interested in hurting children – in fact, Ronnie Mann, who was friends with a younger member of the Dimes clan, suggested quite the opposite – it was just that they looked scary, and were treated with a certain wary respect by all the other 'faces', including my father.

The spivs who hawked a wide variety of black market goodies on street corners and in the pubs and snooker halls sometimes included smutty photographs among the stockings, bottles of booze, tins of Spam and other items that had 'fallen off the back of a lorry'. A timely hiss from a flash geezer in a zoot suit would draw a prospective customer's gaze to a furtive glimpse of a grainy, black and white image of a well-stacked, naked woman. The only requirement for a change of ownership of this, and a few similar pictures wrapped in plain, brown paper, was cash to grease an eagerly outstretched palm and the inclination to part with it.

Sometimes, punters actually got what they had paid for. John Deakin, the *Vogue* photographer, sold explicit 'beaver shots' of Henrietta Moraes, a fellow member of the Soho Boho set, when he was short of drinking money. History doesn't relate whether Henrietta received a percentage of the profits, but I doubt it, given Deakin's reputation as a tightwad and all-round sleazy article.

Other customers were not so lucky. As these transactions were so hurried and clandestine, many a green young – and not so young – man would only discover that he had been stiffed, so to speak, when he opened his treasure in private. He might find himself gazing at ten identical black and white photos of someone's ample, but fully clothed, granny paddling in the sea at Southend, or possibly a wedge of dog-eared playing cards, cast-offs from a local spieler, or a few of Donald McGill's wonderful saucy postcards, which were heavy on innuendo, but light on actual naked flesh. The rapidly flashed photo was simply a hook to draw the customer in. Such rip-offs were all too frequent: after all, who was the punter going to complain to? Censorship was rigorous, and the law would have shown scant sympathy for his plight, especially if it interfered with their own lucrative business of taking bribes for 'turning a blind one'.

The common wisdom of the times was never to buy from street corner Johnnies, but to do business only with men known to you, or recommended by a friend, who plied their trade in premises tucked well away from plain sight down dingy alleys, in basements or up flights of stairs behind an anonymous door. My father ran such a shop from rooms above Parmigiani's delicatessen on the corner of Old Compton Street and Frith Street. Father's shop, and others like it, were highly illegal, but there was an arrangement in place that involved stuffing used banknotes into an envelope and passing it over to one of the policemen who called at regular intervals.

The shops took this duty in turn. If they should fail to hand over the bribes in time, then they were raided and their stock was sold to their competitors. It was all very well organized. One of my earliest memories is of giving a fat envelope to a man who smiled, patted me on the curls and muttered, 'Ta, love. Tell your dad I'll be round next month.' He shoved the envelope, unopened, into his coat pocket, and left as quietly as he had arrived.

Although there were a number of these shops, men were still caught by spivs, because material bought from someone like Father inevitably cost more. This was because rent and bribes had to be paid and, of course, the books, pictures, magazines and flickering Super 8 and 16mm films had to be sourced. In those early days of the fifties, comparatively few of them were made in Britain. The majority of pornography came from France, Denmark and, later, Scandinavia and Holland.

Spivs, on the other hand, were highly mobile, and could take to their toes to evade the law. That way, they only had to cough up hard cash if they were caught. What's more, their material, if it was smutty at all, was likely to be shots of their girl-friends taken with a Box Brownie, which could be developed in a bathroom; if they didn't have one, a walk-in cupboard or a pantry would do. Black and white photographs were incredibly easy to develop. I could do it myself by the time I was tall enough to reach the work surface. All that was needed was a darkroom, a red light, a light box for selecting the right negatives, a few trays of chemicals, photographic paper, a pair of tongs and a washing line, complete with pegs, to hang the photos up to dry. For the spivs' purposes, great art was not needed: any grainy, under- or over-exposed picture would do. Their clientele were in no position to be picky. They drew their customers from casual tourists who had come Up West for a night on the tiles and, of course – in those days of war, conscription and National Service – servicemen on leave. Both types would be here today, gone tomorrow, and would likely be philosophical about being 'had' once they'd sobered up enough to focus clearly on their purchase. Unless they had a mate in the know, these men wouldn't know where to find the 'specialist shops' like Father's, which catered for a more experienced clientele.

One of Father's regulars was the operatic tenor, Gigli. He was a friend of Aldo, Father's business partner. I can remember sitting on Gigli's lap and being sung to while he waited for his friend, or for a preview of the new material recently brought across the Channel. Gigli habitually wore dove-grey, from the crown of his beautiful hat to his spats.

The stock for the shop was smuggled into England in a light aircraft, usually a Tiger Moth, piloted by my father. I often accompanied him on these trips. As a tiny girl with a blonde, curly mop and big blue eyes, I made an excellent smuggler's moll: it looked as if Father was simply taking his little girl for a spin. In those days there was an embargo on taking currency out of the country. I think we were allowed £20 or £25 only, nowhere near enough to pay our suppliers in Le Touquet. It was my job to take the currency out. No matter what the weather, I had to wear a liberty bodice so that the huge, white fivers could be stuffed between it and my body. They prickled and tickled, and the liberty bodice made me sweaty and cranky in hot weather, but at least then the fivers went limp and didn't tickle as much, or rustle as loudly, as they did on brisk autumn or winter days. I felt like a walking crisp packet when the money was new and crackly. My teddy, the hollow bodies of my dolls and my toy handbag were also called into service and stuffed with money – pornography was never cheap, even at wholesale prices.

No Customs officer would suspect the father of a sweetie-pie like me of smuggling smut with his little girl in tow or indeed, any teddy bear of being stuffed to its ears with illegally exported money to pay for the merchandise. How wrong they were, and how right Father was. To my knowledge, we were never searched when I was present. Of course, it's possible that Her Majesty's Customs were as easy to bribe as the West End's policemen in those bleak days when everyone was so heartily sick of shortages and 'making do'. Stiff upper lips were definitely becoming very slack by the early fifties, and even the most upright of citizens was open to the temptation of a few hundred fags and a bottle of brandy.

The drummer, Raye Du-Val, was an equally inventive smuggler. 'I was in the porn game,' he remembers. 'What I used to do was to bring in pictures. When I played on tour in France, I used to paste the packets in my drums. Made sure I didn't have transparent drumskin heads, that's how I brought my stuff in.'

For several fairly obvious reasons, including death, embarrassment and the later acquisition of respectability, it was difficult to find anyone at all who was willing to be interviewed about their part in the pornography trade in the fifties, either as models, performers or retailers. Raye Du-Val mentions his role as a smuggler very briefly, and the only consumer of pornography and customer of shops such as Father's who spoke insisted on anonymity for fear of censure, even in these more enlightened times. I suppose that the stigma of consumers being 'dirty old men' must still cling, even though Tom, as I will call him, was a young man when he first took the train from the genteel town in Surrey where he lived to the West End in search of sleaze. 'I was lingering outside a porn shop in Cambridge Circus,' he remembers, 'summoning up the courage, if that's what it was, to go in. The thing that I was immediately aware of when I went in there, was that I was potentially out of my depth: it seemed to be staffed or manned by what I can only describe as gangster types, it was rather a frightening lesson for a callow youth. They were talking to each other about cars, car engines, but then they stopped the conversation and looked at me. I wondered whether they were going to tell me to bugger off actually, but they didn't, they asked me what I wanted, and as I didn't really know, I was "Er, er"... So they said, "Well, have a look at this." It was American import stuff, and then the price just came and it seemed arbitrary, everyone seemed to be paying a different price from what I could hear, and I thought to myself, "I've got to pay this if I want to leave here", and it was a very rude shock. I felt very intimidated by the whole thing.

'But, on the other hand, I felt that I had gone through a kind of rite of passage. Later, when I went back to buy books – and porn – I was kind of asking myself whether I could handle it or not, and I decided that I could. I wasn't so much worried about the law as frightened somebody would say to me, "Listen, man, give us your money and fuck off." Something like that. But, just as the working girls on the streets seemed to take the business routine in their stride, so the porn guys seemed to take the porn routines in their stride. In fact, they seemed to be thoroughly bored with it, really, because all their conversations were absolutely nothing to do with what they were doing. They were like men on the job, discussing things. You always felt, though, that this could turn a bit nasty.

'What I do remember is that almost all the punters were quite passive, and orderly. They mostly wanted to come in and out, and I was fascinated by that, just in and out. People brought bags in, or wore coats with deep pockets: sums changed hands, then they were gone. There was all this X-rated material, and it was just feet away from where the general public was walking. But the main thing though, the prevailing memory, was what big business it seemed to be. Just so busy, so busy.'

When I asked Tom what had brought him Up West in the first place, I got a very clear picture of how – and why – Soho looked so different from the outside than it did from the inside.

'Soho featured in news broadcasts that I heard,' he remembers. 'It featured in some of the fiction that I read, and then, when I started reading the music papers, I was aware that so much music was based there. Not exactly Tin Pan Alley, but round that area.

'So, all those things – and then there was the *News of the World*. We always had the *People* and the *News of the World*. My father wasn't squeamish about that at all, although my mother certainly was [laughs], but I was intrigued. Some of the *News of the World* reporting was quite blatant; strip clubs, whatever, particularly the court cases involving sexual activity. I never really believed the time-honoured phrase that the reporters trotted out, "I made my excuses and left." [He laughs again.] What red-blooded male would?

'There seemed to be chests full of Danish material or American material, which was very iconoclastic stuff.' Tom recalls. 'I remember that one area of the ground floor, there was a wall given over to photography: on others they seemed to have movies, and there was a maze of shelves going around the shop where there was just material laid out. Another thing I noticed, which was almost something I thought was proverbial about porn sellers, was they all had wads. Wads of cash. Very large sums were involved. There was a man on the till, who sat above everybody else, so he had an overview of the thing, and he had sole charge of the money. One place I went to had this arrangement of mirrors, so from the back of the shop they could see who was coming in the door at any one time, and I suppose manage it from that point. Maybe they'd have five seconds' notice if the police came through the door.'

Personally, I don't think the police would have worried these men at all: they were probably on the payroll. It was thieves after the cash, shoplifters after freebies, or rivals that they had to watch out for. Villains from a rival outfit may have come in looking for trouble, money, or both.

Tom's description of the shops and the men who ran them brought back vivid memories for me, although Father was out of the business years before Tom became a customer. Father always had a wad of notes in his pocket, for example, and so did his fellow shopkeepers. He and I would sometimes visit other shops – a courtesy call, so to speak, for a gossip about the dirty book trade, what was selling, what wasn't, to compare prices and stock or to pass on rumours of a police crackdown. 'Crackdowns' usually only happened after some particularly damning article in a tabloid newspaper that purported to give the inside story of vice in Soho. The police would then have to make a show of being on the case.

Sometimes we went to sell surplus stock, or to deliver items from our most recent trip to Le Touquet. Although I don't remember Father's shop being as Tom described, I do remember some of the others being just like it. In my time, none had a shop window. If they did, it was whitewashed to give the impression that the shopfitters and decorators were in. The only sign that that was not the case was that the whitewash never seemed to disappear. Later, the windows were blacked out, but that was after the law had been relaxed somewhat.

Obviously, being so young, I was shielded from the exact nature of my father's business. As I grew older, and Father had left the trade behind and turned more or less respectable, I was aware of some erotica on his bookshelves at home, and knew that, in the fifties, even *Lady Chatterley's Lover, The Tropic of Cancer* or the works of the Marquis de Sade were considered porn and banned under that archaic 1857 law, but I never really saw the stuff he'd sold.

'In several cases,' Tom remembers, 'there was a sort of anteroom that lured you in: then you went to a sort of hatch, and people seemed to say something and a door at the side opened. Well, I went in the door when someone else went in, and when you went into the back room, there was much more extreme material – full penetration, group sex, lesbian sex, flage. The Danish material mainly seemed to be books of stills from films, but they told some crude kind of story in their way. The girls were always attractive, but the guys were the strange sort of guys you always see in porn movies. Fat hairy guys with moustaches. No child pornography, but stuff involving animals. That always seemed to be Danish or German. Down on the farm... [laughter] You got to look at pigs in a different light.'

Tom tried to explain the appeal of this sleazy life to me. 'The articles in the newspapers fascinated me when I was a teenager. They described a different world; it was forbidden. It kind of magnetized a lot of people like myself, and I thought the nearest I can get to it is to look at it, be a consumer, get some action that way. It was like having a badge. To the men who ran the shops, I was just some kid who spent his money, then got his arse out of there. But to me, I was negotiating my way through that scene without fumbling, without becoming a victim. I had a real sense of accomplishment. I mean, I left much poorer [laughs] but I had more or less what I wanted.'

He pauses and thinks for a moment. 'It was the low life I was interested in. I wanted to investigate that. Because I also found myself talking to a lot of down-and-outs, a lot of people who were peripheral people, marginalized people. It was the porn shop that really conferred that on me, confirmed that it was feasible to get in and out of that life. It was like a hunter coming back with the game. That's how I saw it. The other thing that I remember was that I was aching for the knowledge of it really, and one of the principal reasons for it was that it was exclusively masculine territory. Forbidden territory too. It was a way to be a man.'

Another important part of the sleaze industry were the strip clubs, which thrived in Soho long before they were made legal. The law dictated that if women and men were going to divest themselves of their clothing, they had best do it in the privacy of their own bedrooms, bathrooms or – in the case of men – the locker rooms of their sports clubs, but most definitely not in a theatre or a club in front of an audience.

The famous Windmill Theatre, the one that

kept open during the whole of the Second World War and boasted 'We never closed,' was allowed to display scantily clad and nude women, but only if they formed static 'tableaux vivants'. No exposed jiggling, wriggling or writhing flesh was allowed, lest it inflame the lewd passions of the eager onlookers. If the tableau depicted some kind of mythological or historical scene, so much the better. Then, it could even be considered educational. This harks back to the Victorians again and the hypocritical attitudes enshrined in their laws. When it came to paintings, suitably draped nudes were allowed, providing the picture had a classical or biblical subject. A nude figure simply standing, lolling or doing something everyday like sweeping a floor, wafting a feather duster about or knocking up an omelette, was just plain lewd and therefore disgusting and illegal.

Naturally, the West End club owners didn't let a little thing like the law get in the way of making money. Jack Glicco points out in *Madness after Midnight* that strip clubs were alive, well and thriving as far back as the twenties, and probably before that. They were certainly around in the forties and fifties, despite the ever-present threat of prosecution, fines and subsequent closure. There were, of course, ways around the law, and every dubious club owner knew them. The crudest and simplest method was bribery and corruption, but there was also an elegant legal loophole involving private membership.

The notion that private members' clubs were sacrosanct dated back to the inception of the St

James's gentlemen's clubs in the eighteenth century. Gambling was allowed in those, even when the law forbade the placing of bets by ordinary people – unless they were actually at a racecourse or dog track. Historically, there had long been one set of rules for the rich or titled and quite another for everyone else. It was good old British snobbery of course. A 'gentleman' was deemed to have the money and leisure to indulge himself at his club, while the lesser orders should, in theory, be too gainfully employed serving their betters in one capacity or another, to belong to a private members' club. Besides, members had to be voted in: a working man would never have got as far as being nominated. At one time, even millionaires who'd made their piles in trade were snubbed by the 'best' clubs.

West End club owners changed all that when they took advantage of the system to get strip shows past the censorship laws. Punters became temporary or life members by paying a small sub at the door. The same wheeze was used by those who wanted to show 'adult' films, ones that had been rejected or never seen by the censors, to a paying public. The first of these, the Compton Cinema Club, opened opposite the 2I's at 56 Old Compton Street in 1960. The law, trained by previous generations never to bother a gentleman at his club, had no real provision for this new twist, and backhanders ensured that the local police made discretion their byword, unless the bribes were too small or there was trouble at a club that they were unable to ignore.

The owners of strip clubs did their best not to give the police any excuse to declare their houses disorderly. Jack Glicco often earned his money playing at strip clubs as a musician, as did Raye Du-Val, and both agree that messing with the girls was not wise, thanks to the men behind the clubs. As Raye remembers, 'I did the strip clubs, played all night. The girls in the clubs, you worked behind them, but you weren't allowed to fool around with them, even in the seediest of clubs.'

Things began to change radically when Paul Raymond (real name Geoffrey Anthony Quinn) opened the doors of the Raymond Revuebar on 14 April 1958. Before that, he had run a touring variety show that featured naked girls, who, like those at the Windmill Theatre, were not allowed to move. Rumour has it that Raymond handed out pea-shooters to some members of his audience so that well-aimed, hard little peas would produce some titillating action for the punters to enjoy, even if the poor bruised girls were less than thrilled. Tired of the law's restriction, he took up the lease on the Doric Theatre in Walker's Court, which joins the southern end of Berwick Street to Brewer Street, and opened his Revuebar using the private members scam operated by many small clubs before him.

The difference was that in those clubs the scam was something that passed on a nod, a wink and lots of pound notes between club owners and the police, while Raymond advertised, and openly charged a guinea on the door for a lifetime membership. Within two years, Raymond's Revuebar boasted amongst its vast membership, 'Ten MPs, eight millionaires, more than sixty knights, thirty-five peers and enough businessmen and captains of industry to drain dry the Stock Exchange and the Savoy Grill.' This information comes from a 1960 issue of the *Spectator*, appropriately enough.

Like the Windmill, Raymond's Revuebar prided itself on the lavishness of its sets, its costumes and, once the girls were permitted to move, its choreography, which may account for its incredible popularity with wealthy clients and its membership lists. The girls who worked in both places were seen as a cut above the rest, and a few went on to greater things – although most simply slipped down the scale to work in seedier joints as their looks faded.

Perhaps because his was not a private arrangement between him and the police, but a blatant one with his customers, Raymond was prosecuted in 1961. A barrister for the prosecution was heard to wonder how it was possible for all these people to be members of a private club when not one of them had been proposed and seconded by existing members and voted in by the membership, as was the usual practice at the clubs in St James's, while the judge described Raymond's enterprise as 'filthy, disgusting and beastly' when he heard how punters rang the three bells that made up the entire costume of Bonnie Bell, the Ding Dong Girl. He was also profoundly shocked by the image presented of Julia Mendez, the Snake Girl, swallowing her snake. He fined Raymond £5,000. This was a vast sum for the times – equivalent to six figures today – but it represented a fraction of the entrepreneur's profits.

Raymond carried on regardless, and where the Revuebar led, lots of other little clubs followed: there was certainly no shortage of punters. Victor Caplin paints a charming picture of the scene in the early sixties: 'I remember visiting strip clubs like the Carnival on Old Compton Street. There were at least twenty clubs dotted around a very close area, and the girls would run from one to another, click-clacking hurriedly in their high heels, usually wearing toreador pants and perhaps an animal skin print blouse. They all carried one of those boxy little make-up cases. They would be fined if they were late for their spot.

'It used to be so funny: these places were tiny, perhaps eight or ten rows of seats, maybe only six across and some standing room at the back. They were filled with guys with either a raincoat or a newspaper on their laps. There was always a few minutes to wait between each girl, and as people left, there would be a mad scramble over the seats to get to the front and a better view. The girls all looked so bored. They would prance across the stage, squinting as they moved into the spotlights towards some tawdry prop, the odd piece of clothing falling to the floor. They would make a big deal about placing their own towel on the scuzzy chair that would support them as they finally revealed all, for one split second, as the curtains closed ... and then the mad scramble for a better place and the wait for the next chance to see what all the big fuss was about.'

I also remember those scuttling girls, who wore heavy make-up and yards of false eyelashes, dashing from one venue to another, goose-pimpled and breathless as they hurried. Sometimes they'd have a cigarette on the go, dying for a gasper between shows.

The Revuebar not only opened the way to legal striptease clubs, but it also had the first sign openly offering STRIPTEASE in bright neon lettering. Raymond didn't stop there; he revolutionized the other sector of the 'glamour' market too. Harrison Marks, a 'glamour photographer' with studios in Gerrard Street, had begun publishing the 'nudie mags' *Spic* and *Span* in the late fifties, but in the sixties Raymond upped the ante with the launch of such barely legal 'girlie' magazine titles as *Men Only, Escort, Razzle* and *Club International.* He made enough money from his various enterprises to buy up large chunks of Central London real estate, and was able to claim that his was the only private London estate to be formed in the twentieth century.

As in the best morality tales, though, Raymond's great financial success did not bring him ultimate happiness. He died in March 2008, a lonely, unhappy recluse whose beloved only child had predeceased him, thanks to a heroin overdose. Still, perhaps the last word on glamour and sleaze is best left to the self-styled 'King of Soho' who built an empire on it: 'There will always be sex – always, always, always.'

17

Taking a Chance

When people talk about vice and the West End they are usually referring to the sex trade, but in the mid twentieth century, gambling was also considered a serious vice, and the public was protected from it – in theory anyway – by a series of restrictive laws passed in the nineteenth century that reflected Victorian morality and rampant snobbery. You could legally play cards and casino games for money only in private homes and licensed gentlemen's clubs. Bookmakers could legally take bets only at 'pitches' on the racecourse or dog track. The only form of lottery was the weekly football pools, and even there, maximum prizes were set by law throughout the fifties.

The law's repressive attitude ensured that gambling was equated with crime. Even where it was legal, it had a criminal following. In the twenties and thirties, for example, the typical criminal organization in Britain was the 'race gang', which had nothing to do with racism, as the name would suggest today, but everything to do with preying on 'the racing fraternity'. Members of the gangs subsisted – and often lived very well – on the proceeds of mugging punters, shaking down bookmakers, gaining control of pitches and charging extortionate rents, and influencing the result of the odd race or two. It was activities like this that sustained underworld figures such as Jack Spot and the Sabini gang in much the same way that Prohibition in America had sustained Al Capone and his chums. Although the Sabini brothers were indeed Italians from Clerkenwell, our home-grown mob substituted a good duffing up with coshes, fists, razors and shivs (knives) for the Mafia's more murderous machine-guns.

Knives were much in fashion in the forties and fifties, and according to my father one was used on him during the Soho Fair. I was never able to verify the tale, and Father did have a tendency to elaborate fancifully – or indeed, tell outright porkies – but he swore that Frankie Fraser stabbed him in the back over an altercation about the outcome of a horse race. It was true that he did have a scar, and it was also true that he knew Frankie Fraser, but as my mother was wont to say, 'If your father tells you it is raining, it's wise to check.'

It might seem odd, even quaint, to the modern eye but betting on a horse race in the forties and fifties was perfectly acceptable if the transaction involved the punter and bookmaker meeting face to face on the racecourse; otherwise it was frowned upon. This meant that the working classes were effectively largely excluded from legal gambling during the working week and, if the racecourse was hard to get to, at weekends as well. And it created two shady professions that no longer exist, the street bookie and the bookie's runner. Some street bookies actually collected money on the streets, while others maintained fairly swish offices, called themselves 'turf accountants' and took bets over the phone from posh types who couldn't get away from the office.

There were plenty of well-heeled gamblers. As Owen Gardner remembers, 'The founder of Page's, Harry Bradbury-Pratt, was a great gambler. He lost three fortunes in his lifetime, but when he died in about 1949, he still left about £75,000, which was a lot of money in those days. He was an owner, too. When his horse was running, and it was running to win, he'd send a memo round the shop, to say there's ten shillings on for everybody in the firm. He'd put a bet on for everybody and pay everybody out, if it won, at the end of the race.'

Janet Vance's father, Charlie Blyghton, was the sort of street bookie who rarely dealt with high rollers. 'His pitch,' she remembers, 'was on the street in Bateman Buildings, just opposite where we lived. He had lookouts, one at the Soho Square end and one at the corner of Greek Street. They would blow a whistle or something to let him know if the police were around. He had a phone connected to the racecourse actually in our flat, so he got all the results there and then. He used to pay out in the Carlisle Arms in Bateman Street. All the winners would know to go there. And it was good for the pub, too, because while they was in there with their winnings, they'd be buying drinks. That was part of the deal. Let me pay out here, and they'll buy drinks with the money.'

Charlie Blyghton was essentially a local businessman, serving the local community. 'His customers were all sorts – regulars, locals, people who came to work who wanted their sixpence or shilling on. He wouldn't go up to them, they would come to him. It was all word of mouth.' Other people, especially people with jobs that brought them into contact with the general public, would join in for a small fee. Henry, the Swiss Italian on the door at La Isola Bella, where Janet's mother worked, used to take bets for her dad.

Like the majority of street bookies, Charlie Blyghton had a legitimate status, too. 'He had a legal pitch at the dogs and the races. He went to White City and Harringay for the dog-racing, and he had someone go to Catford on a Saturday. For horse racing he went to Alexandra Park and Sandown, any place you could get to by train at Victoria. He went under the name of Jackie Pye.'

Charlie Blyghton's double life as a legitimate and illegitimate bookie – not to mention running an illegal gambling club in the basement of the house where they had a flat – was far from one of luxury and ease. 'He would be out on the street in the mornings about ten or eleven until the first race, whenever that started,' Janet recalls, 'and again from about five to six in the evenings for the dogs and the night racing in the summer. And of course if there was dog-racing in London he would be off to his pitch at White City or wherever, and then back to the spieler until the early hours. He was a hard worker, he kept going.'

He had two full-time employees, who worked as runners and lookouts as well as helping him on his legal outings at the dog tracks and race-course. They were a father and son team. 'Matt Jones, who was in his eighties, and Charlie lived in Red Lion Square,' Janet remembers. 'Matt used to go around on a bike, but his son could run a bit faster. They would use Alfie Binks's shop [a greengrocer's in Frith Street] to hide in if they had to get away. He had a basement, and they would go down there to get away.'

Bookies' runners apparently got their name because they would 'run errands' for the book-maker, visiting clients to collect bets and that sort of thing, rather than for their ability to have it away on their toes at the sight of a policeman bearing down on them. Not that it did any harm to be able to show a clean pair of heels to the coppers. My late friend, Terry Pizzey, used to tell me stories of his childhood in Marylebone between the wars, when he knew a bookie's runner who had been christened Florence, but whose fleetness of foot when confronted with the law led to her being nicknamed 'Scarper Flo'.

Another example of this vanished breed was one of the more wonderfully eccentric characters in my own young life, a man called Fred Potter, who spoke entirely in slang. He was a very good friend of my father, and at one point combined being a bookie's runner with a job as a beat copper in South London. Unfortunately, the constabulary took a dim view, and gave him the elbow, which prompted Fred to become a full-time member of my father's netherworld of pornographic bookshops and illegal gambling.

Bookies and their runners were a fairly common sight on the streets in the fifties. Often, as with the working girls, the police would turn a blind eye to their activities, provided they weren't too blatant about it, although there were exceptions. Olga and Graham Jackson's father was a policeman who was nicknamed 'Snakey', as in 'snake in the grass'. One reason he got his name was that, unlike ex-Constable Potter, he particularly disliked brasses (prostitutes) and bookies, and made it his business to arrest as many of them as possible on his beat in Covent Garden.

Occasionally there were general clean-ups, or some enthusiastic new recruit got carried away by the sport of it, and Charlie Blyghton would get lifted. 'Once,' Janet remembers, 'during the summer holidays, myself and Liz, a mate that lived in Greek Street, saw Dad being led off by two men. I went up to him and said "Can I have money for ice cream?" and he said "No, go away", but gave me this sort of look that I should follow him. He always wore this gaberdine mac. As the plainclothes coppers led him along to West End Central, he was screwing up the bets and dropping them through a hole in his pocket. By the time they got to Meard Street, he had dropped all the bets he had, and me and my mate, following on behind, picked them all up and took them home. By the time he got to the police station, he had nothing, so they couldn't nick him for anything.' And I expect he managed to get the bets laid and the punters paid out as a result of the girls' timely help as well; I hope they got their ice cream for their efforts.

'Another time,' Janet went on, 'a copper

spotted him, and he dodged into the French baker's in Greek Street, where they baked bread on the premises, and flew upstairs. The copper didn't know if he'd gone up or down, so he stood in the door, to make sure he couldn't slip out. Dad had gone upstairs, and dumped a bag of flour out of the first floor window on to the copper. While he was dusting himself off, my dad was down the stairs, out the door and away.'

Every now and then the coppers won one. 'He got pinched a few times and landed up in Great Marlborough Street magistrates' court. He'd go up there and be fined, and then he would go back and do it again. They'd fine him a few quid and then he'd go back and earn it. He used to ask for time to pay.'

Several other bookies operated in Covent Garden and Soho. 'There was another Charlie for a start,' says Janet. 'Charlie Fordham used to have pitches in Gerrard Street, Newport Street, down that end. There were probably others, all with their pitches. You could always get a bet on.'

When I was very young, I remember a line of rather drunken looking telephone boxes – the Blitz had shaken them up a bit – outside a post office which was either in, or near, Marshall Street. It was a place where bookies and runners who operated without the luxury of a private phone would hang about, gossiping and jiggling their pennies, waiting to call in bets or to get results. Father and I would go there if he wanted to place a bet in a hurry, or to track down his mate Fred. Soho Square was another place to put a few bob on; Prince Monolulu, tipster, street bookie and childminder *extraordinaire* could usually be found there.

Jeff Sloneem remembers a bookie who spent less time in the streets: 'I had a friend who lived in Wardour Street. His mother was a good friend of my mother, and his father was a bookie. He didn't work on the streets, but he had a bookie's office in his flat. This was obviously completely illegal, although I didn't know that at the time. I used to go there a lot because they had a television and we didn't.'

The street – and flat! – betting scene changed dramatically after the passage of the Betting and Gaming Act in 1960. This made it legal to run gambling premises – from bingo halls to Mayfair mini-casinos – as private member clubs, and for bookmakers to accept off-course bets in licensed premises, which soon came to be known as betting shops. Casinos were so restricted by the 1960 Act that it was only when this was reformed in 1968 that they really took off, but a rash of betting shops opened on high streets everywhere. Bookies went from being shady characters who operated largely outside the law, to slightly less shady characters, who operated not only within the law, but also indoors in the warm.

Charles Hasler, who policed the Soho Streets in the fifties, did not think the new law was an improvement. 'Street bookmaking was less harmful than betting shops, because the punters had to put all their bets for the day at the same time. They couldn't, if they had a win, put it all back again, because the runners used to disappear off the street to get their slips and money to the boss man before racing started. All sorts of people picked up these slips and took them in – milkmen, for instance. I never thought street bookies did any harm, although sometimes there was trouble if someone interfered with someone else's pitch.'

Of course, the majority of the new licensed betting shops were opened by people with experience in the field, as it were. 'People were often running credit bookmaking elsewhere as well as their ready money betting, and all that happened with betting shops was it legitimized their business,' Charles Hasler points out. The course and street bookies alike took some of the outdoor ambience into the shops, which were often little more than basic dives, very rough and ready. One of those early punters described one to me, but asked for his name not to be used. 'There were no TVs, of course, often nowhere to sit,' he remembers. 'The runners and form were torn out of one of the morning newspapers and stuck on the wall with drawing pins, there were cheap pens and paper to write in your selection, and a counter to pass your cash over. Behind the counter there was someone scribbling the odds for the next two or three races on a big blackboard. That was it for decor. The windows were painted over, fluorescent lights. Blokes hanging around smoking and looking fed up, occasionally getting excited as the Extel feed from the courses described a race rather than the prices. You hardly ever saw a woman in there. It was all blokes, always full of smoke and stinking a bit of beer sweat.'

Mike O'Rouke left school in 1962 to start work chalking the boards in a betting shop belonging to his uncle, James Keith. 'He had about four or five shops in the West End, and I went to work for him in Great Newport Street. There was another shop in New Row, one up in Drury Lane, which is now a hotel, on the corner of Shorts Gardens, and another one down in Exeter Street. My uncle started out as a runner. That's where most of them started. All the big firms started out in the streets.'

Not all of the former street bookies prospered, however. 'When the Act came in,' Janet Vance remembers, 'my dad went legit with two shops. One was in Old Pye Street, Victoria, and one in Kilburn High Street. He went broke. From there, he went into the film business, in Soho Square. He'd got to know people from the BBC, customers. He used to do voice-overs. He had a rough and ready London voice – he'd curse and swear at you without even blinking.' Mine too! I always said Father was bilingual, fluent in English and Anglo-Saxon. His accent was middle class, as he had been an actor briefly in his youth, but he retained his command of the colourful language associated with a London street urchin, which is how he started out in life.

Although there were street bookies in every town and city, gambling clubs were generally thin on the ground, except in Soho. This was mainly because many of the nationalities that made their homes in the West End – the Maltese and the Chinese, for example – had very different views about gambling than the British legislature. Spielers were often frequented by crooks, who had an easy come, easy go attitude to their cash. Some were definitely dens of iniquity – but not all of them, as Leo Zanelli recalls: 'When my father retired from running the restaurant, he opened the Tosca in Newport Place, just over the road from where we lived. It was an old-fashioned Italian drinking club, mainly for men, with cards, drink and betting on horses.'

Janet Vance also remembers how her mother 'used to work for Joe Cohen at his club in Greek Street. That was a drinking and gambling club. The gambling went on behind curtains; it was a legal drinking club and an illegal gambling club.' This was a common arrangement, but Janet's father's club, in the basement of the building where they lived, had no pretence to legality. In fact, it had very few pretensions of any kind. 'The club was just a basement room, quite small. You could get tea, coffee, and you could have a drink – but under the counter, sort of thing – and play cards. Dad didn't take a cut, you just paid to play and for your drinks. It was open of a night until quite late in the morning. He was on the streets during the day, then did his bits down there. He worked hard for his money.'

Charles Hasler recalls that 'Down the end of Old Compton Street toward Charing Cross Road, there was a court that had a gaming club in it which used to get raided quite regularly. The owners didn't take any notice, it was no more than rent to them. They paid the fine and carried on. Once, at West End Central police station, we shoved them all in an accommodation cell while we were trying to decide what to do with them.

While they were in there, they continued their dice game in the cell. Some people who had several quid on them when we booked them in had nothing when they went out. They were incorrigible.'

You could always find a card game – pontoon, brag and solo as well as poker – in Soho, if you knew the right people, whether it was at unlicensed clubs like the one Charlie Blyghton ran, or at even less formal venues. You didn't really need much to run a card game, after all; just a room, tables and chairs. Owen Gardner, who worked next door to the Empire Snooker Hall, remembers that 'There was a blanked-off section in there where they used to play cards. In the heyday of the 2I's, there was a whole string of rock and rollers playing cards in there, all afternoon, gambling behind that screen.'

I remember card games going on late into the night at our kitchen table. One morning I woke up to a shower of big, white fivers being dumped on me, and the instruction to 'Count them, it'll teach you to count in fives.' Father had, apparently, found a high-stakes poker game and had done well. We were in the clover, for a little while at least.

Cards and horses weren't the only things you could bet on. There was always some action to be found in the snooker halls. 'My father was a very good snooker player pre-war, when Joe Davis was world champion,' Owen Gardner recalls. 'Joe used to tour the country to play the best snooker players in each area, and my father scored most against him, or came closest to beating him, and as a result won a cue. He used to go to a Cypriot barber, just at the back of Seven Dials, and they would say "Oh, you should go to the Empire if you're that good, make some money." But my father steered clear of it: if people are gambling on you, it's like boxing or anything else, you win when you have to win, and you lose when they tell you to lose. He stayed right out of it.'

Although snooker was a minority sport in those days, there were people who were prepared to back their own skill, or someone else's, with hard cash. Father was one of them: he liked to play snooker for fun, but he'd bet on other players. Even now I can see the smoke-filled air at the Empire snooker hall, smell the cigars and hear the sharp click of ivory balls crashing into another. I remember it as an almost entirely masculine place, apart from me and one or two women who came in with their men friends: the women didn't play.

Like the Americans, with their 'bathtub gin' joints that sprang up during the Prohibition years to give your 'average Joe' a drink when he wanted one, the would-be punter showed boundless resourcefulness in getting in on 'the action' during the years of repressive gaming laws in Britain. The message is clear: men and women will drink and they will bet and nothing the authorities do will stop them.

Tolerant of human frailty to the last, the West End in general, and Soho in particular, has always been willing to accept people's foibles and to exploit them where possible. Gambling is no exception. Even on the Sabbath day in the fifties, when everything of a mercantile nature, save for pubs and restaurants, went quiet, and attending church was the big event of most people's day, a body could get a punt on if he knew where to look. Alberto Camisa remembered how, after Mass, his family would take a stroll around Soho and frequently came across an extracurricular Sunday activity. 'Up at the top of Berwick Street, behind the pub, the Blue Posts, there was a dead end alleyway, and they used to do hare coursing there. With rats. Because they had all the market stalls there, in lock-ups, with fruit and veg on them, there was always rats. The stallholders caught them during the week, kept them in boxes. Sunday morning people come along with little terrier dogs, and they used to release the rats, and release the dog, and obviously money changed hands.'

I can't help but find in this bloody activity a faint echo from Soho's distant past, when hounds regularly chased hapless hares across Soho Fields.

18

The Criminal Element

The West End in general, and Soho in particular, has long been associated with crime. Certainly the words 'Soho Slaying' on a news-stand in the fifties and sixties sold more papers than 'Hoxton Homicide', 'Marylebone Murder' or 'Camden Carve-up'. It didn't matter how sensationalist the facts of the case were; the mere mention of Sinful

Soho suggested juiciness.

This may have been because certain sorts of criminal – pickpockets, con men, black market dealers, jewel thieves and fur thieves (a crime far more fashionable in the forties than it is today) – always gravitated towards the West End. It's where crowds, money and luxury goods have met and mingled for generations, and where that lot linger, thieves are never far behind. The crimes these people committed could be seen as particularly urban ones, and the West End is, of course, the epitome of urban. The thronged pavements and shops of the West End have ever been a busy dip's natural habitat. Jewellery shops and furriers clustered in the same few shopping streets were too much temptation for smash-and-grabbers, as well as more sophisticated thieves, who specialized in lifting sparklers and minks and knew just where to off-load them.

In Soho, the hardcore criminals fell largely into two categories: those who ran and worked in the local rackets, and those who came to spend the fruits of their labours rather unimaginatively on drink, gambling and women. Very few criminals actually lived there. They had their own manors south of the river, like the Richardsons, or in the East End, like the Krays: when they got really successful they rented apartments in Bayswater and Knightsbridge, or moved to the stockbroker belt in Surrey, like Charlie Richardson. According to my father, who knew and drank with Richardson, this upscale relocation wasn't a success. Once he'd settled into his new home in Virginia Water, Charlie thought it would be nice to invite the neighbours in for a cocktail and a 'getting to know you' party, and duly sent out the invites. When the great evening came, not one neighbour graced the Richardson party with their presence. Sensing a hint of snobbery in this snub, Richardson vacated the house and let it for a peppercorn rent to a large, extended family of immigrants. I hope the locals found it in their heart to offer a friendly welcome, but in the times when this is supposed to have happened, I doubt it.

Some criminals targeted Sohoites who were operating beyond the law and so were unlikely to report them to the police. Such criminals might run a regular 'protection' racket, pocketing fixed sums each week to leave an illegal drinking club unmolested; or they would simply crash in and take what they wanted when they felt like it. This method was particularly popular with British criminals, who would victimize the Maltese community, seeking easy money.

Tommy 'Scarface' Smithson was typical, as his sometime henchman, Jim Barnett, remembered in a TV interview. 'The Maltese were frightened of Tommy. If they opened a drinking club, spieler, whatever, they'd always be frightened that we'd walk in. Every club, every street, is full of weapons. A wall is a marvellous weapon. You ram somebody's head into a wall, that's a pretty heavy thing to hit them with. Tables? Just look around you. Heavy ashtrays? Chairs? Your hands, your feet, your elbows? Your head?' In the same programme, Barnett offered a defence of Smithson's behaviour: 'I think that a bully is somebody that hurts little people just for his own gratification. Tommy

Smithson hurt people, bloody right he did, but he hurt people who were going to hurt him, or he hurt them for money.'

In the late forties and fifties, there were criminal types you simply do not find today, such as 'peter men' – safecracking burglars, with the expertise to use a stethoscope to crack a combination or choose the right amount of 'jelly' to open a safe's door without destroying its contents – smash and grab boys, and 'jump-up men'. Smash and grab particularly appealed to young thieves who were in it as much for the adrenaline as the money. All they needed was a fast car – usually nicked for the purpose – and a brick. The latter would be heaved through a jeweller's window, then a gloved hand would grab everything within reach before a tyre-squealing getaway through what were then relatively empty streets. In certain circumstances, you didn't even need a car, as Charles Hasler, who joined the Metropolitan Police after serving in the Second World War, remembers: 'The London fogs were thick, dirty, yellow. You couldn't see across the road. The minute you got the fogs, you started getting more smash and grabs. Anybody could heave a brick through a shop window and disappear in the gloom.' It didn't have to be a jeweller's window: 'In the forties and fifties, everything was scarce, so everything had a value. Whatever they could lift, they could sell. So they did.'

The same principle applied to jump-up men, who worked in teams. They drove around looking for a delivery lorry, then followed it, waiting for the driver to get out and go into a shop. As soon as he was through the door, one or two would swarm up over the tailboard, grab cartons of cigarettes or anything else they could sell on the black market, and chuck it down to their mates below, who threw it into their car and zoomed away while the jump-up men legged it. Jump-up men often graduated to hijacking lorries – sometimes waiting for the driver to get out of the cab and sometimes simply dragging him out – and driving them off to a pre-arranged spot for swift unloading.

Crime thrived in certain places in the West End simply because of the presence of another, legal activity. In the forties and fifties second-hand car dealers operated largely out of Warren Street, where cars were displayed in the street and business was done on the pavements. Where better to trade in dodgy petrol coupons, stolen parts, tyres and so on? Most of the car dealers operated on the far-flung fringes of legality anyway, and some weren't too fussed about leaving it behind altogether.

And then there was the little matter of the recent war. The Blitz and the blackout proved heaven-sent for opportunistic thieves and fraudsters, while the black market in rationed and just plain unavailable goods transformed London. Just as Prohibition had done in America, it made everyone who resorted to buying 'on the black' a criminal. Although policemen were never called up to fight, many volunteered, depleting the force, while deserters and those fleeing the call-up swelled the ranks of the gangs that were springing up to loot the capital. As Frankie Fraser wrote, wartime London 'was a thieves' paradise, and everyone was a thief'. The Blitz also ensured that there were empty buildings available at London's heart to provide shelter to these runaways, as well as bases from which to commit the crimes that funded their life on the run. Nothing was safe, and there was a market for everything, as any enterprising spiv could tell you.

And just as rationing continued after the war, so did the crimes associated with it, which were mainly fraud and theft. Another thing the war gave criminals was the chance to update their weaponry, as Charles Hasler remembers. 'Virtually every one of us had a service pistol. Of course you brought back souvenirs from the war. I've known blokes have a sub-machine-gun in their kitbag. Also there were an awful lot of souvenirs from the First World War floating around, especially the German Luger, with the long barrel. They were all over the place, in people's drawers and so on.'

Despite the availability of firearms, high profile cases, such as the murder of a motorcyclist, Alec de Antiquis, after he attempted to block the get-away of some jewel thieves in Fitzrovia in 1947, or the killing of a police officer by a sixteen-year-old gunman in Croydon in 1952, were high profile largely because they were so shockingly unusual. In the latter case, a 'gun battle' between a teenager with a few rounds of modified ammunition and some armed police who supposedly never fired a shot brought headlines such as 'Chicago comes to Croydon' in the newspapers.

'Criminals did use firearms,' Charles Hasler remembers, 'but not as much as now. The penalty if you got caught with them was pretty stiff. You could expect double the sentence for a robbery involving firearms than for an ordinary blagging. But they were certainly using them. My first two years, there were two police officers killed, shot, in London.' Perhaps it was these heavy sentences that kept the razor or knife, the cosh and the knuckleduster as the weapons of choice for most villains. They were easy to get, for one thing. Coshes were typically made from cut-down starting handles sleeved with rubber, while cut-throat razors and knives could be bought in any high street. One way to tell who had been a criminal in Soho for some time was the scars on their faces; they were almost a badge of honour.

An event that has taken a leading place in the criminal history of the West End is the Spot–Dimes fight. Two old-school villains, associated with rival racetrack gangs, Jack 'Spot' Corner and Albert Dimes (born Dimeo) cut each other up in a fight that had dozens of witnesses. Later, however, no one could agree about what had gone on, although all concurred that it ended in the Continental Fruit Store on the corner of Frith Street and Old Compton Street. The small shop belonged to 'Hymie' and Sophie Hyams and it was Sophie who brought some order to the proceedings by bringing the heavy metal pan from the potato scales down on Spot's head, while demanding that they should 'Stop it, you silly boys.' Eventually, Dimes was whisked off to hospital in a taxi and Spot tottered into a barber's shop up the road and told the nervous barber to fix him up.

Everyone who was in Soho at the time, no

413

matter how young, has some memory of the fight, which shows just how rare any serious unpleasantness actually was, despite reports to the contrary. I did not see it, but heard about it from Father and his friends. John Carnera had a similar memory. 'I was there in the street when it was going on, but I didn't exactly see what happened, because there was all crowds all round. I was a kid: I couldn't see anything.' Owen Gardner believes that Jack Spot bought the knife used in the fight that very day at Page's.

The one closest to the action was probably Leo Zanelli, but he didn't see anything either. 'I was in the Bar Italia when there was a big commotion, and in the Bar Italia was a fellow called Bert Marsh, a very nice fellow, but tough, he was an enforcer for one of the Italian gangs. I was a young lad, and I wouldn't go up and talk to him. I remember someone coming in and saying Albert Dimes was in trouble in the grocery place on the corner. I saw Bert rush out and hail a taxi, and I understand he took him to the Middlesex Hospital. Marsh and Albert Dimes were part of the same racetrack gang. Marsh had been a boxer, and eventually got in with a bad crowd... If he hadn't, let's face it, he would probably have ended up sweeping the streets. It was Bert who put the first fruit machine in my dad's club in Gerrard Street.'

A blade wasn't enough for everybody. According to my father, Frankie Fraser, whom he knew through Richardson, liked to tell people that he always carried five bob. When asked why, he'd explain that it was the price of an axe, one of his favourite tools when he was called upon to frighten people into submission or to teach them a lesson. How true this is, I couldn't say, but what I can say is that as a small girl I found Frankie Fraser's eyes very scary, especially as my father used to say that it didn't do to attract this man's attention, and if his eyes were on you...

Among the really hard men, gunplay was always a possibility. Leo Zanelli remembers a double shooting that took place in January 1963. 'Next to the French House, on the first floor, was Tony Mulla's club. Tony Mulla, the Lone Wolf. It was called the Bus Stop, a clip joint, but there was an authentic club up there as well, the villains used to go up there. Now Tony Mulla... Years before, a gang had put him in hospital really badly. The rumour was that they'd stuck an open razor up his backside. He was always saying what wonderful people nurses were. Anyway, he was a real hard villain.

'The story goes that Mulla goes into the club, and walks toward the manager, Alf Melvin, pointing a finger and saying, "You, you've been fiddling me." The manager responds by reaching under the bar, pulling out a revolver and shooting him in the chest once or twice. Tony Mulla just stops, looks down, turns around, and walks towards the stairs. I don't know whether Melvin thought, God, he's gone for a shotgun or something, but as Mulla walked down the stairs, the manager walked after him, assured himself he had shot Mulla then shot himself. Actually, Tony Mulla was probably thinking, I've got to get to a hospital, but he got to the pavement outside, collapsed and died.'

Raye Du-Val remembers the day another of these guys, called One-eyed Danny, let him in on what it meant to be a hard man. 'He once said to me, "Do you know what? It's all right, this life, but there's always someone after you. When I go 'ome, you never know who's waiting round the corner. Even now. You might do this, you might do that, but it's the unseen you've got to be very frightened of."'

Pepe Rush did some work for James Humphries. 'He was a real villain,' Pepe remembers, 'had a loaded shotgun behind his door, but to deal with he was always very polite to me and my family. They were all like that, those real villains, not like the sickos like the Krays and the Richardsons and the modern scummy ones. Most of them were very professional. I used to go to a drinker in D'Arblay Street, on the corner of Berwick Street. There were villains there. Once they knew I was in electronics they would come up and ask me if I knew how to get round the security phone things for banks and I said no. "If you ever learn, there's a good little earner in it for you," one said. "You could retire on the money you get for that."'

All the hardcore criminals had come up from the streets, and Raye Du-Val was well on his way to emulating them before he diverted his energies to drumming. He had lived the life of a teenage tearaway in the late forties. There was something vaguely Dickensian about it, as Raye acknowledges. 'I was the Artful Dodger. I was no good at pickpocketing, but I'd nick anything. I'd nick apples off a stall. Wheeling and dealing on the street. I was a cocky little bastard, acting older than I was, talking like an adult, trying to be a big man, doing the bebop talk, while I was only a little lad. I had a little gang, you know. I was a Ted, black drape coat, big shoulders, bootlace tie. Oh yeah, all of that. We used to carry a nail file in our lapel, because that was a weapon. And the other great weapon was crêpe soles. If you rubbed them over a geezer's face they'd tear it to shreds. They were a big weapon. Proper thick crêpe soles.'

Raye's escapades earned him some time in an approved school. Violent criminals often received a more violent retribution. Coshboys could expect the cat or the birch in the late forties, while twelve months and twelve strokes was the standard punishment for street robbery – or mugging, as it's now called. The police were not averse to dishing out the deterrents, either, as Ronnie Mann remembers. 'If you got caught nicking stuff down the market, you'd get a wallop by the coppers, who'd smash you round the head. I mean, open fist. Fair enough, they'd send you home. There was no nicking you. They knew you'd nicked an apple, what's the bleeding point? Everybody's nicked apples as long as they grew on trees.

'But you always knew what would happen if you got caught. If you got caught for thieving as an adult, you went to prison. You knew that if a copper told you to bugger off, you buggered off, because if you didn't, you'd get hit. I remember when I was about fourteen in Trafalgar Square, firework night, and some coppers came and said "Go home," and one of my mates was, "Why should I?" He was in that Black Maria like eyes that are winking. Out about ten minutes later, bloody nose, black eye, tooth bleeding...

'I'm not saying it was right, but you knew, as far as I was concerned, where the boundaries were. Same as if you swore in school, you got expelled. The police was the authority. I'm not saying it was right, but if you knew the rules, that was what it was all about. If they said to you, "Don't do it," there was no good you saying, "These are my civil rights," as far as I was concerned.'

Most teenagers would probably have preferred a bang round the ear from a copper to what awaited those whose lawlessness went beyond that kind of rough justice. 'When I was fourteen,' Ronnie remembers, 'two mates of mine, Fred and Cyril, were caught lifting stuff out of the Civil Service Stores – combs, toothpaste, little amount of cash. Fred got off because his dad had been in the RAF. Cyril was branded a bad apple, although he wasn't; funnily enough, he was probably the least bad apple of the lot. He got a month in Borstal or whatever it was at the time, approved school, wherever, and came out after two weeks. They had to discharge him because he was so frightened and so scared. That guy never committed another offence. He said it was horrific, he started to eat soap and stuff to make himself ill, to get out of the main drag.'

Andy Pullinger was another one who learned the hard way that the police were not for cheeking. 'Not far from the 2I's was a pub where we would go to cool off after a couple of hours crammed in the basement. One night there was a fight inside the pub (not with us). The police

418

arrived and asked everyone to move on. I was stubborn and asked the officer to repeat what he had said. He said to f– off, to which I asked again what he had said.

'His reply was "George, grab him". George grabbed me and they carted me off to Broadwick Street police station for obstructing a policeman in the course of his duty. Next day it cost me ten shillings at Bow Street magistrates' court.

'Another time I was arrested for impersonating a policeman. We had bought some helmets at a surplus store and were parading them around on Wardour Street. I was taken off to Broadwick Street again and charged. Later, they proved the helmets were surplus and should have let me go, but instead I was charged with insulting a policeman. He said I shouted out, "All coppers are bastards." Later, in the cell, he told me that it was one of my friends who had said it. Another ten shillings at Bow Street and advised to get rid of the helmet.'

As the children of a beat bobby from Bow Street, Olga and Graham Jackson both remember the rather ambivalent way the police were viewed in the community. 'Some people didn't have a lot to do with us because our father was Snaky Jackson, and it could be their father that he'd knocked off, as they used to call it. And if their father's been knocked off, and is in prison, because of your father, you'd get this stigma. Our brother Arthur got a bit of stick, and so did Mum. She used to get called names across the road.'

Graham remembers how his father 'used to take me through Covent Garden after he'd retired from the force, and you'd get these comments: "Hello, you old bastard, ain't you dead yet?" "Look who it isn't." And each time I'd say, "Who's that?" and he'd say, "Oh I nicked him" – usually for illegal betting. But there was a respect. He was a copper, and he'd nicked him, but there was still that respect.'

I don't think that respect extended to the more hardened criminals, but the sight of a uniform definitely gave the more timid or would-be miscreant pause. 'Dad kept his helmet hanging behind the door,' Graham recalls, 'so when Mum opened the door to a stranger, they saw the policeman's helmet. That would have frightened someone then; today, it would be a challenge. I remember he'd say he would go down the street wearing his helmet, and turn the corner, and everybody would go [scarpering noises], and the prostitutes would [same scarpering noise, only quicker and more high-pitched]. He didn't have to do anything. What he'd do was, creep round the other way and nick 'em. [laughter]'

Bow Street, where Constable Jackson spent his whole working life, looked after the Covent Garden area, but the main police station was West End Central, where Charles Hasler was a sergeant. He was on the desk, and on the beat, for what he describes as 'three happy years' in the early fifties. He lived in Islington, but many others at the station lived in the heart of the West End, in Sandringham Buildings in Charing Cross Road or the police section house in Broadwick Street. 'As a sergeant,' he told me, 'you get to spend a lot

420

of time at the station. I never got to know the area intimately in the three years I spent there in the way I did in thirteen years at Marylebone. Of course, in West End Central, there was a hell of a lot to get to know. It took in the whole length of Oxford Street, right down Charing Cross Road to Trafalgar Square, right around the Square to Pall Mall, along Pall Mall up to Green Park, then back up to Piccadilly and right round to Marble Arch.'

The police were as likely to be involved in crowd or traffic control as catching villains, Charles remembers. 'In those days, Oxford Street would be even more crowded than nowadays with shoppers. Crowd control was necessary particularly before Christmas. There were so many, they couldn't stay on the pavement. You'd have bodies sent down from as far away as Haringay just to keep people off the road, literally shoving them off the junctions so the traffic could get through.'

The bobbies on the beat spent much more time out nicking fly-pitching spivs and barrow boys than they did chasing down gangsters. 'We had to go round checking these guys' licences, and if they didn't have one they'd be wheeled down to the station and charged with obstructing the highway. Down Oxford Street, nearly every corner would have somebody with a barrow. Especially in the festive season, they'd come out selling anything on their barrows. Or from a suitcase, the suitcase boys.

'People used to earn a living standing outside Selfridges, selling jewellery, anything. There were whole families involved in it,' Charles says. 'There were others down around Oxford Circus, another group, basically Italians from Clerkenwell, and they specialized in lingerie or stockings. I don't know where they got them from, but they were reasonable stuff, sold in suitcases outside John Lewis.'

Graham Jackson's work in the funeral trade meant he dealt with the send-off of several members of the more colourful reaches of the underworld, and he confirmed that minor villainy was often a family business. 'There was a family in Drury Lane, a well-known dodgy family, and I remember going home one day and saying so-and-so was dead, and Dad said, "At last." He'd been a thorn in his side.' He also remembers a funeral of one of these local villains at 'one of those little houses off Drury Lane. They had this thing about lying at home. They chose this big lead-lined casket, all polished and shiny and that sort of thing, and they wanted him to lie at home. Well, it was only a narrow stair, and a big casket, so someone suggested taking him upstairs first, and then taking the casket up. To get it up, they tipped it sideways, not thinking it's got to come down. So we've all gone in there, to pick it up, and I'll always remember my old governor has measured the width of the banisters, and it's like an inch too narrow. We can't just tip it up and bring it down because you've got, you know, Rent a Crowd outside.

'And one of these guys comes in, big guy, like the Mafia or something, and says, "Got a problem?" "No, no, no. No problem." "Well there must be a problem. Tell me, and we'll sort it out." "Well, the stairs aren't wide enough." So he got hold of the banisters and went [crunching, tearing, splintering

422

noise] took the banisters right off the stairs.

'There was always a bottle of whisky and six glasses sitting in the room for the pall-bearers [at these funerals]. Dare we touch it? No-o-o-o.'

There was a certain tolerance of petty villainy, providing no one got hurt. 'A lot of the criminals in those days were characters,' Graham Jackson remembers. 'Dad knew them. They knew they were nicked, they went to the court, paid their fine, ten shillings or whatever, and off they'd go again, and that was it.'

Ronnie Mann remembers that 'Chris Pussy had a bent second-hand shop in Monmouth Street. She was the local fence. I don't know whether Pussy was a surname or a nickname. The family were Irish. If you wanted anything cheap... It was just a little old junk shop, but when you walked into the back it was like Aladdin's Cave. I remember buying my first suit there, a Daks suit, that was about a quarter of the price. She must be dead and buried now. It can't be far short of fifty years ago.'

Some people simply could not resist a scam. Owen Gardner remembers 'a guy who had a restaurant called Gilbert's, Chez Gilbert he called it, and he was always in trouble with the law. In one case, he was accused by the police of getting his wife to knock him on the head, tie him up and rob his own safe. That old story.'

And then, of course, there were the specialists. The West End is full of bookshops, marching up both sides of the Charing Cross Road, scattered in side streets around the British Museum and clustered by the University. Gary Winkler who ran the Nucleus coffee bar, particularly remembers 'Nooky, who was famous for his long overcoat, two arms out that weren't his arms tucked into his pockets, and on the inside of the overcoat long pockets.' Nooky was a striking figure, with jet black hair and a hooked nose. He'd take orders for books from interested parties, then stroll around Foyles and other bookshops in Charing Cross Road looking for his orders. While apparently browsing the shelves, Nooky's real hands would snake out of the front of the coat, grab the books he wanted and tuck them snugly into the many pockets. To the casual onlooker, and even to the store detective, it seemed as if his hands were still safely tucked into his pockets. Amazingly, he was never caught.

Peter Southon wrote and told me that Nooky – or someone very like him with a similar garment – also used to come into the Sam Widges coffee bar in the late fifties to take orders for textbooks from hard-up students from London University, with a sliding scale of charges depending on the size of the book and its cover price. Then again, it's possible that there were several men wandering up and down Charing Cross Road with poachers' pouches sewn into their overcoat and prosthetic arms disappearing into its pockets. That's certainly what Ronnie Mann believes: 'There was quite a few of them around, people who used to nick books. A bloke who's dead now, I used to know at school, that was his game. He used to have the overcoat, with the arms in the pocket, and the false pockets inside the thing as well, so he could slip things inside them.'

The West End had some problems to overcome that weren't shared by the rest of the capital. 'Other places in London might have had rough people, but they were all local rough people,' Ronnie Mann told me. 'The problem with the West End was all the people coming in. You had the Nuffield Centre down by St Martin's Lane, which was the forces, Americans, Canadians, New Zealanders, British, and they used to fight like hell. Down in Bedfordbury, you had the Welsh Harp at the corner, the Marquis of Granby, the Black Horse. Now the Black Horse, there was always fights with the soldiers, right up through the forties to the early fifties, there was still loads of people stationed over here.'

Charles Hasler agrees. 'The West End was always full of people from all over. In my day, in the early fifties, you couldn't move for American servicemen. In Piccadilly Circus or Leicester Square, you would always find up to three, sometimes four, West End Central police officers, four or five American Snowdrops [military police officers] with their white helmets walking around, and a couple of pairs of our Redcaps. I mean, I was there when the Korean war was going on, and the number of people over the wall [Absent Without Leave or AWOL] from various places was tremendous.'

Another place you could more or less be guaranteed to find a good punch-up was the South Bank. 'After the Festival of Britain was on in 1951, that area all became derelict,' remembers Ronnie Mann. 'It was like a huge gladiatorial fighting

ground. Gangs used to come from, well, everywhere, it seemed to me, like Roman legions
fighting each other. On reflection, it was this
macho image from the war. There might have
been gang violence, punch-ups, but it was macho,
rather than gang. When you had a fight, it was to
prove you were tougher. You didn't have to kick
the shit out of someone or stick the knife in, that
was beneath you.'

Andy Pullinger was a Ted, but one with a re-
strained, even genteel side to his violence.
'Compared to today's gangs, we were a calm
bunch. There were quite a gang of us. Coming
from all over. Some from the Elephant & Castle
area, others from Camden Town and Knightsbridge. There was Sweetpea, Glen Cardno, Tom
Mathers, Spider, who was very short, and Willy,
who was tall and thin. Willy carried around large
quantities of change because, as he said, if he got
rolled they would only look for the pound notes.
There was an occasional fight at the pub around
the corner on Dean Street. No weapons were
used apart from putting the boot in.'

Pubs formed the focus for many a fight; the line
between a knees-up and a punch-up is an easy
one to cross. 'One New Year's,' Mike O'Rouke
remembers, 'we were down the Mercer's Arms,
my old man's playing the piano, and this gang,
they're in their late twenties, had come in, and
the old girl says, "No, I'm not serving you." They
came up to where I'm standing in the pub,
talking, holding a pint of beer, and this guy
barges into me, drink all over me, and I said
something, and he said, "Right, outside." As he

426

went out, Wallop, my dad's chinned him.

'Within seconds the bloody place was in uproar. My sister's saying "Don't hit him, dad, don't hit him," and the poor little sod, my old man's chinning him left and right. All the geezers who'd been drinking and were tight as lords had come out, and there was punch-ups galore in the street. Somebody said to call the police. They phoned for help and they said we can't come, there's nobody left in Bow Street. You can never get a policeman on New Year's Eve.'

While most people knew the rules about violence, things could escalate, if someone was reckless enough to ignore the warning signs, as Ronnie ruefully remembers. 'When I had my teeth knocked out down the Lyceum, it was my fault. I should have known better. I was a bit cocky. I was working in the market, I was fairly fit, fairly strong, I'd done a bit of boxing when I was a kid. I got knocked out twice in successive fights, so I wasn't very good, but I was still cocky enough to think I could handle myself. It was a lunchtime, and there was this girl I fancied, so I went over and danced, and I should have known then there was a group of guys she'd been dancing with, but I couldn't give a shit. When I come off, they all come around me, and I could still have got away, but I was just "F off" and all that.

'Thinking back, the guy who done it was two or three years older, a lot tougher and stronger and bigger, and in a one-to-one he'd probably have won in any case, but as soon as he slipped a knuckleduster on, and there was three or four of them, you knew what was going to happen. Most people thought I deserved it, because of what I'd done, and when the bouncers turned up afterwards, they didn't want to get involved with this guy. I didn't know him, but he was obviously a lot tougher, and had a rep. Those bouncers were tough, too: I saw them in a fight and they opened up the exit – you know, "Push Bar to Open" – with this guy's head, banged it on the bar then literally flung him out.'

While Ronnie's childhood gang from the Bedfordbury would take on the other Peabodyites from Wild Street in great mêlées, others found different reasons to take sides. John Carnera steered clear, but his brother did not. 'He did get involved in a little bit of gang warfare, because there were rival gangs, you know. For example, in those days, my brother and his mates were all up in arms against Greeks. There were a lot of Greek kids. There were one or two big fights down in Golden Square. Pitched battles. Fists and other things flying about as well. This was the mid fifties. He was involved in that, I was a bit young. Kids at that age wanted to show off who they were, so they formed gangs and then went looking for other gangs. That's the way it happens.'

Sometimes outside events intervened to give street fights a particularly vicious edge, as Chas McDevitt remembers: 'There was quite a lot of trouble at the Freight Train, because around the corner from us, in one of the mews behind Berwick Street was a Cypriot club, and this was at the time of the Cypriot–Greek troubles in Cyprus, so there were often fights. I saw a bloke stagger up the road and actually die outside the

428

coffee bar. Fell on the pavement and died from stab wounds.'

Another problem at the Freight Train was the occasional run-in with 'Curly King and his gang, a bunch of East End gangster layabouts who always used to cause trouble in the West End. There was one black member, they called him "Omo", and he was the only black guy I ever remember coming in the coffee bar. They were quite evil lads, always looking for a fight, getting into running fights in the West End, throwing bricks through windows. We just got the edge of it all, the fracas: our windows would go in, something like that. Wally Whyton crossed swords with the gang for some reason, and for protection, he used to carry a crowbar down his trouser leg.

'The Curly King gang were an unsavoury mob. Their girlfriends – they used to call them the Blackies, all dressed in black, black hair – would go up to a stranger in the street and ask him the time, and he'd get his watch out and they'd grab it, or they'd ask him for change for a note and just grab his wallet and run.'

Yet although there were people like the Curly King mob and the Blackies around, the locals rarely came across them as they went about their daily business. 'I spent a lot of time in the area, and you could walk through it at night without any worries,' Owen Gardner told me. 'If you were an innocent person, you stayed an innocent person. If you wanted to find trouble, you could find it.'

Sometimes, however, trouble found you. 'My brother David was one of the Krays' first victims,' Owen recalls. 'He would have been eleven or twelve, so this was about 1949, 1950. On the way to Sunday School in Kingsway, my younger brothers walked through Covent Garden, and on the way back they picked up all these orange wrappers. Each individual orange had its own wrapping to keep them fresh, printed with different coloured designs. My little brothers would collect them like stamps.

'So, this one time these lads came up to David and said, "What have you got there?" and he just said "Orange wrappers." They started razoring David's school blazer. He came home looking like a tramp, with it all shredded, and in one place they had cut through, and there was a cut on his back.

'Anyway, we were one of the few places in those days who had a phone, and my father was friendly with the police in Bow Street, so he rang them. They found this whole mob of boys in Kingsway, I don't know how many, six to eight maybe. The police grabbed two of them, sat them in the back of the car, and told them that they'd severed an artery in my brother's back, and that he was in Charing Cross Hospital, and could die, and that they wanted to know who did it. The lads caved in and gave out the names of the Krays, and they were arrested. My father went to court with my brother. The Krays' father, or someone, came up to my father, who was fuming, and said "I'm sorry that this has happened," and offered him a lift home. I thought my father was going to hit him, but he resisted the temptation.'

Owen Gardner's father had a special relationship with the police at Bow Street because 'There was a flat roof on Page's warehouse, where we were living, and we used to let the police go up there at night. From there, with a pair of binoculars, they could see what was going on all the way round. They were always up on the roof if they wanted to watch somebody.'

Ronnie Mann was another to find out that it did no harm having the police owe you a favour. 'Me and Keithy Clarke were going down to the Mercer's Arms in Mercer Street – we were about seventeen, underage – and saw this copper getting beaten up by some bloke he'd tried to arrest. He was on the deck – only a young copper – and he was getting a right kicking. He was pleading for us to help him, and I was a bit wary, because this other guy was a bit tasty, although there were two of us, so I said, "Do yourself a favour, fuck off, because you're only going to get yourself up shit creek, you'll end up doing bird" – because that was what happened if you got done for assault on the Law. And he run off. The copper blew his whistle, and Bow Street come, and whether they got the bloke or not I dunno, but the reality of it was that we were there, and he said "Thanks for helping."'

Ronnie realized how grateful the police had been for his help a year or two later. 'Where I worked at Monroe's, in the market, there was apparently quite a few blokes nicking off lorries and that. They had quite a thing going on one of them. The lorry would turn up and they would tell the driver to bugger off, and take as much stuff off as they could, and he'd come back and say he'd been nicked [robbed].

'The first I knew about it, this policeman came up and asked if I was involved with this guy, so I said no. "If you are," he said, "do yourself a favour. Lose yourself for the next couple of hours." I wondered what he was on about. Well, it turned out they came in and nicked the whole lot, about six of them. They all done about two or three years in prison. I wasn't involved, but if I had've been, I'd have ended up doing two or three years, and my whole life would have changed completely – except I would have got away with it because I stopped someone beating up a copper.'

Generally, even in the thick of the West End, Ronnie's experience was the limit of most people's contact with crime and criminals, as John Carnera explains. 'They never bothered us, or worried us, because we were like civilians, if you like, and they were soldiers. If you were a civilian, you didn't cross their paths.'

Alberto Camisa agreed with John, and was keen to express the dual nature of life in the West End. 'There were two sides. There were the residents, who were law-abiding and well-behaved, and then there was the nightlife, the strip clubs, Revuebar, Sunset Strip, all of that. There was obviously some rough stuff, with the Maltese, the night-clubs and so on, but the residents didn't get involved, and the two kept separate. People ask me about the protection racket, but there were no protection rackets with the ordinary shops. Just among themselves. The strip clubs, gambling clubs, they were all illegal, they paid protection. Normal residents had no problem with it.'

Despite what Alberto says, every now and then

the two worlds, of the more or less law-abiding locals and the much less law-abiding incomers, did collide, and then there was trouble. Sometimes the outcome was unexpected. The Mann family's picture-framing shop in Monmouth Street was next door to the Nucleus coffee bar, which Gary Winkler ran in the fifties. By the time Ronnie joined the family business in 1962, Gary was long gone, and the ambience in the Nucleus had taken a dive from the bohemian to the seedy. The Manns saw it as a haunt of druggies and general lowlife: 'It stunk, and all the dossers used to come out in the morning. They'd stay there all night and when they come out, the smell was awful.'

Then, one day, 'A mob turned up team-handed to sort out the guys that owned the Nucleus. Someone had let off these shotguns at the club in the morning, and my uncle and my dad were a bit pissed off about that. My uncle's nickname was Tiny, and you can imagine why, and my dad was also a big geezer. They both done physical training, and they had big arms and were very fit.

'I'd been down to the Seven Dials to get some stuff off the ironmongers, and as I was coming back, these guys have turned up, and they're doing a lot of commotion, and one geezer said something to my old man, and he's gone Bang! hit him right across the beak. Another one's come haring up, and as he's going by, my uncle's gone Wallop, hit him into a parked car. Another one's coming and I've got hold of him by the back, I'm kneeing him in the back, my dad's chinned him, and there's all these people in the street cheering, because they are all pissed off with the Nucleus, which by this time was a drug dealers' den.

'We had the police called, there were bodies everywhere. One kid turned round to me and gone "You", and he's gone like that [gestures] with a razor. As he's done that my dad's turned round and gone Wallop, and he's gone down again, bodies everywhere.'

It sounds like a scene from a Western. An Up Western.

Endpiece

When I set out to write this book, my main aim was to show that, contrary to popular belief, there's far more to West Enders than a motley collection of gangsters, prostitutes, perverts, weirdos, bohemians and legions of the bewildered. I wanted to introduce you to some West Enders who don't fall into any of those categories, and whose families have managed to live industrious lives alongside eccentrics and seamier citizens with very little trouble, plenty of humane understanding and no hint of the ersatz outrage so beloved of the tabloids.

Although there are acres of print about the lives of the plucky East Enders who stood up to everything poverty and that ratbag Hitler could throw at them, few seem to associate the West End with equally plucky locals bringing up families in tenements, dodging doodlebugs and dealing with the daily triumphs and disasters of life. I have always been proud of – and grateful for – my association with Soho in particular, and the West End in general, and I know that other locals feel the same.

As the book took shape, and I listened and read more, I realized that it was about more than the communities that exist in the heart of the West

End. I was astounded at just how often I found myself beginning a sentence with some variation on, 'It's hard for people today to imagine...', and to realize how things that were commonplace just fifty short years ago are now downright *historical:* public baths, gas mantles, one-man bands, street vendors, mangles, horses and carts, lamplighters – it's a long list.

Listening to the testimony of my generous contributors reminded me of so much that has disappeared virtually without trace, including such everyday conventions as calling a woman a lady, even when they so obviously were not. It was downright rude and patronizing to refer to females as 'women'. The term was used by the well-heeled when talking about their charlady, or cleaner, and even then, never to her face: and, of course, there were derogatory references to 'scarlet women' or 'the other woman'. There is also much about today that was beyond our imagining then, such as mobile phones, the fact that households without at least one television and at least one car would become the exception rather than the rule, that washing machines, fridges and even bathrooms would be a fixture in the vast majority of homes, that divorce would become common and that we'd be showing off our underwear to all and sundry as a fashion statement. It really is extraordinary.

The second thing that struck me was how far ahead of its time the West End was in the period covered by the book. I originally chose the post-war years because it was such a fascinating era. Before the two world wars, British society did change, of course it did, but slowly for the most part. The great majority of British people lived their whole lives in very small areas, but after the debris of the Second World War had been cleared away, the pace of change accelerated. Communities started to break up and young people were no longer content to become carbon copies of their parents and grandparents. Most cultural commentators look at the sixties as the time everything changed, but between 1945 and the early sixties, the West End was way ahead of the pack when it came to more enlightened attitudes towards sexuality, censorship, race, religion and the class system, among other things.

One reason for this is that the West End has long been an important centre for the performing arts, and where there are comedians, writers, musicians, theatres and clubs, there are dissenting voices who bring their subversive views to the notice of the public. Another factor was that many West Enders were refugees of one sort or another – political, religious, economic, sexual or simply unwanted elsewhere – and people who have suffered discrimination and repressive laws tend not, for the most part, to want to oppress anyone else. When you couple this general liberalism with the means of spreading the word, you have two of the major ingredients for change. It is no accident that the satirical magazine *Private Eye* and the Establishment Club, which also poured scorn and derision on our politicians and the ruling classes, were born in Soho in 1961. The West End was a safe place to be out of step with the masses: the avant-garde knew it, and flocked there.

Not only was the West End a place that positively celebrated difference, it did its best to accommodate those differences by producing the fashions that became the uniforms of the trendsetters and the music that they marched to. Modern and Trad jazz, skiffle, rock 'n' roll, R & B and the clothes that marked you out as a devotee of one or the other lured the young Up West. And they, in turn, took their new-found tastes, styles and music back to their towns, villages and suburbs.

In the freewheeling sixties, the rest of the country caught up with what West Enders had taken for granted for, in some cases, decades. The iron grip of censorship slackened a bit with the court case concerning publication of D.H. Lawrence's *Lady Chatterley's Lover*, a book banned not only because it had explicit sexual content but because it was about an extramarital affair between a lady out of the top drawer and a gamekeeper from a drawer very near the bottom. Back in the West End, of course, people like my father had been flogging the book on the sly for years and lords and ladies had been seeking illicit pleasure with 'lesser breeds' for centuries. How we laughed at the judge who was so out of touch with the new world that he asked if the jury would want their 'wives and servants' to read such a disgusting book.

The Wolfenden Report of 1957 eventually led to a reform of the laws forbidding homosexual acts between consenting adults and slowly, slowly it became relatively safe to be gay outside of the

West End.

Young adults became teenagers in their own right and rebelled in every way they could think of against a system that had always seemed to value class above ability and talent. They 'turned on, tuned in and dropped out'; they made love, not war; and they stuck two fingers up at senseless rules, the establishment and the status quo – something that West Enders had been doing ever since they defied their monarch and built their hovels on Soho Fields and their ramshackle market on the Duke of Bedford's posh piazza, and welcomed the gamblers, rakes, cross-dressers and all comers into their midst.

What came shining through overall, though, was that despite all the changes Up West, the voices of its natives show that some really important things have not changed at all, namely their warmth, humanity, tolerance, generosity and good humour. Long may they continue.

Sources

Quentin Crisp, *The Naked Civil Servant* (Cape, 1968)

Dan Farson, *Soho in the Fifties* (Joseph, 1987)

Frankie Fraser, *Mad Frank's London* (Virgin, 2001)

Jack Glicco, *Madness after Midnight* (Elek, 1952)

Roy Harrison, *Blitz Over Westminster* (Westminster Libraries, 1990)

Matt Houlbrook, *Queer London: Perils and Pleasures in the Sexual Metropolis 1918–1957* (Chicago University Press, 2005)

Kelly's Directories, selected volumes from 1946 through to 1959

Peppino Leoni, *I Shall Die on the Carpet: with a Foreword by Fabian of the Yard* (Frewin, 1966)

Fergus Linnane, *London's Underworld* (Robson Books, 2004)

Fergus Linnane, *London, The Wicked City* (Robson Books, 2003)

Chas McDevitt, *Skiffle: The Definitive Inside Story* (Robson, 1977)

Frank Norman & Jeffrey Bernard, *Soho Night & Day* (Secker & Warburg, 1966)

John Richardson, *Covent Garden Past* (Historical Publications, 1995)

Nigel Richardson, *Dog Days in Soho: One Man's*

Adventures in 1950s Bohemia (Gollancz, 2000)

Penelope Seaman, *Little Inns of Soho* (St Catherine's Press, 1948)

Judith Summers, *Soho: A History of London's Most Colourful Neighbourhood* (Bloomsbury, 1989)

Richard Tames, *Soho Past* (Historical Publications, 1994)

Marthe Watts, *The Men in My Life* (World Distributors, 1962)

Duncan Webb, *Crime is My Business* (Frederick Muller, 1953)

Peter Wildeblood, *Against the Law* (Weidenfeld & Nicolson, 1955)

Picture acknowledgements

Every effort has been made to trace copyright holders, those who have not been contacted are invited to get in touch with the publishers.

Map on pages 14–15 by Encompass Graphics

Photo section
Bomb damage, Newport Dwellings, 17 April 1941: City of Westminster Archives Centre

Bedfordbury kids: © Len Mann, courtesy Peabody Trust; Coronation Day at Bedfordbury (three photos), 2 June 1953: private collection courtesy Linda Rockey and Nicola Duckworth; St James's and St Peter's School, July 1955: Getty Images

Making ballet shoes at Gamba, 1966: © Henry Grant Collection/Museum of London; waitresses, 1955; Covent Garden Market, 1957; bookshop, June 1956; brothel, Soho, July 1956; street betting, May 1955; all Getty Images

Chas McDevitt, Freight Train Coffee Bar, 1959, and opening night, spring 1958: both courtesy Chas McDevitt; the 2I's, 1955: General/PA

The publishers hope that this book has given you enjoyable reading. Large Print Books are especially designed to be as easy to see and hold as possible. If you wish a complete list of our books please ask at your local library or write directly to:

Magna Large Print Books
Magna House, Long Preston,
Skipton, North Yorkshire.
BD23 4ND

This Large Print Book for the partially sighted, who cannot read normal print, is published under the auspices of

THE ULVERSCROFT FOUNDATION